SPECIAL EDUCATIONAL NEEDS AND THE LAW

AUSTRALIA
LBC Information Services
Sydney

CANADA AND USA
Carswell
Toronto

NEW ZEALAND
Brooker's
Auckland

SINGAPORE AND MALAYSIA
Thompson Information (S.E. Asia)
Singapore

SPECIAL EDUCATIONAL NEEDS AND THE LAW

BY

John Friel,
Barrister

AND

Deborah Hay,
Barrister

LONDON, DUBLIN, HONG KONG
SWEET & MAXWELL
1996

Published in 1996 by
Sweet & Maxwell Ltd of
100 Avenue Road, Swiss Cottage,
London, NW3 3PF
Computerset by
Tradespools Ltd, Frome, Somerset
Printed and bound in the
United Kingdom by
Butler and Tanner Ltd of Frome
and London

A catalogue record for this book is available from the British Library

ISBN 0-421-510307

Acknowledgement

The Authors would like to acknowledge the contribution made by Pat Wilkins, whose work forms virtually the whole basis of the Chapter on Legal Aid. Both Authors who are members of the Bar, thought it was inappropriate for them to write about the practicalities of Legal Aid and we are extremely grateful to Pat for her assistance in this respect. In addition, we would like to thank Tamala McGee and Clive Rawlings for their assistance in the preparation of this book.

Contents

Chapter 3
ASSESSMENT AND IDENTIFICATION

Chapter 4
STATEMENTS OF SPECIAL EDUCATIONAL NEEDS

Chapter 5
TRIBUNAL PRACTICE AND PROCEDURE

TABLE OF CASES

TABLE OF STATUTES

All references are to page numbers

TABLE OF STATUTORY INSTRUMENTS

All references are to page numbers

Chapter 1
The Duty to Educate

The statutory duty to provide education and make policy

The Education Act 1944 represented a further development of the system of public education which had been established by statutes going back to 1870. The purpose and overall policy of the 1944 Act is contained in section 7:

> **"7 Stages and purposes of statutory system of education**
> The statutory system of public education shall be organised in three progressive stages to be known as primary education, secondary education, and further education; and it shall be the duty of the local education authority for every area, so far as their powers extend, to contribute towards the spiritual, moral, mental, and physical development of the community by securing that efficient education throughout those stages shall be available to meet the needs of the population of their area."

Since its original enactment, the system has changed considerably. The specific duty to provide schools and education is provided for in section 8; this is a target duty.[1] The section as now amended is:

> **"8 Duty of local education authorities to secure provision of primary and secondary schools**
> (1) It shall be the duty of every local education authority to secure that there shall be available for their area sufficient schools—
>
> (a) for providing [primary education, that is to say, full-time education suitable to the requirements of junior pupils who have not attained the age of ten years and six months, and full-time education suitable to the requirements of junior pupils who have attained that age and whom it is expedient to educate together with junior pupils who have not attained that age]; and
> (b) for providing secondary education, that is to say, full-time education suitable to the requirements of senior pupils,... [and full-time education suitable to the requirements of junior pupils who have attained the age of ten years and six months and whom it is expedient to educate together with senior pupils];
>
> and the schools available for an area shall not be deemed to be sufficient unless they are sufficient in number, character, and equipment to afford for all pupils

[1] *R v. 1 LEA, ex p. Ali* [1990] C.O.D. 317, *per* Woolf L.J.; [1992] Admin L.R. 882.

opportunities for education offering such variety of instruction and training as may be desirable in view of their different ages, abilities, and aptitudes, and of the different periods for which they may be expected to remain at school, including practical instruction and training appropriate to their respective needs.

(2) In fulfilling their duties under this section, a local education authority shall, in particular, have regard—

(a) to the need for securing that primary and secondary education are provided in separate schools;
(b) . . .
[(c) to the need for securing that special educational provision is made for pupils who have special educational needs; and]
(d) to the expediency of securing the provision of boarding accommodation, either in boarding schools or otherwise, for pupils for whom education as boarders is considered by their parents and by the authority to be desirable:

Provided that paragraph (a) of this subsection shall not have effect with respect to special schools.

[(3) In fulfilling their duty under subsection (1)(b) above a local education authority shall have regard to any facilities for full-time education—

(a) provided for senior pupils by any educational institution maintained or assisted by the authority in exercise of their functions under section 41 of this Act; or
(b) otherwise secured for such pupils by the authority in exercise of those functions.]"

The duty under section 8 must be read with the duty placed on parents. Section 36 of the 1944 Act imposes a duty on the parents of every child of school age to cause him to receive efficient full-time education suitable to his age, ability and aptitude and to any special needs he may have, either by regular attendance at school or otherwise.

These are the basic statutory provisions which create the general duty on local education authorities to provide education for children of compulsory school age in their area, and thereafter for those who wish to stay in school and upon parents to ensure attendance or receipt of education.

Provision for special educational needs

It is often not fully appreciated that the 1944 Act introduced a system, which was an expansion of an earlier system, to provide education for children with special educational needs. However, the system was neither adequate nor comprehensive.

The Warnock Report

As a result of general concern about the failure of the system to cater adequately for children with special educational needs, a Committee of Inquiry into Education of Handicapped Children and Young People was set up under the chairmanship of Mrs Warnock (now Baroness Warnock), "the Warnock Report".[2]

The Warnock Report was largely adopted by the Government, and became the foundation of the Education Act 1981. The report remains compelling and sensible reading. The Education Act 1981 introduced a system of assessment for all children with special educational needs. It created a special system for unusual or severely affected children with special educational needs, and for those who required help which was not normally available without specific recognition of their needs. The Act introduced the new concept of a statement of special educational needs. The original approach to statements of special educational needs was that they were required in cases where the need was severe or complex (not severe *and* complex). This was an accurate reflection of the recommendations of the Warnock Report, and a sensible approach. This approach was reflected in the original DFE circulars on the Act.[3]

The Act, like Warnock,[4] envisaged that most children would be assisted in ordinary schools. This was a major change of direction. Only where necessary due to the need for specialist intervention outside the capabilities of an ordinary school, would a statement be made. The structure of the Act was to set up a system of assessment which depended on parental representation and negotiation and the goodwill and efficiency of local authorities. It created an advisory system of appeals at local level, with a written appeal to the Secretary of State. This system, was dependent on guidelines, not on specific rules. The appeal to the Secretary of State was binding on all parties.

The Education Act 1993: Part III; Education Act 1996: Part IV

Unfortunately, local authorities often proved unable to assess children with special needs as quickly or efficiently as the statute and the Warnock Report envisaged. Local appeals could be and were often ignored by education authorities. This led to great dissatisfaction. The written appeal to the Secretary of State was subject to a number of valid criticisms, not least maladministration and delay. A number of local authorities and the Secretary of State made substantial improvements between 1991 and 1993. However, considerable dissatisfaction led to a reform of the system by the 1993 Education Act Part III, which effectively replaced the 1981 Education Act with a system of statutory rights and duties. The 1993 Act introduced the concept of a National Code of Practice[5] in order to increase standards of practice and awareness in ordinary schools and will be replaced in

---

[2] *Special Education Needs*, Cmnd. 7212 (1978).

[3] Education Act 1981, DES Circular 8/81; W.O. Circular 59/81, December 7, 1981; finally DFE Circular 22/89.

[4] See above, n.2.

[5] s. 157.

November 1996 by the Education Act 1996, Part IV, which largely consolidates the legislation.

General duty to make provision in ordinary schools

Section 316 of the Education Act 1996 provides a qualified duty to secure the education of children with special educational needs in ordinary schools.[6] It reads as follows:

> "**316.**—(1) Any person exercising any functions under this Part in respect of a child with special educational needs who should be educated in a school shall secure that, if the conditions mentioned in subsection (2) are satisfied, the child is educated in a school which is not a special school unless that is incompatible with the wishes of his parent.
>
> (2) The conditions are that educating the child in a school which is not a special school is compatible with—
>
> (a) his receiving the special educational provision which his learning difficulty calls for,
>
> (b) the provision of efficient education for the children with whom he will be educated, and
>
> (c) the efficient use of resources."

This section is derived from section 2 (2) and (3) of the 1981 Act. However, there are modifications. The old section 2 required education in an ordinary school, subject to the provisors of seeking parental views, that the making of provision in an ordinary school would be compatible with meeting the child's special educational needs and not disruptive to the efficient education of other children in the school, and that it would be an efficient use of resources. The wording of section 316 appears to impose a veto if the parents do not wish such education. The Minister of State, Baroness Blatch, stated in a third reading in the House of Lords:

> "the crucial considerations determining the LEA's decision are that a placement should be appropriate to the child, appropriate to his peers and compatible for the efficient use of public resources. We cannot allow parents' views to override these wholly reasonable considerations; we cannot give the parents a veto."

Latham J. considered this section in an appeal against the decision of the Special Educational Needs Tribunal.[7] In his judgment, he took the opposite view to Baroness Blatch. Clearly section 316 imposes a duty to integrate where practical and possible. It does, however, give parents a greater say in relation to the future of their child. Latham J. decided that if the parents did not consent, the duty "falls away".

The correct approach to section 316 would appear to be that the duty is disapplied if educating a child in this way is incompatible with the wishes of the parents. One then looks elsewhere in the Act for guidance as to parental choice. [8]

---

[6] This principle was emphasised in the White Paper, "Choice and Diversity", Cm. 2021.

[7] *S v. Special Educational Needs Tribunal and Another* [1995] 1 W.L.R. 1627; [1996] E.L.R. 102.

[8] Sched. 27, para. 3(1) and (2). See also [1995] 1 W.L.R. 1627 at 1636—1639.

The two categories of pupils with SEN

The 1981 Education Act created a duty upon local education authorities to make provision for two categories of pupils. Those for whom the local authority determine provision is necessary are subject to a statement of special educational needs. They are very carefully protected. Those who are not subject to a statement are provided for in the ordinary school. The introduction of these two categories was a new development in the 1981 Education Act.[9] The Education Act 1996 continues these two different categories, namely those children with a statement of special educational needs who receive considerable protection, and those for whom the ordinary school makes provision. In the latter cases there is less protection. Those in the ordinary school with no statement constitute the larger category.

Duties of governing bodies of schools in relation to pupils with special educational needs

Section 317 determines the duties of the governing bodies of all schools which are in the public sector, whether they be county, voluntary or grant maintained schools. Maintained nursery schools are managed by the local education authority itself.

> **"Duties of governing body or LEA in relation to pupils with special educational needs**
>
> **317.**—(1) The governing body, in the case of a county, voluntary or grant-maintained school, and the local education authority, in the case of a maintained nursery school, shall—
>
> (a) use their best endeavours, in exercising their functions in relation to the school, to secure that if any registered pupil has special educational needs the special educational provision which his learning difficulty calls for is made.
> (b) secure that, where the responsible person has been informed by the local education authority that a registered pupil has special educational needs, those needs are made known to all who are likely to teach him, and
> (c) secure that the teachers in the school are aware of the importance of identifying, and providing for, those registered pupils who have special educational needs.
>
> (2) In subsection (1)(b) "the responsible person" means—
>
> (a) in the case of a county, voluntary or grant-maintained school, the head teacher or the appropriate governor (that is, the chairman of the governing body or, where the governing body have designated another governor for the purposes of this paragraph, that other governor), and
> (b) in the case of a nursery school, the head teacher.

[9] *R. v. The Secretary of State for Education and Science, ex p. Lashford* [1988] 1 F.L.R. 72.

(3) To the extent that it appears necessary or desirable for the purpose of co-ordinating provision for children with special educational needs—

(a) the governing bodies of county, voluntary and grant-maintained schools shall, in exercising functions relating to the provision for such children, consult the local education authority, the funding authority and the governing bodies of other such schools, and
(b) in relation to maintained nursery schools, the local education authority shall, in exercising those functions, consult the funding authority and the governing bodies of county, voluntary and grant-maintained schools.

(4) Where a child who has special educational needs is being educated in a county, voluntary or grant-maintained school or a maintained nursery school, those concerned with making special educational provision for the child shall secure, so far as is reasonably practicable and is compatible with—

(a) the child receiving the special educational provision which his learning difficulty calls for,
(b) the provision of efficient education for the children with whom he will be educated, and
(c) the efficient use of resources,

that the child engages in the activities of the school together with children who do not have special educational needs.

(5) The annual report for each county, voluntary, maintained special or grant-maintained school shall include a report containing such information as may be prescribed about the implementation of the governing body's policy for pupils with special educational needs.

(6) The annual report for each county, voluntary or grant-maintained school shall also include a report containing information as to—

(a) the arrangements for the admission of disabled pupils;
(b) the steps taken to prevent disabled pupils from being treated less favourably than other pupils; and
(c) the facilities provided to assist access to the school by disabled pupils;

and for this purpose "disabled pupils" means pupils who are disabled persons for the purpose of the Disability Discrimination Act 1995.

(7) In this subsection "annual report" means the report prepared under the articles of government for the school in accordance with section 161 or, as the case may be, paragraph 7 of Schedule 23."

The governing body is therefore required to use its best endeavours to secure that the special educational provision which the learning difficulty calls for is made for a child with special educational needs. The duty extends not only to identification of children but to circumstances where a child has been identified by the local education authority, but does not require a statement. The phrase "best endeavours" has not been considered in any case law. It is clearly not a mandatory duty but it is higher than a discretion. The words equate best with a duty on the governing body to make reasonable efforts to ensure provision is made. The Code of Practice provides some guidance on this duty. This is considered in Chapter 2.

Definition of "responsible person"

A "responsible person" outlined in subsection 1 is defined in section 317(2) as, in the case of a county, voluntary and grant maintained school as the head teacher or the appropriate governor (which means the chairman of the governing body or a governor designated for that purpose) and in the case of a nursery school, the head teacher. They have specific responsibility for those who have special educational needs and who require special educational provision.

Definition of special educational needs and learning difficulty

Section 312 (1) defines special educational needs in the following terms:

> "**312.**—(1) A child has 'special educational needs' for the purposes of this Act if he has a learning difficulty which calls for special educational provision to be made for him."

This definition is continued from section 1 of the 1981 Act.

The definition is quite simple. A child has special educational needs if he has a learning difficulty which calls for special educational provision to be made. This definition refers to the whole child, it is immaterial whether a child has one learning difficulty or more than one.[10] The definition of learning difficulty, contained in subsection 2, is as follows:

> "(2) Subject to subsection (3) (and except for the purposes of section 15(5)), a child has a 'learning difficulty' for the purposes of this Act, if—
>
> (a) he has a significantly greater difficulty in learning than the majority of children of his age,
>
> (b) he has a disability which either prevents or hinders him from making use of educational facilities of a kind generally provided for children of his age in schools within the area of the local education authority, or
>
> (c) he is under the age of five years and is, or would be if special educational provision were not made for him, likely to fall within paragraph (a) or (b) when of or over that age."

This definition is also in the same terms as under section 1 of the 1981 Act. The categories of children with learning difficulties are extremely wide and cover all possible disabilities which create difficulties falling within subsection(3). Taylor J. commented in *R. v. Hampshire Education Authority*[11] that this definition is extremely wide,[12] and that it was intended to expand the number of categories of

[10] *per* Balcombe L.J. in *R. v. The Secretary of State for Education and Science, ex p. E* [1992] F.L.R. 377.
[11] *ex p. J* (1986) 84 L.G.R. 547.
[12] *ibid*, see p. 566.

disability falling within this definition into a wider range of difficulties than were covered by the 1944 Act.[13] Balcombe J. in *R. v. The Secretary of State for Education, ex p. E*[14] stated "the 1981 Act looks at the whole child. A child has special educational needs if he has a learning difficulty which requires special educational provision. Of course a child may have more than one learning difficulty".[15] The duty therefore arises if the child has a learning difficulty which calls for special educational provisions to be made for the child.

Special educational provision

Special educational provision is defined by section 312(4) as meaning:

> "(a) in relation to a child who has attained the age of two years, educational provision which is additional to or otherwise different from the educational provision made generally for children of his age in schools maintained by the local education authority (other than special schools or grant-maintained schools in their area); and
>
> (b) in relation to a child under that age, educational provision of any kind."

For those under two years of age, any educational provision is therefore special educational provision. Where they have attained the age of two years, the phrase "made generally for children of his age", means provided to the majority of children. It has been stated that Greek tuition or music lessons may be additional to the provision made generally for the majority of children in schools, but such tuition could not be special educational provision because the definition must be read in conjunction with subsection 1. It must be a provision which is called for by the learning difficulty.[16]

Problems have arisen in relation to what is or is not special educational provision. In *R. v. Lancashire County Council, ex p. M*[17] it was contended that speech therapy was not special educational provision because it is medical and not educational provision. The Divisional Court and the Court of Appeal,[18] however, held that speech therapy is usually educational provision, although it could in certain circumstances be solely medical. Stewart-Smith L.J., in the Divisional Court utilised the definition of education to be found in the *Oxford Dictionary*. That is:

> "1. The process of nourishing or rearing.
>
> 2. The process of bringing up.
>
> 3. The systematic instruction, schooling or training given to the

[13] [1992] 7 F.L.R. 337.
[14] *ibid*, see p. 388F.
[15] [1988] 2 F.L.R. 279.
[16] R. *v. Hampshire, ex p.* (1986) 84 L.G.R. 567 at 555—556.
[17] [1988] 2 F.L.R. 279.
[18] See judgement of Balcombe L.J., p. 378.

> young... in preparation for the work of life. Also the whole course was scholastic instruction."

This approach was continued in the Court of Appeal by Balcombe L.J.

In *R. v. London Borough of Lambeth, ex p. MBM,*[19] the issue arose as to whether the local education authority was bound to construct a lift to deal with the special educational needs of a child who suffered from muscular dystrophy. Owen J. decided that the provision of the lift was necessary to assist mobility but that it was not a special educational provision. He said "The installation of a lift would be no more special educational provision than the provision of a wheelchair", thus the Respondent was under no statutory duty to provide the lift. Owen J. also pointed out, after citing Stewart-Smith L.J.'s approach in the *Lancashire* case (above) that "Education" is defined in relation to the words special educational provision as "pertaining to education". The definition will therefore include not only speech therapy, but also such needs as physiotherapy, in an appropriate case.

The enforcement of the duty to educate by the individual

In a long line of authorities starting with *Wilford v. West Riding of Yorkshire County Council*[20] to *R. v. Inner London Education Authority, ex p. Ali,*[21] the Courts have considered whether a right of action arose where education was not being provided or adequately provided to a child. In *Gateshead Union v. Durham County Council*[22] the Court of Appeal decided that an injunction was available to enforce the obligation to provide education. In particular, the famous observations of Scrutton L.J. have been considered in many later cases. Scrutton L.J. said:

> "but it seems to me that a statutory obligation to provide education without fee and without religious restriction, if broken, gives a right of action to any person specially injured by breach of such an obligation though he is not expressly mentioned in statute. The parent is the person specially injured by any unauthorised exclusion of his child of the free education to which he is entitled, and therefore a person entitled to sue for such a breach of statutory obligation."[23]

In the cases of *E (a minor) v. Dorset County Council, Christmas v. Hampshire County Council; Keating v. Bromley London Borough Council,*[24] the Court of Appeal considered all the authorities extensively.[25] The Court of Appeal unanimously rejected the claim that damages could arise from a breach of statutory duty.

These cases were appealed to the House of Lords. The appeals succeeded on the point of the existence of a cause of action for negligence. In the House of Lords these cases were heard together with two Children Act cases. All five cases involved the joint issues of breach of statutory duty and the existence of a cause of action for

---

[19] [1995] E.L.R. 374.
[20] [1908] 1 K.B. 685.
[21] [1992] A.L.R. 882.
[22] [1918] 1 Ch. 146.
[23] *ibid* 3 W.L.R. 853.
[24] [1994] 3 W.L.R. 853.
[25] *ibid*, see pp. 886—872.

negligence. The cases are reported as *X (minors) (Appellants) v. Bedfordshire County Council (Respondents) and Others.*[26]

The unanimous opinion of the House of Lords was given by Lord Browne-Wilkinson V.-C. On the issue of breach of statutory duty he stated, "I cannot improve on the Master of the Rolls' analysis and gratefully adopt it." Having referred to some of the best-known cases, including the *Gateshead* case (above), Lord Browne-Wilkinson V.-C. stated "the cases were concerned with the enforcement of public law rights by way of declaration and injunction and do not establish any private law claims for damages for breach of duties imposed by the Education Acts."

Judicial review is therefore the appropriate remedy where there is a breach of statutory duty. For children with special educational needs in an ordinary school and without a statement, who have a complaint about the failure to make special educational provision, the governing body of the school would be the appropriate respondent in most cases. Where a statement of special educational needs is maintained and provision is not being delivered, the respondent will be the education authority in the judicial review proceedings.

LEA and school policy on special educational needs

Section 315 requires local education authorities to keep under review the arrangements made by them for special educational provision, and in doing so, they shall, to the extent that it appears necessary or desirable for the purpose of co-ordinating the provision for children with special needs, consult the funding authority (for grant-maintained schools) and the governing bodies of county, voluntary, maintained special and grant-maintained schools in their area. The governing bodies of schools within the area are also required, to the extent that it appears necessary or desirable to them, for the purpose of co-ordinating provision for children with special educational needs, to consult the local education authority, the funding authority and the governing bodies of other such schools. In the case of maintained nursery schools the duty to review is that of the local education authority.[27] The duty to consult and keep under review the provision for children with special needs represents a considerable improvement as between the 1996 Act and the 1981 Act. A further improvement is the requirement in section 317(5) and (7) for the annual report for each county, voluntary, maintained special or grant-maintained school to include such information as may be prescribed about the implementation of the governing body's policy for pupils with special educational needs. The annual report is the report prepared under the articles of government for the school as required by section 30 of the Education (No.2) Act 1986 or, as the case may be, para. 7, Schedule 23 of the 1996 Act. The Education (School Information) (England) Regulations 1994[28] provide for the publication of relevant information, in Part 2 by the head teacher, in Part 3 by local authorities

---

[26] [1995] W.L.R. 152.
[27] s. 161.
[28] S.I. 1994 No. 1421.

and in Part 4 by governing bodies. The Regulations provide for the publication of general information, particulars of admission arrangements, examination results in school prospectuses. Most importantly, local education authorities are required to publish details of the arrangements in respect of special educational provision. Part 2 of Schedule 1 and in Part 3 (Regulations 14 to 18) require the local authority to publish detailed arrangements and policies in respect of:

1. the identification and assessment of children with special educational needs and the involvement of parents in that process;

2. the provision made in the county, voluntary and special schools maintained by them for pupils with special educational needs and of such provision in special schools maintained by other authorities; and

3. the special educational provision provided otherwise than at school.

The authority's arrangements and policies in respect of grant maintained, grant maintained special and non-maintained special and independent schools must also be published. Furthermore, careers advice in relation to special needs and further education must be published. Details of transport and arrangements for persons over compulsory school age are also required to be published.

The publication of information about special educational needs by schools is governed by the Education (Special Educational Needs) (Information) Regulations 1994.[29] These Regulations require the governing body of each county, voluntary, or grant–maintained school to publish information about the matters set out in Schedule 1 of the Regulations. Regulation 4 requires the annual report of such schools to include information about the governing body's policy for pupils with special educational needs as specified in Schedule 4 of the Regulations.

The requirements for the publication of information by schools falls into three categories:

1. basic information about the school's special educational provision;

2. information about the school's policies for the identification, assessment and provision for all pupils with special educational needs;

3. information about the school's staffing policies and partnership with bodies beyond the school.

By Schedule 4, the annual report must also contain information on the success of the governing body's special educational needs policy in the last year, significant changes in the policy and the outcome of any consultation carried out under section 317(3). It must also contain information as to how resources have been allocated to and amongst pupils with special educational needs since the last report.

[29] S.I.1994 N. 1048.

Duties as to consultation

Increased duties as to consultation are imposed on local education authorities and the governing bodies of schools by the Regulations. These changes, which also apply to the Grant Maintained Funding Council, must be considered in the light of the Code of Practice.

Agency co-ordination and co-operation

Agency co-ordination and co-operation is an important principle in the field of special educational needs. In practice, a major difficulty may occur in obtaining help from a different agency, for example the health service. Under the Code of Practice, it is the responsibility of the school special educational needs co-ordinator to liaise with external agencies, including educational psychologists, other support agencies, medical and social services, together with voluntary bodies. The Code also recommends that social services departments should designate an officer or officers to be responsible for working with schools and LEAs on behalf of children with special educational needs. In this context the Children Act 1989 has sought to foster greater co-operation between agencies concerned with the welfare of children, in particular between social services authorities and LEAs.

LEA's are required by section 27(1) to (3) of the Children Act to comply with the request for assistance from welfare authorities in respect of functions concerning support for children and families in Part 3 of the Children Act. These functions include duties to safeguard and promote the welfare of children within their area who are in need. A child defined as being in need under the Children Act may also have special educational needs. A child "in need" is unlikely to achieve or maintain, or have the opportunity of achieving or maintaining, a reasonable standard of health or development without the provision for him or her of services by a local authority, or (a) if he is disabled[30] (b) if his or her health or development is likely to be significantly impaired or further impaired without the provision to him or her of such services. "Development" is defined as physical, intellectual, emotional, social or behavioural development. "Health" covers physical and mental health. "Disabled" under the Children Act is defined as being blind, deaf or dumb or suffering from a mental disorder or being substantially and permanently handicapped by illness, injury or congenital deformity, or any other such disability as may be prescribed.[31] Section 21 (4) of the Children Act provides that local authorities (i.e. welfare authorities) shall assist L.E.A.s in making provision for children with special educational needs.

---

[30] s. 17(10).
[31] s. 17(11).

Duties of district health authorities or other local authorities to help the child's local authority

Section 322 of the Education Act 1996 allows an LEA to request help from a district local authority or a local authority other than itself, in connection with any of its functions under Part IV of the Education Act 1996. Similar powers existed under the 1981 Act, and the intention of the provision is to give statutory force in situations in which a local education authority would normally expect a health authority or alternatively another local authority to assist, for example in cases where a child attended school in the area of another authority. The request for assistance must be complied with, save on the following specified grounds set out in the section.

1. The authority to which the request is made considers the help is not necessary for the purpose of the exercise by the requesting LEA of its functions under Part III of the Education Act, Part IV of the Education Act 1996.
2. In the case of a district health authority only, that a district health authority, having regard to resources available to it for the purposes of exercising its functions under the National Health Service Act 1977, considers that it is not reasonable for it to comply with the request.
3. In the case of a local authority only, the authority considers that the request made to it is not compatible with its own statutory or other duties and obligations or unduly prejudices the discharge of its functions.

The Education (Special Educational Needs) Regulations[32] perscribes time limits for responding to such requests. They are normally six weeks.

In conclusion, the Education Act 1993 bought into force a far more extensive and supportive system for children with special educational needs, now contained in the Education Act 1996, Part IV.

[32] S.I. 1994 N. 1047.

Chapter 2
The Code of Practice on the Identification and Assessment of Special Educational Needs

The 1981 Education Act was implemented in the light of a series of ministerial circulars. The last and most comprehensive of which was Circular 22/89. Useful though the circulars were, they were not a comprehensive guide to the identification and assessment of children with special educational needs. A major change introduced by the 1993 Act was the introduction of the Code of Practice.[1]

Section 313(1) of the Education Act 1996 provides that the Secretary of State shall issue, and may from time to time revise, a code of practice giving practical guidance in respect of the discharge by local education authorities, the governing bodies of all state schools and the Funding Council for grant-maintained schools of their functions under Part III of the Act. This means that the guidance applies to all those who work in the state system. Section 313(2) provides that it shall be the duty of

"(a) local education authorities, and such governing bodies, exercising functions under this Part, and

(b) any other person exercising any function for the purpose of the discharge by local education authorities, and such governing bodies, of functions under this Part
to have regard to the provisions of the code."

The new Tribunal established by the Act is also required to have regard to the Code of Practice.

Section 313(4) requires the Secretary of State to publish the Code which is in force at that time. Section 314 deals with the making of the Code. The Secretary of State is required to prepare a draft Code or a revised draft Code. Having prepared such a draft the Secretary of State shall consult such persons as he things fit and consider any representations made by them. If the Secretary of State determines to proceed with the draft either in its original form or a modified form he shall lay it before both Houses of Parliament. By section 314(4), if the Code is approved it shall come into effect on the day the Secretary of State may by order appoint.[2]

[1] s. 313(1).
[2] The Education (Special Educational Needs Code of Practice) Appointed Day Order 1994 (S.I. 1994 No. 1414) as appointed September 1, 1994 for the coming into effect of the Code of Practice, the Code having been published on May 25, 1994.

The status of the Code of Practice

There was some important debate in the House of Lords Committee and in the Lords' consideration of Commons amendments of the meaning of "have regard to". An amendment to change this wording so that the Code would be binding in law failed in Parliament.

During the Committee stage in the House of Lords, the Minister of State, Baroness Blatch, explained at some length the Government's thinking in relation to the Code which, together with the Act and Regulations, would set the framework for special education. She stated that the Code was intended to deal with matters where an element of judgment is always required and that it was to reach much wider than merely giving guidance to the education authority or the special educational needs tribunal. This is because of the affect on health service and social service functions. No doubt these were considerations which led the Government to oppose the amendment to make the Code legally binding.

The Code is intended to promote a consistent approach to special education across England and Wales. Equally, it is intended to deal both with those who will need a statement and those who will not need a statement. Baroness Blatch also stated, as the foreword to the Code explains, that the effect of having regard to the Code may vary according to the circumstances and over time.[3]

The Special Educational Needs Tribunal and the Code of Practice

The Special Educational Needs Tribunal is also under a duty to have regard to the Code. This serves as an added incentive to LEAs to have regard to the Code. The statement in the draft foreword to the Code was quoted by Baroness Blatch: "the Tribunal will expect LEAs to be able to justify any departure from the Code where such a departure was relevant to the decision in question." However, an LEA could properly depart from the Code providing the departure was justifiable.

"Have regard to"

There is some case law on the words "have regard to". In *R. v. Police Complaints Board, ex p. Madden and Rhone*[4] a decision of the Complaints Board was quashed. The Board were required to have regard to guidance from the Secretary of State, which it had followed exactly. It was held that the phrase "have regard to" required the Board to take the guidance into account, but did not mean that the Board was obliged to comply. The guidance of the Code is therefore not of direct statutory effect, and can be departed from in an appropriate case.[5] The Tribunal in a number

---

[3] *Hansard*, H.L. Vol. 554, No. 83, paras. 14. 13 and 14. 17. Code of Practice published May 25, 1994 and came into force September 1, 1994.

[4] [1983] 2 All E.R. 353.

[5] *De Falco v. Crawley B.C.*[1980] 1 All E.R. 913.

of decisions which are published in its first two Digests has frequently applied the Code.[6]

On a practical basis, everybody working in this field must be familiar with the Code.

Defects of the Code of Practice

The main defect of the Code, which is a good document, is that it is silent on the issue of what happens if a child has special needs but where provision is not being made as the school or the local education authority has not the resources available, or these are not made available. This situation does arise in practice but is clearly a politically controversial area. Equally, the Code expects the ordinary school to have experience in many areas of disability, which may be unrealistic.

The Code contains a great deal of statements of good intention, rather than firm advice.

Basic principles of the Code

The fundamental principles of the Code are set out in the introductory section and are as follows.

- The needs of all pupils who may have special educational needs either throughout, or at any time during, their school careers must be addressed. The Code recognises that there is a continuum of needs and a continuum of provision, which may be made in a wide variety of different forms.
- Children with special educational needs require the greatest possible access to a broad and balanced education, including the National Curriculum.
- The needs of most pupils will be met in the mainstream, and without a statutory assessment or statement of special educational needs. Children with special educational needs, including children with statements of special educational needs, should, where appropriate and taking into account the wishes of their parents, be educated alongside their peers in mainstream schools.
- Even before he or she reaches compulsory school age, a child may have special educational needs requiring the intervention of the LEA as well as the health services.
- The knowledge, views and experience of parents are vital. Effective assessment and provision will be secured where there is the greatest possible degree of partnership between parents and their children and schools, LEAs and other agencies.

The practices and procedures essential in pursuit of these principles are as follows.

[6] See, also 1996 *Education Law Reports*.

- All children with special educational needs should be identified and assessed as early as possible and as quickly as is consistent with thoroughness.
- Provision for all children with special educational needs should be made by the most appropriate agency. In most cases this will be the child's mainstream school, working in partnership with the child's parents: no statutory assessment will be necessary.
- Where needed, LEAs must make assessments and statements in accordance with the prescribed time limits; must write a clear and thorough statement, setting out the child's educational and non-educational needs, the objectives to be secured, the provision to be made and the arrangements for monitoring and review; and must ensure the annual review of the special educational provision arranged for the child and the updating and monitoring of educational targets.
- Special educational provision will be most effective when those responsible take into account the ascertainable wishes of the child concerned, considered in the light of his or her age and understanding.
- There must be close co-operation between all the agencies concerned and a multidisciplinary approach to the resolution of issues.

Assessment and provision

The guidance in the Code is drafted subject to the principles set out above which must be borne in mind. The Code envisages five levels of support for children with special educational needs. The first three stages are based in the school, which will where necessary call upon the help of external specialists. At stages 4 and 5 the LEA is expected by the Code to share responsibility with schools. Stages 4 and 5 are basically the assessment stage and, if a statement is necessary, the statement stage. The stages are described in the Code as follows.

- *Stage 1*: class or subject teachers identify or register a child's special educational needs and, consulting the school's SEN co-ordinator, take initial action.
- *Stage 2*: the school's SEN co-ordinator takes lead responsibility for gathering information and for co-ordinating the child's special educational provision, working with the child's teachers.
- *Stage 3*: teachers and the SEN co-ordinator are supported by specialists from outside the school.
- *Stage 4*: the LEA considers the need for a statutory assessment and, if appropriate, makes a multidisciplinary assessment.
- *Stage 5*: the LEA considers the need for a statement of special educational needs and, if appropriate, makes a statement and arranges, monitors and reviews provision.

Need for immediate referral

Neither the Act nor the Code contemplates that children who require over and above that which is normally available in the ordinary school will have to wait to go through the stages as outlined in the Code. The Code recognises that there are children who need an immediate referral for statutory assessment; however, the examples given are somewhat limited as the Code has confined itself to the more obvious and severe problems.[7]

In relation to the criteria for making an assessment in such circumstances: detailed guidance is given by the Code, and it is likely that the Tribunal will order an assessment in the following circumstances:

1. Where the disability is obviously one that needs extra help and resources are not normally available in an ordinary school.
2. Even where the school is of the view it can cope, where the parent can show that the school has not adequately coped and/or does not adequately understand the child's needs and problems, so that intervention is necessary.
3. Where there is an obvious need for immediate action such as emotional problems developing into a severe difficulty, development of medical or psychiatric problems, where the child refuses to attend school, having become school-phobic, or where the needs are misunderstood or undetected and the child is far behind.

These illustrations are not, of course, exhaustive. An important consideration is the availability of adequate expertise or provision or both.

It should be borne in mind that for most children, it is only after the school's resources, with some extra help from the authority, have been tried that it can be seen whether the child needs more help.

The Code and The Warnock Report

The Code's five stages of assessment generally follow the stages used by the Warnock Report. However, the Code in Chapter 2, paragraph 2 does sound a note of caution in relation to the Warnock Committee's estimate of the number of children with special needs. The Warnock Committee made a "guestimate" that 20 per cent of children may at some time during their schooling have special educational needs. Of those children it was reckoned that about two per cent nationally would require a statement.

These figures were reiterated in the ministerial circulars, and in some local authorities appear to be applied as a form of undefined but rigid policy. The 1981 Education Act and the 1993 Education Act did not look at percentages of children. Both the 1981 Act and the 1996 Act, together with the Code of Practice, are looking at the child's needs and requirement for provision on an individual basis.

[7] Code of Practice, paras. 3:24 to 3:26.

The idea of two per cent being treated as a carefully researched, relevant figure to be applied nationally has caused great concern; it was never intended that this be applied as some form of rigid rule.

From statistics available for some counties and local authorities, it seems that the actual number of children who should be statemented was always greater than two per cent. Whether that be so or not, the Code makes it clear that this is a broad national estimate, and the proportion of children with special needs will vary significantly from area to area. The Code gives a strong warning against using these figures.

Responsibilities of the governing body

The Code is drafted on the basis of the respective responsibilities of the governing body[8] and the local education authority. The governing body must:

- do their best to secure that the necessary provision is made for any pupil who has special educational needs;
- secure that, where the "responsible person"—the head teacher or the appropriate governor—has been informed by the LEA that a pupil has special educational needs, those needs are made known to all who are likely to teach him or her;
- secure that teachers in the school are aware of the importance of identifying, and providing for, those pupils who have special educational needs;
- consult the LEA, as appropriate, the funding authority and the governing bodies of other schools, when it seems to them necessary or desirable in the interests of co-ordinated special educational provision in the area as a whole;
- report annually to parents on the school's policy for pupils with special educational needs;
- ensure that the pupil joins in the activities of the school together with pupils who do not have special educational needs, so far as that is reasonably practical and compatible with the pupil receiving the necessary special educational provision, the efficient education of other children in the school and the efficient use of resources;[9]
- have regard to the Code of Practice when carrying out their duties toward all pupils with special educational needs.[10]

It is the responsibility of the governing body to decide how best to provide for children with special educational needs. The Code of Practice recommends that the governing body delegate their responsibility to an individual member of the body, the head teacher or the co-ordinator of the special education needs (SEN) team. The

[8] Education Act 1996, s. 317.
[9] *ibid.*
[10] Education Act 1996, s. 313.

Code expects, however, that arrangements are made for the governing body to closely monitor the work of the school in relation to pupils with special educational needs. The Act reinforces the duty on the governing body by requiring the following prescribed issues to be addressed in the school's policies.[11]

Basic information about the school's special educational provision

- the objectives of the school's SEN policy;
- the name of the school's SEN co-ordinator or teacher responsible for the day-to-day operation of the SEN policy;
- the arrangements for co-ordinating educational provision for pupils with SEN;
- admission arrangements;
- any SEN specialism and any special units;
- any special facilities which increase or assist access to the school by pupils with SEN.

Information about the school's policies for identification, assessment and provision for all pupils with SEN

- the allocation of resources to and amongst pupils with SEN;
- identification and assessment arrangements; review procedures;
- arrangements for providing access for pupils with SEN to a balanced and broadly based curriculum, including the National Curriculum;
- how children with special educational needs are integrated within the school as a whole;
- criteria for evaluating the success of the school's SEN policy;
- arrangements for considering complaints about special educational provision within the school.

Information about the school's staffing policies and partnership with bodies beyond the school

- the school's arrangements for SEN in-service training;
- use made of teachers and facilities from outside the school, including support services;
- arrangements for partnership with parents;
- links with other mainstream schools and special schools, including arrangements when pupils change schools or leave school;

[11] Education (Special Educational Needs) (Information) Regulations 1996 (S.I. 1996 No.1048) reg. 1 and Sched. 1.

- links with health and social services, educational welfare services and any voluntary organisations.

The Code expects there to be an SEN co-ordinator responsible for the day-to-day operation of the school's SEN policy, advising class and subject teachers, taking the lead in managing provision for keeping records of all pupils with special educational needs, working with the parents of the children, and liaising with external agencies. It is doubtful whether before the 1993 Act, these tasks were adequately addressed in all schools. The Code certainly requires a substantial change in practice by schools.

Partnership with Parents

The Code accepts[12] that the relationship between parents and the school has a crucial bearing on the child's educational progress and on the effectiveness of any school-based intervention. The Code expects the attitude of the school to be a working partnership with the parents and that this will be a practical and effective scheme. The Code of Practice sets out the following matters.[13]

Information—information should be provided:

- on the school's SEN policy;
- on the support available for children with special educational needs within the school and LEA;
- on parents' involvement in assessment and decision-making, emphasising the importance of their contribution;
- on services such as those provided by the local authority for children "in need";
- on local and national voluntary organisation which might provide information, advice or counselling.

Partnership—the school should create:

- arrangements for recording and acting upon parental concerns;
- procedures for involving parents when a concern is first expressed within the school;
- arrangements for incorporating parents' views in assessment and subsequent reviews.

[12] Code of Practice, paras. 2:28—2:30.
[13] See para. 2:33.

Access for parents—the school should, where appropriate, provide:

- information in a range of community languages;
- information on tape for parents who may have literacy or communication difficulties;
- a parents' room or other arrangements in the school to help parents feel confident and comfortable.

The involvement of the child

The Code equally recognises that the effectiveness of any assessment and intervention will be mainly influenced by the involvement and interests of the child and young persons concerned.[14] Thus, the child or children have a right to be heard and should be encouraged to participate in decision-making about provision to meet their needs. The school should make every effort to identify the ascertainable views and wishes of the child and young person about his or her current education. The Code invites all concerned to consider how they:

1. involve pupils in the decision-making processes;
2. determine the child's level of participation, bearing in mind the age, ability and past experiences of the child;
3. record the pupil's views in identifying their difficulties, setting goals, agreeing a development strategy and monitoring and reviewing progress;
4. involve pupil and implement individual education plans.

Involvement of health services

In appropriate places, where the difficulties seen at school involve medical conditions (whether related to the educational needs or whether the disability itself involves a medical condition), the child health services are required to be involved.[15] In particular, where the case gives rise to cause for concern to the general practitioner, health visitor, school health service, or the community paediatrician, whichever is the appropriate expert, the relevant advisory teacher should be consulted. If parents make an expression of anxiety about an aspect of development they should be involved and the relevant professional consulted. Where such advice is necessary, useful and relevant, the SEN co-ordinator should ensure its confidentiality and keep an effective system operated by the school for:

1. keeping any medical records of children with SEN;
2. drawing together any information available from the general

[14] Code of Practice, 2:34—2:37.
[15] Code of Practice, 2:41—2:52.

practitioner, school health service, health visitor, community paediatrician, child and adolescent mental health service or hospital children's department;

3. the transfer of relevant medical information between phases for ensuring thorough co-operation with the relevant professionals, and the elimination of medical causes as a possible explanation for observable learning and behavioural difficulties;

4. identifying early signs of depression and abnormal eating behaviour and substance misuse.

Social services and education welfare service

Schools should be aware of the range of social services provided by the education welfare service and the social services department to support children regarded as being in need.[16] They should also be aware of the duty of social services departments under section 17 of the Children Act 1989:

> "(1) It shall be the general duty of every local authority (in addition to the other duties imposed on them by this Part)—
>
> (a) to safeguard and promote the welfare of children within their area who are in need; and
> (b) so far as is consistent with that duty, to promote the upbringing of such children by their families,
>
> by providing a range and level of services appropriate to those children's needs.
>
> (2) For the purpose principally of facilitating the discharge of their general duty under this section, every local authority shall have the specific duties and powers set out in Part 1 of Schedule 2.
>
> (3) Any service provided by an authority in the exercise of functions conferred on them by this section may be provided for the family of a particular child in need or for any member of his family, if it is provided with a view to safeguarding or promoting the child's welfare.
>
> (4) The Secretary of State may by order amend any provision of Part 1 of Schedule 2 or add any further duty or power to those for the time being mentioned there.
>
> (5) Every local authority—
>
> (a) shall facilitate the provision by others (including in particular voluntary organisation) of services which the authority have power to provide by virtue of this section, or section 18, 20 or 24; and
> (b) may make such arrangements as they see fit for any person to act on their behalf in the provision of any such service.
>
> (6) The services provided by a local authority in the exercise of functions

[16] *ibid.* para. 53.

conferred on them by this section may include giving assistance in kind or, in exceptional circumstances, in cash.

(7) Assistance may be unconditional or subject to conditions as to the repayment of the assistance or of its value (in whole or in part).

(8) Before giving any assistance or imposing any conditions, a local authority shall have regard to the means of the child concerned and of each of his parents.

(9) No person shall be liable to make any repayment of assistance or of its value at any time when he is in receipt of income support, family credit or disability working allowance under the Social Security Act 1986.

(10) For the purposes of this Part of the Children Act a child shall be taken to be in need if—

(a) he is unlikely to achieve or maintain, or to have the opportunity of achieving or maintaining, a reasonable standard of health or development without the provision for him of services by a local authority under this Part of the Children Act;
(b) his health or development is likely to be significantly impaired, or further impaired, without the provision for him of such services; or
(c) he is disabled,

and 'family', in relation to such a child, includes any person who has parental responsibility for the child and any other person with whom he has been living.

(11) For the purposes of this Part of the Children Act a child is disabled if he is blind, deaf or dumb or suffers from mental disorder of any kind or is substantially and permanently handicapped by illness, injury or congenital deformity or such other disability as may be prescribed; and in this Part of the Children Act—

'development' means physical, intellectual, emotional, social or behavioural development, and
'health' means physical or mental health."

Requirements of the Code of Practice

The Code requires schools to provide an integrated approach to the education, health and welfare needs of children with special educational needs. It also requires schools to co-operate with the social services department where it is considered that the child is at risk of abuse or neglect.

A social services department should designate an officer or officers to be responsible for working with schools.[17] This officer should be available so that schools and the LEA can refer cases for advice. Schools are required to have suitable arrangements for:

1. liaison with social services;
2. registering concern about a child's welfare;

[17] Chap. 2, para. 2:54.

3. putting into practice any local procedures relating to child protection issues;
4. liaison with the local authority when a child is accommodated by that authority;
5. obtaining information on services provided by the local authority for children in need.

Summary of school-based stages of assessment

The school-based stages should be seen as a continuous and systematic cycle of planning and intervention. There should be the necessary review within the school to check progress. It is intended to enable the child with special educational needs to learn and make progress. As Baroness Blatch made clear in the Lord's debate, it is unlikely at the present moment that all schools will be able to apply such a sophisticated and careful system of assessment in a uniform manner in accordance with national accepted standards. Nevertheless it is obviously the intention of the Code that, as time goes on, standards should improve, particularly as schools become more familiar with the system and its requirements.

Stage 1

This envisages class or subject teachers consulting the SEN coordinator and identifying the child's special educational needs, assembling information and putting into place any special arrangements to meet those needs and informing the head teacher.

Stage 2

The SEN co-ordinator now takes the lead responsibility for managing the child's special educational provision, working with the child's teachers to devise a more comprehensive set of strategies, and informing the head teacher.

Stage 3

The SEN co-ordinator continues to lead responsibility and should always consult and inform the head teacher. Specialist staff from outside the school, such as the educational psychologist, and advisory teachers with special qualifications, are brought in to help the school support a child with more complex needs. Should the child still not progress satisfactorily, a specialist will help the school consider whether the child is likely to meet the criteria for statutory assessment.

Review

At the end of each stage, the Code indicates that the progress of the child should be reviewed.[18] The class teacher and the SEN co-ordinator will decide whether they are applying each stage to:

1. continue the child's current educational arrangements;
2. seek further advice; or
3. draw up a plan using the expertise within the school, initially and at the end of each stage;
4. review the progress made by the child;
5. review the effectiveness of the education plan;
6. review the updated information and advice available in the light of the child's progress or lack of progress; and
7. decide on future action.

At each stage the decision will involve either a decision that no further help is needed, or that the child remains at the same stage, or that the child should move forward to the next stage.

Each stage requires an education plan for the child, as well as review of any decision-making process. Stage 2, the more sophisticated stage, involves consideration of non-curriculum issues such as the pastoral care arrangements, medical requirements and the like.

Stage 3

Stage 3 is the stage which can be regarded in most cases as the threshold to a statement. If stage 3 does not work, one would expect certainly an assessment, and very possibly a statement. However, stage 3 is not simply a stage that should be used following stages 1 and 2.

The Code makes it clear that in some cases children will need intensive intervention, but not necessarily an assessment or statement. In the cases of such children the SEN co-ordinator, having consulted the head teacher, can put into place early intensive intervention and bring in external support where it is immediately necessary.

Such support will come from teachers in learning or behaviour support services, peripatetic teachers, the educational psychologists, child health or mental health services, social services and advisors or teachers with knowledge of information technology. Equally, where help is available from special publications, or from organisations which deal with particular problems of the disabled, such as the National Council for Educational Technology, this should be sought. The SEN coordinator is expected by the Code to be familiar with relevant information and local practices.

[18] Code of Practice, paras. 2:82, 2:83, 2:96 and 2:97.

Stage 3 is therefore also an alternative form of assessment on a less sophisticated basis to the assessment procedures envisaged by statute and regulation. The SEN co-ordinator will review the position, assuming the child has gone through stages 1 and 2. This will include information gathered at that point and the report compiled for the review at the end of stage 2.

Equally, stage 3 should lead to consideration as to whether an assessment is necessary at this stage; the decision made should include consideration of whether further advice is necessary, and the drawing up of a new education plan, including the involvement of support services. The Code at this stage requires a much more detailed individual education plan, which is reproduced below.

Stage 3—individual education plan

- nature of the child's learning difficulty;
- action – the special educational provision;
- school staff involved, including frequency and timing of support;
- external specialists involved, including frequency and timing;
- specific programmes/activities/materials/equipment;
- help from parents at home;
- targets to be achieved in a given time;
- any pastoral care or medical requirements;
- monitoring and assessment arrangements;
- review of arrangements and date.

It is important that a review date be set; this may be within half a term, but should always be within a term. The SEN co-ordinator should agree with the pupil's teachers and the external specialists who are involved in arrangements about the means of monitoring the child's progress against the objectives which are established in the plan. The SEN co-ordinator should convene a review meeting at the end of the review period and it should focus on:

1. progress made by the child;
2. effectiveness of the education plan;
3. whether a child is likely in the future to be referred for statutory assessment, an important part of the decision-making process;
4. updated information and advice;
5. future action.

Obviously, the outcome of the review can be a continuation at stage 3 if progress is satisfactory or non-proven, a reversion to stage 2 if progress is at least satisfactory, or at this stage the head teacher may consider referring the child to the

LEA for a statutory assessment if progress is not satisfactory. The Code expects the head teacher to work together with the SEN coordinator on this issue.

Reference for statutory assessment

The Code expects the following information to be available should there be a reference for a statutory assessment:

- the recorded views of parents and, where appropriate, children on the earlier stages of assessment and any action and support to date;
- evidence of health checks—for example, relevant information on medical advice to the school;
- when appropriate, evidence relating to social services involvement;
- written individual education plans at stages 2 and 3 indicating the approaches adopted, the monitoring arrangements followed and the educational outcomes;
- reviews of each individual education plan indicating decisions made as a result;
- evidence of the involvement and views of professionals with relevant specialist knowledge and expertise outside the normal competence of the school.

If the school does not keep the required documentation some LEA officers believe this is a reason to refuse an assessment. Equally, the school may not strictly apply the Code. However, if a parent appeals, the real issue will be the child and the child's education, not whether the school has applied the Code. The Practice Direction of the President of the SEN Tribunal[19] confirms this view.[20] In *Burbridge v. Birmingham City Council*,[21] Dyson J. held that the correct approach to a decision, as to whether a statutory assessment was required, was to consider the whole child and each of his or her needs.

The Code also requires a head teacher to consider disapplying exemptions to certain parts of the National Curriculum under section 19 of the Education Reform Act 1988 and to give directions modifying the National Curriculum. These exemption provisions are an important route to assist children with special needs.

Stages 4 and 5 are the statutory assessment and the decision to make a statement. These stages are considered in the light of the statutory provisions in more detail.

[19] March 15, 1995.
[20] [1995] E.L.R. 335.
[21] CO/3769/95, unreported, May 14, 1996.

They also arise in considering the types of appeal. The remainder of the Code is considered in the context of assessments, reviews, statements and the law.

Children under the age of five years

The Code of Practice deals with the children under the age of five years. In its consideration of such children it is a very comprehensive document. Section 331 of the Education Act 1996 deals with assessments for children under the age of two. By section 331 (1) , if the authority is of the opinion that a child under the age of two has special educational needs and it is necessary to determine the special educational provision (subsection 2,) then they may, with the consent of the parents, or at the request of the parents, make an assessment of the child's needs. Obviously, they will in practice not need such consent if a parent first makes the request.

Section 331 reflects the old law in this way: the assessment is made in such a manner for young children of this nature as the authority considers appropriate. The statement is also maintained in such a manner as considered appropriate. Bearing in mind that these provisions are to help the more severely disabled child, it is entirely appropriate to have such generalised provisions so that some specific help can be given by way of early intervention.

For children under five in a maintained nursery, the provisions of section 317 require the LEA to use its best endeavours to see that provision is made for registered pupils with learning difficulties. For children of this age group attending a maintained nursery school class, the Code states that the LEA may normally expect that a school-based assessment process will be used. However, the Code of Practice seems to be somewhat optimistic in this view as it is really designed to deal with children who are in an ordinary school after the age of five. Nevertheless, many children will be attending pre-school education with provision made by social services, health authorities or from a voluntary or independent charitable sector. In the more obvious cases of disability or problems which have emerged from birth or as a result or accident after birth, assessment should take place. The Code of Practice in para. 5:16 provides useful guidance setting out the criteria for such an assessment.

> "**5:16.** When a child under five is already attending a maintained nursery school or class the LEA may expect that the broad principles of the school-based stages of assessment, action and review, adapted as appropriate in the light of the circumstances of the school concerned, will be followed as for older children. However, many young children will be attending provision made by the social services, the health services or the voluntary or independent sectors when concern about a possible special educational need is first raised. Because early identification should lead to a more timely assessment and intervention which in turn should avoid the escalation of a difficulty into a significant special educational need, it is important that any concern about a child's development and progress should be shared at the earliest possible moment."

Procedures for assessment

The Code of Practice points out that where children between the ages of two and five have complex needs, statutory procedures may be essential in order to maximise their opportunities. It also makes the obvious point that contributions from non-educational services such as medical or social services are likely at this stage to be of key importance. The relevant part of Chapter 5, paras. 20 to 24, gives good guidance on these issues:

"5:20. Where children between two and five have such complex needs that statutory procedures may be essential in order to maximise their opportunities, the statement will follow the same format as for any other children. The contributions of non-educational service providers are likely to be of key importance.

5:21. LEAs should note that parents of children under five may express a preference for a maintained school to be named in their child's statement and may make representations in favour of a non-maintained or independent school for their child. The LEA should ensure that parents have full information on the range of provision available within the authority and may wish to offer parents the opportunity to visit such provision and discuss any aspect of the provision with the Named Officer within the LEA. LEAs must provide parents with lists of independent schools approved under section 189 of the Act; all non-maintained special schools; and of all LEA-maintained and grant-maintained schools in the area of the LEA which cater for children of the appropriate age. They may also inform parents of such schools in neighbouring areas.

5:22. LEAs should informally review a statement for a child under five at least every six months to ensure that the provision is appropriate to the child's needs. Such reviews would complement the statutory duty to carry out an annual review in accordance with the Regulations but would not require the same range of documentation so long as they reflected the significant changes which can take place in the progress of a child under the age of five.

Special educational provision for children under five

5:23. For very young children, access to a home-based learning programme or the services of a peripatetic teacher for the hearing or visually impaired may provide the most appropriate help. In the case of a child with a behavioural difficulty, the advice of the clinical psychologist at a child development centre or an educational psychologist may enable the child to remain within an existing service. In some instances there may be a decision that a child should attend nursery class or school (either within a mainstream or special school setting), playgroup or opportunity playgroup.

5:24. All services working within a local authority with young children, including home-based learning programmes, should have clearly articulated arrangements for access to their services. Those arrangements should be readily understandable by parents of children with special needs; indicate the kind of support which can be provided; and state any priority admission arrangements for such children.

Assessment and statements for children under five

Section 331 provides for a statement for children under five if the child has special educational needs and it is necessary for the authorities to determine the special educational provision. Where this is contemplated, the child will have a severe problem. It may be that the child is born and diagnosed after birth as disabled or handicapped, or it may be apparent that there are obvious disabilities such as those that would include hearing and speech problems.

In such cases, either the parents or the child's health services or social services or all three will have identified the child as having special needs.

A decision to make a statement will usually be either because the child has complex needs, or to allow access to a particular service. This could be a home-based teaching service or a developmental play programme.

The Code of Practice stresses a number of factors. LEAs should explain to parents of children under five with special needs their rights in relation to requesting a statutory assessment and the implications of a statement. The parental perspective is particularly important for such children. Such children should be assessed in a place where the child and the family feel comfortable. Access to other parents, family centres, local services, play and opportunity groups are important in such cases.

Where a child is in the nursery class or school, the schools in the LEA are expected to follow broadly the same procedure for identifying and meeting the special needs of children under five as in the case of older children of compulsory school age. If the education/developmental progress of the child under five gives rise to concern, the child's teacher, if the child is at school, should prepare a written report setting out the child's strengths and weaknesses and noting the evidence for concern.

Notification of concern

Section 332 provides that district health authorities and national health service trusts must inform the parents and the appropriate LEA when they form the opinion that a child under the age of five may have special educational needs. They must also inform the parents if they believe a particular voluntary organisation is likely to be able to give the parents advice or assistance in connection with any special educational needs that the child may have.

It is likely that this method of notification will be by far the most important for such young children. With such children, contact with the child health services is obviously going to be important, so that proper medical advice and professional advice is received to deal with the child's disabilities and behaviour. Where the health authority or trust consider that the child does have special needs they must inform the parent of their views and give the parents the opportunity to discuss those views with an officer of the health authority or of the trust. Only after this takes place must the LEA then be informed. Health authorities and trusts must give parents the name of any voluntary organisation which might be of assistance, if they consider that a child under five may have special needs. The health services should give parents information on the full range of local statutory and voluntary services. For children under five, statements will be rare. The Code of Practice very wisely directs LEAs to first consider programmes of support according to the child's particular needs. There is no statutory framework for this area, and the Code of Practice in para. 5:5 indicates that where parents actually request an assessment, this indicates that the support is inadequate.

The Code of Practice considers separately children under the age of two[22] and those up to five.[23] One would expect there to be more information available on a child attending a nursery school, or a nursery class. The Code of Practice expects LEAs to adopt similar (but adapted) procedures for these younger children to that used for older children.

In any event, many young children will be attending provision made by social services, health services or voluntary independent sectors within this category. Intervention will lead to a more timely assessment and provision, which will prevent escalation of the difficulties or, indeed, in some cases eliminate them as the child enters school.

Criteria for statutory assessments

1. Where the child is at school, what difficulties have been identified by the school?
2. Has the nursery class or school developed full broad-based strategies to assist the child?
3. Where the child is attending health services, social services, voluntary or private provision, have any concerns been raised about his or her development, has any outside advice been sought regarding the child's:
    - (a) physical health and function?
    - (b) communication skills?
    - (c) perceptual and motor skills?
    - (d) self-help skills?
    - (e) social skills?
    - (f) emotional and behavioural development?
    - (g) responses to learning experience?

The Code of Practice states that the LEA will then assess the evidence and decide

[22] Paras. 5:5 and 5:8.
[23] Paras. 5:16 to 5:18.

whether the child's difficulties or developmental delays are likely to be resolved only through a multi-professional approach which will require monitoring and review over a period of time.[24]

The basic test should be whether a child has severe or complex needs so that the statutory procedures are necessary at this young age in order to maximise their opportunities for the future, prevent lack of development or reduce the handicap or problem. Non-educational services at this age are likely to be essential.

It must be remembered that such non-education staff do not necessarily supply non-educational provision. Speech therapy is likely to be educational as well as non-educational, and in cases of more severe disability, occupational therapy and physiotherapy will be as much educational as medical.

Parental preference

The parental right to express a preference for a maintained school to be named in the statement is stressed in the Code of Practice. Parents are likely to regard this as important, as they will see the provision of the statement for a very young child as the first part of the child's future developmental plan. The existence of an appropriate school once a child is of compulsory school age is going to be an important factor in any parental considerations, as it will be for the LEA itself in planning for the future.

Provision of help

For these very young children, access to specialised help is going to be an important part of the special educational provision. Access to a home-based learning programme and the services of a peripatetic teacher for the hearing or visually impaired in those cases will be the help required. Equally, for those who have speech impairments which constitute either the major problem or an associated part of their problems, the importance of speech therapy cannot be underestimated.

The services working within a local authority with young children, including home-based learning programmes, should be clearly specified in the statement, together with the arrangements for the provision made by the local education authority. Parents should be able to understand the statement, and what help is actually being offered and intended to be given. Where services are provided under the Children Act, whether because the child is on the child protection register or more likely because the child is defined as disabled within the terms of section 17(10) of the Children Act, social services are obliged to provide statutory assistance. It is important that the LEA and the social services department should jointly agree arrangements and ensure there is a proper plan for provision for all the child's needs, including those which are non-educational. In some instances children under five will have received considerable support without a statement. This could well be the situation even though the provision is sufficient to justify a statement in the cases of children of compulsory school age.

---

[24] Para. 5:19.

If a child requires a statement prior to entering primary school at the age of five, careful attention should be paid to the parent's views and information available from all relevant sources. Particular attention is required to be given to the child's health and development and home environment to ensure that learning difficulties do not relate to wider family problems, in order to promote appropriate support for parents.

Where the child is of compulsory school age, despite the fact that the authority may be intending to assess a child's needs, and there will be no question that a statement of special educational needs will eventually be supplied, practitioners may well advise a request for a statutory assessment by the parents themselves. This will enforce the time limits set out in the chapters dealing with statements and the assessment regulations, and ensure that adequate provision including non-educational provision is made to meet the child's needs.

If the child requires speech therapy and does not have it at school, or does not have adequate speech therapy, it is obviously advisable that the parents request a statutory assessment in order to ensure that adequate speech therapy is available. The same comment applies to occupational therapy and physiotherapy and also to all children who require specialist help by specialist teachers or from other sources.

Arrival at primary school

For those children who do arrive at an ordinary primary school, even those who may have had considerable help already but not a statement, it is important that the parents liaise with the head teacher and the relevant school staff to obtain an assessment of the child's special educational needs, if this is either arguably or certainly required.

The Code of Practice[25] draws the attention of schools to the need to assess pupil's current levels of attainment on entry in order to ensure they build upon their earlier years. Where a child is identified as having or potentially having special educational needs, the head teacher, the SEN coordinator and the child's class teacher should:

1. use information arising from the child's early years experiences to provide starting points for curricular developments for the child;
2. identify and focus attention on the child's skills and highlight areas for early action to support the child within the class;
3. take appropriate action—for example, developing an individual education plan, and monitoring and evaluating strategies to maximise development and alert any relevant support or external professionals at the earliest possible age;
4. ensure that ongoing observations and assessment provides regular feedback to teachers and parents about a child's achievements and experiences and that the outcomes of such assessment form the basis for planning the next steps of the child's learning;

[25] Para. 5:29.

5. use the assessment process to allow children to show what they know, understand and can do, as well as to identify any learning difficulties;
6. involve parents in developing and implementing learning programmes at home and in school.

The Code of Practice draws attention to the fact that where children are suffering from a developmental delay, where parents do not speak English (or Welsh) as a first language, they are likely to be particularly disadvantaged, if they are not identified at the earliest possible age. Equally, there is likely to be a category of pupils, where the parents have a lack of command of the English language and knowledge of the system, who may well be at the greatest disadvantage. Such parents are less likely to know about the child's statutory rights, or to appreciate the full situation. In conclusion, it is probably right to observe that, even for children with severe problems, in practice the question as to whether they will be statemented prior to their coming of compulsory school age rather depends on how a local authority and the local health service operate its identification system.

Chapter 3
Assessment and Identification

The Education Act 1993 (now the Education Act 1996) created specific duties requiring local authorities to identify and assess children with special educational needs who may require a statement of special educational needs. Those duties are directed towards children at the severe end of the spectrum of needs. However, to define the severity of need or the extent of provision required in a way which attempts to restrict the circumstances in which an assessment can be made, would be unwise. Although it is expected that children with the more severe or complex difficulties will normally be the subject of an assessment or statement, clearly it is not intended that children with specific needs are to be excluded.

The statutory duty provides for a pragmatic and practical approach. Section 321(1) provides:

> "**321.**—(1) A local education authority shall exercise their powers with a view to securing that, of the children for whom they are responsible, they identify those to whom subsection (2) below applies."

The key issue in section 321(2) is that it is "necessary" for the authority to determine the special educational provision which any learning difficulty a child may require. In relation to the Education Acts the word "necessary" was considered in *R. v. Devon County Council, ex p. G*,[1] when section 55 of the Education Act 1944 was considered. This case involved a local education authority considering arrangements for the provision of transport or otherwise as they considered "necessary . . . for the purpose of facilitating the attendance of pupils at schools". At p. 604E to F, Lord Keith of Kinkel defined necessary as being "really needed". He referred to the definition of Lord Griffiths in *Re an Enquiry Under the Company Securities (Insider Dealing Act)*.[2] Clearly it is for the authority to determine whether a statement or an assessment is really needed, however, this is not an open-ended discretion. If on a practical basis the required help is not available, the statutory test would require the authority to act, as it would then be necessary.

[1] [1981] A.C. 573.
[2] [1988] 1 A.C. 660 at 704D.

Jurisdiction

By section 321(3) the local authority is responsible for a child who is in its area and:

"(a) he is a registered pupil at a maintained, grant-maintained or grant-maintained special school,
(b) education is provided for him at a school which is not a maintained, grant-maintained or grant-maintained special school but is so provided at the expense of the authority or the funding authority,
(c) he does not come within paragraph (a) or (b) above but is a registered pupil at a school and has been brought to the authority's attention as having (or probably having) special educational needs, or
(d) he is not a registered pupil at a school, is not under the age of two years or over compulsory school age and has been brought to their attention as having (or probably having) special educational needs."

This definition covers all children who attend a school within the area of a local authority, including those who are either educated at home or in the independent sector.[3] Such children must have been brought to the authority's attention as having or probably having special needs. Section 321 re-enacts section 4 of the 1981 Act, the duty of the LEA to identify among those children in their area those who require a statutory assessment.

Upper age limit of LEA responsibility

A local education authority ceases to be responsible for a child, under section 321 firstly, when the child reaches the age of 19 years [4]or secondly, after the child has left school. Once the child has reached the age of 16, consideration will be given in some cases to transfer to further education. If a child transfers and goes to a college of further education, then they are no longer within the jurisdiction of the local education authority.

However, there is a right of choice at the age of 16 as to whether a child stays at school or leaves.[5] In *R. v. Dorset County Council, ex p. G*,[6] Auld J. decided the local education authority was funded on the basis that it would remain responsible until the age of 19, and that local education authorities could not simply divest themselves of responsibility by ceasing to maintain a statement, particularly where the child and parents wanted the LEA to continue to exercise their statutory duty.

---

[3] s. 321(3)(c).
[4] s. 321(3)(a).
[5] s. 8 of the Education Act 1944.
[6] [1995] E.L.R. 109.

Assessment statutory provisions

Section 321 defines the area of a local education authority's responsibility. The assessment of a child's special educational needs referred to in the section means a statutory assessment. Non-statutory assessments are carried out normally within the ordinary school at stages 1 to 3 of the Code of Practice; such children are not subjected to the statutory assessment provisions.

The statutory assessment can be commenced by two routes. The first is where a local education authority is of the opinion that a child for whom it is responsible has special educational needs, and it is necessary or probably necessary for the authority to determine the special educational provision which any learning difficulty the child has may call for.[7] The second is where the parents themselves request an assessment. Section 329 provides for a parental request where no statement is maintained by the authority and no assessment has been made within the period of six months up to the date upon which the request is made. If it is considered necessary by the authority for an assessment to be undertaken, the authority "shall comply with the request". Additionally the governing body of a grant-maintained school can request an assessment, in the rare case where they have been directed to admit the child.

In all cases it must be "necessary" for the authority to assess. The authority must be of the opinion that the child falls or probably falls within this criterion and the criteria set out in the Code of Practice 3:46—3:59. Whilst the Act itself continues the two categories of pupils—those with statements and those without—the test under the Education Act 1996 is different from that considered under the Education Act 1981, which gave a wide discretion to the local education authority. The old statute was considered in *R. v. The Secretary of State, ex p. L*,[8] however, that authority provides no assistance in relation to the new statutory provisions.

Criteria for deciding to make a statutory assessment, Code of Practice

The Code of Practice envisages a child in an ordinary local authority school. It also envisages that the child will go through stages 1 to 3 of the Code. It does, however, accept that some children will need an immediate referral for statutory assessment. Such children are dealt with in paras. 24 to 26 inclusive. For those children who are out of school as they are too young, separate considerations arise and they are dealt with separately in the Code.

The Code of Practice accepts that in a minority of cases schools may consider that statutory assessment is necessary even though no action has been taken at stages 1 to 3.[9] Para. 25 of the Code defines urgent situations as follows:

> "**3:25.** Where there is agreement between the school, the child's parents and any relevant consultant or adviser about the child's need for

[7] s. 167(2).
[8] [1988] 1 F.L.R. 26.
[9] Chap. 3, para. 3:6 of the Code.

further multi-disciplinary assessment or there is concern that any delay might further damage the child's development, the child may be referred immediately to the LEA for consideration for statutory assessment. It is in such circumstances that assessment and emergency placements may be appropriate – see paragraphs 4:13 – 4:16."

Clearly, there will be urgent situations, either when children enter school, due to the severity of their disability, or as a result of a condition which develops medically, or for other reasons, which will include failure to appreciate that a child has severe learning difficulties which has led eventually to a crisis point that requires rapid intervention.

The guidance in the Code of Practice on making a statutory assessment is that when there is evidence that, despite the school, with the help of external specialists, taking relevant and purposeful action to meet the child's severe or complex learning difficulties, those difficulties remain or have not responded sufficiently, this may require the LEA to determine the child's special educational provision. It is important to note the use of the word "may". An LEA does not have to be satisfied that the child will ultimately need to be the subject of a statement. The Code of Practice draws attention to the school's assessment of the child. In addition, attention is drawn to evidence of the child's academic attainment in the school and the child's potential ability. LEAs are expected to ask questions of that evidence in order to understand why the child has achieved the levels shown. (Perhaps the Code should here have simply referred to failure to make adequate progress). The Code recognises that the criteria for a statutory assessment will vary considerably according to the child's problems and learning difficulties.

In looking at the overall situation the Code of Practice in Chapter 3 paras. 3:50 and 3:51 draws attention to the child's potential, the child's known ability as established by standardised tests and the child's actual performance in the National Curriculum and in class work. The Code in particular gives guidance in Chapter 3, describing comprehensively a number of recognised learning difficulties. This part of the Code is very helpful, but it should be remembered it is by no means exhaustive. While it includes a number of recognised learning difficulties such as speech and language difficulties, medical conditions, sensory impairment and visual difficulties, emotional and behavioural difficulties, physical disabilities and specific learning difficulties (for example, dyslexia), it omits a number of other recognised conditions, *e.g.*: autism is completely omitted.

Procedure

Where the local education authority is of the opinion, whether as a result of parental request or through its own investigations, that a child falls within the statutory criteria, they are required to serve a notice on the child's parents in the following terms:

(a) that they propose to make an assessment of the child's educational needs;
(b) of the procedure to be followed in making the assessment;

(c) of the name of the officer of the authority from whom further information may be obtained; and

(d) of the parent's right to make representations, and submit written evidence, to the authority within such period (which shall not be less than 29 days beginning with the date on which the notice is served) as may be specified in the notice.

Once such a notice has been served, and the specified period has expired, the authority will normally proceed to assess. In practice, because parents normally wish an assessment, authorities can be asked to waive or indicate they will waive this period of delay. If, however, a parent wishes to make representations, the authority must consider these representations and if, having taken into account any representations or evidence submitted to them in accordance with the notice and they are still of the same opinion, they should then proceed to make an assessment of the child's special educational needs. Where they decide to make an assessment they must serve notice in writing.[10] The notice must include the reasons for the making of the assessment.

Once an assessment has commenced, by section 323(6), a local education authority may at any time after serving the notice decide not to assess the child's needs but must give notice in writing to the parent of their decision. This decision gives rise to an appeal.

Statutory assessment procedure and time limits

In summary, the time limits for making assessments and statements are as follows:

- considering whether a statutory assessment is necessary: the period *from* the issue of a notice under sections 167(1) or 174(2) or the receipt of a request for a statutory assessment from parents *to* the decision as to whether to make a statutory assessment must normally be no more than: **6 weeks**

- making the assessment: the period *from* the LEA's decision to make a statutory assessment *to* the LEA's decision as to whether to make a statement must normally be no more than: **10 weeks**

- drafting the proposed statement or note in lieu: the period *from* the LEA's decision whether to make a statement *to* the issue of a proposed statement or of a notice of the LEA's decision not to make a statement, giving full reasons, preferably in the form of a note in lieu, must normally be no more than: **2 weeks**

- finalising the statement: the period *from* the issue of the proposed statement *to* the issue of the final copy of the statement must normally be no more than: **8 weeks**

Total 26 weeks

[10] s. 167(4).

The conduct of the assessment and the time limits are governed by Education (Special Educational Needs) Regulations 1994.[11] These regulations mean that in the statutory assessment which must be made, the LEA must seek parental, educational, medical, psychological, and social services advice. If any other advice is considered appropriate it too must be obtained, and the local education authority and its psychologists must consult those who may have relevant information.[12] The full regulations are considered in more detail below.

Service of documents

Service is effected on a parent or any other person who requires written notice under the regulations. The document is served or sent by properly addressing, prepaying and posting a letter containing the document on notice.[13]

For the purposes of the regulation the proper address of a person is:

1. in the case of a child's parents, the last known address;
2. in the case of a head teacher or other member of staff of the school, the school's address;
3. in the case of any other person, the last known address of the place where he carries on his business, profession or other employment.

Service is effected as being the second working day after the date of posting unless the contrary is proved.[14] If second class post is used it is to be the fourth working day.[15]

By regulation 4 (5) the date of posting shall be presumed, unless to the contrary is shown, to be the date shown on the postmark of the envelope in which the document is contained. This will apply if there is no evidence as to whether first or second class post was used. These service regulations may be important in considering whether or not an appeal has arisen, or to calculate the time limits for an appeal.

By regulation 5, where an authority has decided to make an assessment it must give notice to a child's parent of its decision. It shall send copies of the relevant notice to:

1. the social services authority;
2. the district health authority; and
3. if the child is registered at a school, the head teacher of that school.

Where the parent has requested an assessment, the authority are required to give notice in writing of that request to the above bodies informing them of the request and telling them what help that they are likely to request of the body.

---

[11] S.I. 1994 No. 1047.
[12] Reg. 6(3) and 9(2).
[13] Reg. 4(1).
[14] Reg. 4(3).
[15] Reg. 4(4).

Advice to be sought

Regulation 6 provides for the following advice to be sought:

"(a) advice from the child's parent;
(b) educational advice as provided for in regulation 7;
(c) medical advice from the district health authority as provided for in regulation 8;
(d) psychological advice as provided for in regulation 9;
(e) advice from the social services authority; and
(f) any other advice which the authority consider appropriate for the purpose of arriving at a satisfactory assessment."

The advice referred to above shall be written advice relating to the educational, medical, psychological or other features of the case which appear relevant to the child's educational needs including his likely future needs or according to the nature of the advice sought, how those features could effect the child's needs, and the provision which is appropriate for the child in the light of the child's case, to provide special educational provision or non-educational provision. The advice should not extend to the naming of the school.

The person from whom the advice is sought may consult such persons as it appears to him expedient to consult, and must consult such persons, if any, as are specified by the authority as persons who have relevant knowledge of all information relating to the child.

When seeking the advice the authority shall provide the person from whom it is sought with copies of representations made by the parents and any evidence submitted by or at the request of the parents under section 323(1)(d).

In cases of reassessment, if the authority has obtained advice in the preceding 12 months and if the authority, the person from whom the advice was obtained and the child's parent are satisfied that the existing advice is sufficient for the purposes of arriving at a satisfactory assessment further advice is dispensed with. However, the LEA must obtain further advice from the child's parents.

Educational advice

By regulation 7(1),

"(a) [educational advice must be sought from]: The headteacher of each school at which a child is currently attending or at which he has attended at any time within the proceeding 18 months; or
(b) advice can be obtained from a headteacher of a school at which a child is currently attending or person who the authority know has experience of teaching children with special needs or knowledge of the differing provision which may be called for in the different cases to meet those needs.
(c) If the child is not attending the school and if the advice under

Sub-paragraph b) is not advice from such a person advice is needed from the person responsible for the educational provision to him.

(d) If any of the child's parents is a serving member of Her Majesty's Armed Forces, the Services Children's Educational Authority."

Educational advice must be sought from a qualified teacher. Where a head teacher has not himself taught the child within the preceding 18 months the advice must be given after consultation with a teacher who has taught the child. The advice sought from the head teacher shall include advice relating to steps which have been taken by the school to identify and assess the special educational needs of the child to make provision for the purpose of meeting those needs. If it appears to the authority that the child is :

1. hearing impaired;
2. visually impaired;
3. both hearing and visually impaired,

they must obtain advice if the person giving the advice under regulation 7 (1) is not properly qualified, after consultation with a person who is so qualified, such a person being employed at school as a teacher of a class of pupils who are so impaired, otherwise than to give instruction in a craft, trade, or domestic subject.

Medical advice

Regulation 8 provides that the advice given shall be sought from the district health authority, who shall obtain the advice from a fully registered medical practitioner.

Psychological advice

Psychological advice referred to in regulation 6 shall be sought from a person:

1. regularly employed by the authority as an educational psychologist; or
2. engaged by the authority as an educational psychologist in the case in question.

An authority can elect therefore to use employed psychologists or to specifically instruct psychologists. Regulation 9 (2) provides that when the advice is sought from a person in para. 1, if that person has reason to believe that another psychologist has knowledge of or information in relation to the child, the advice should be given after consultation with another psychologist. There is therefore a specific obligation to consult with another psychologist under this regulation.

Social services advice is not subject to any more than the requirements of regulation 6, and is not governed by a separate regulation.

Time limits

The 1993, now 1996 Act substantially differs from the 1981 Act in that it set out statutory time limits. These are provided for by regulation 11, the effect of which is summarised below.

The timetable for the process

The LEA initiates the process. The first task for the LEA, having notified the parents that the statutory assessment might be necessary or having received a request from the parents or a grant maintained school, is to decide whether a statutory assessment must be made. The timetable in each case is as follows:

1. The LEA concludes that it is necessary to make an assesment and serves the statutory notice giving 29 days to make representations. Six weeks after issuing a notice under section 323(1) the LEA must tell parents whether they will or will not make a statutory assessment.
2. Parents request a statutory assessment under either section 328(2) or section 329(1). The LEA must decide within six weeks of receiving the request whether they will or will not make a statutory assessment and inform the parents.
3. The governing body of grant maintained schools, where there exists a section 431 direction to admit a pupil, request a statutory assessment under 329(1). The parents must be informed within 29 days, and the LEA must, within six weeks of receiving the request, tell the parents and the governing body whether they will or will not make a statutory assessment.
4. **Making the assessment:** the period from the LEA's decision to make the statutory assessment and the LEA's decision whether or not to make a statement must normally be no more than 10 weeks.
5. Drafting the proposed statement or a note in lieu of a statement: the period from the LEA's decision whether to make a statement to the issue of a proposed statement must be no more than two weeks.
6. Finalising the statement: the period from the issue of the proposed statement and the final copy of the statement must normally be no more than eight weeks.

Total: 26 weeks.

Exceptions to the limits

Regulations provide for the following exceptions to the time limit in regulation 11.

1. When having received full advice as requested by the LEA, further advice or reports are needed as a result of exceptional circumstances.

2. Where the parents want to provide advice for an assessment more than six weeks after the LEA's request.
3. Where district health authorities or social services departments have had no relevant knowledge of the child prior to receiving a copy of the LEA's proposal to make an assessment or from notice that the child's parents have requested an assessment.
4. Where the LEA and the district health authority or social services department are aware of exceptional personal circumstances affecting the child and his parents following the process of assessment or the making of a statement.
5. Where the parent or child are absent from the LEA's area for a continuous period of more than four weeks.
6. Where a child fails to attend for an appointment for an examination or test.
7. Where the LEA issues a request for educational advice during the period beginning one week before the school closes for a continuous period of more than four weeks, ending one week before it re-opens.
8. Where the parents, having received a proposed statement, want to make representations about the content of the statement after the 15-day period allowed for, or seek more than one meeting under para. 4 of Schedule 27.
9. Where the LEA has sent a written request to the Secretary of State seeking his consent under section 347 to the child being educated in an independent school which is not approved by him and such consent has not been received by the LEA within two weeks of the date on which the request was sent.

In practice, delays are likely to occur where the parents want to submit their own evidence in relation to assessing the child's needs by an independent expert, if they have not obtained expert advice in advance of the decision to assess, or where they wish to make representations in relation to the draft statement. A proposed statement must be served prior to a final statement.

The diagram below represents this process.

Matters to be taken into account when making an assessment

Regulation 10 provides that when making an assessment, an authority shall take into consideration:

1. any representations made by the child's parent under section 323(1)(d);
2. any evidence submitted by or at the request of the child's parents under section 323(1)(d); and
3. the advice obtained under regulation 6.

Therefore having obtained the advice under regulation 6 and received representations from the parents, and any evidence submitted by them, the

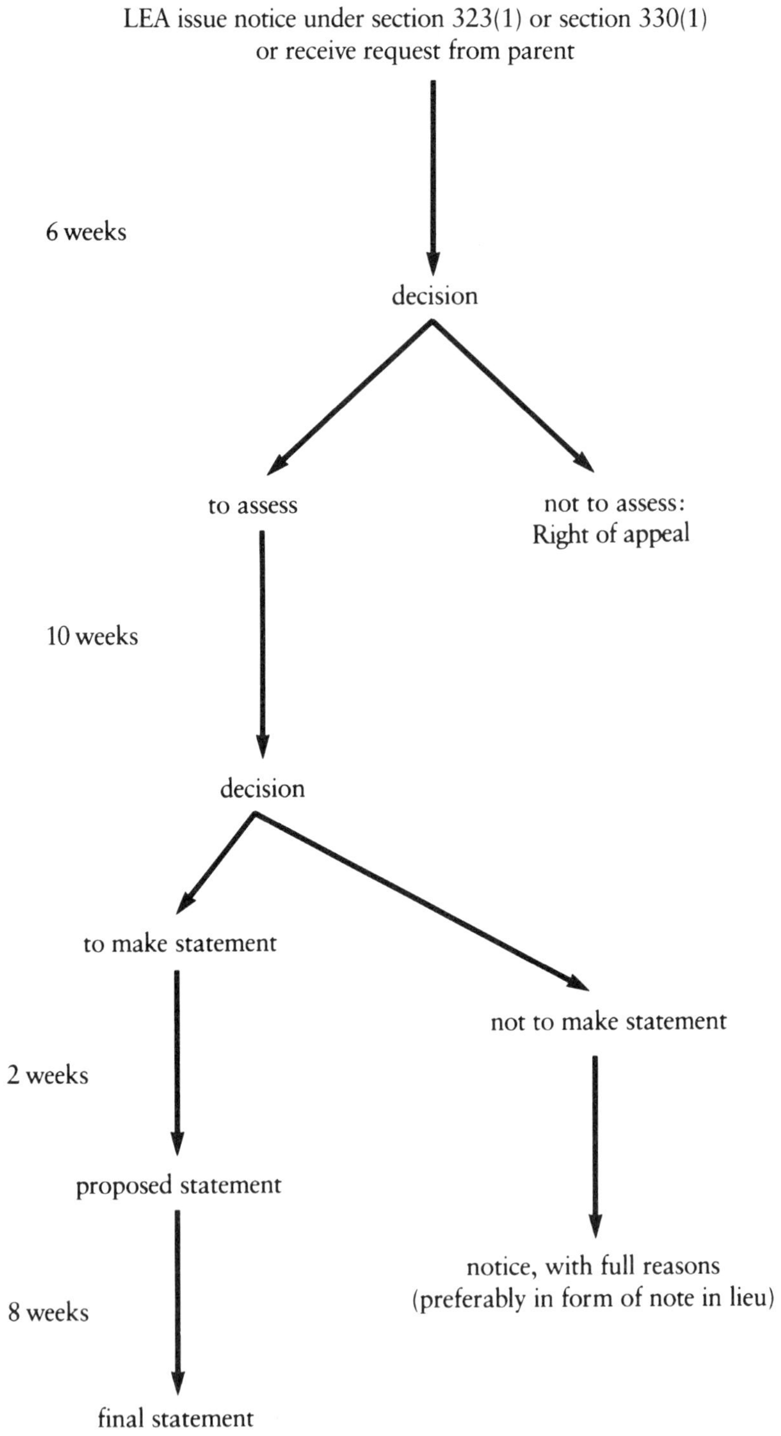
LEA issue notice under section 323(1) or section 330(1)
or receive request from parent
6 weeks
decision
to assess
not to assess:
Right of appeal
10 weeks
decision
to make statement
not to make statement
2 weeks
proposed statement
notice, with full reasons
(preferably in form of note in lieu)
8 weeks
final statement

authority must decide whether or not to make a statement. The statutory test uses the same wording, namely that it is "necessary".[16] A question can arise as to whether the LEA has conducted the assessment lawfully for the purpose of the statute, if it does not have before it all the required reports prior to making its decision under regulation 10 and section 324. This issue came before the Divisional Court in *S v. The Special Educational Needs Tribunal and the City of Westminster*[17] Latham J. stated that, so far as the appellate system before the Special Educational Needs Tribunal was concerned, the process of appeal operated on the premises that a statement is a valid statement which can be amended in accordance with the findings of the Tribunal. However, he stated on this issue:

> "I can see that there might be an argument in some circumstances that the failure to obtain a particular report was so fundamental that no decision could be reached as to the nature and extent of the child's special needs until it was obtained, and therefore no conclusion could be reached as to the way in which those needs were capable of being met. But that was not the situation in the present case."

Whether an assessment is at the end of the day lawful will depend on whether the authority has obtained reports in accordance with the regulations, and having made its decision, whether those reports address the fundamental issues. Clearly, if there is a failure to address a fundamental and known issue, Latham J. envisaged that a statement might be unlawful. That may be a matter for judicial review, not an appeal to the Tribunal. The Tribunal lacks power to order a particular report, but can order a statement to be amended.[18] The omission of an essential report may be a defect, which cannot be cured on appeal.

Decision not to make a statement

If the authority considers no statement is necessary and they do not propose to make a statement, they must give notice in writing to the child' s parents, and in such cases the child's parents may appeal against the decision.[19] Where an LEA has carried out an assessment it is obliged within two weeks of the conclusion of the assessment to serve a notice either that it has decided not to make a statement, or the proposed statement.[20] In such cases the Code of Practice provides that local education authorities should consider issuing a note in lieu of a statement.[21] In such a note the LEA should set out their reasons for their conclusions with supporting evidence from the statutory assessment of the child. All advice collected as part of a statutory assessment should be sent to the parents and, subject to their agreement, the child's school and to other professionals who gave the advice during the assessment process. It is the intention that this information can be used by those working with the child in the school to help the child and make provision. It is

[16] ss. 323 and 324 which deal with the statement of special educational needs.
[17] [1995] 1 W.L.R. 374.
[18] s. 326.
[19] ss. 325 (1) and (2).
[20] Reg. 14.
[21] Chap. 4, para. 4:18.

suggested by the Code[22] that a note in lieu should follow broadly the statutory form of a statement. Therefore the first part might describe the child's needs with supporting evidence. The second might set out the LEA's reasons for declining to make a statement and offer guidance as to special educational provision. The Code also provides for the LEAs to deal with non-educational provision.

Through the statutory appeal process, the Tribunal will certainly seek to examine the facts carefully. An LEA which fails to comply with the Code of Practice, and has no good explanation put on appeal, can expect difficulty.

Assessment under five

The second part of Chapter 2 'Code of Practice' considers the assessment of these young children.

[22] Chap. 4, para. 4:21.

Chapter 4
Statements of Special Educational Needs

Section 324 of the Education Act 1996 governs the making of a statement and its form and contents. It provides in subsection 1:

> "**324.**—(1) If, in the light of an assessment under section 323 of any child's educational needs and of any representations made by the child's parent in pursuance of Schedule 27, it is necessary for the local education authority to determine the special educational provision which any learning difficulty he may have calls for, the authority shall make and maintain a statement of his special educational needs."

The statement must in particular:

1. give details of the authority's assessment of the child's special educational needs;
2. specify the special educational provision to be made for the purpose of meeting those needs, and include particulars required by section 324(4).

A statement must also be in the prescribed form and contain such information as may be prescribed.[1] Part 3 of the Special Educational Needs Regulations[2] provides under regulation 13 that a statement will be in a form substantially corresponding to that set out in Part B of the Schedule of the regulations, shall contain information therein specified, and shall be dated and authenticated by the signature of a duly authorised officer of the authority concerned.

> PART B
>
> STATEMENT OF SPECIAL EDUCATIONAL NEEDS
>
> **PART 1: INTRODUCTION**
>
> 1. In accordance with section 324 of the Education Act 1996 ("the Act") and the Education (Special Educational Needs) Regulations 1994 ("the Regulations"), the following statement is made by [*here set out name of authority*]("the authority") in respect of the child whose name and other particulars are mentioned below.

[1] Education Act 1996, s. 324(2).
[2] S.I. 1994 No. 1047.

Child

Surname	Other names ....
Home address	....
....	Sex ....
....	Religion ....
....	Home language ....
Date of birth	

Child's parent or person responsible

Surname	Other names ....
Home address	....
....	Relationship to child ....
....	....
Telephone No.	

2. When assessing the child's special educational needs the authority took into consideration, in accordance with regulation 8 of the Regulations, the representations, evidence and advice set out in the Appendices to this statement.

PART 2: SPECIAL EDUCATIONAL NEEDS

[*Here set out the child's special educational needs, in terms of the child's learning difficulties which call for special educational provision, as assessed by the authority.*]

PART 3: SPECIAL EDUCATIONAL PROVISION

Objectives

[*Here specify the objectives which the special educational provision for the child should aim to meet.*]

Educational provision to meet needs and objectives

[*Here specify the special educational provision which the authority consider appropriate to meet the needs specified in Part 2 and to meet the objectives specified in this Part, and in particular specify—*

(a) *any appropriate facilities and equipment, staffing arrangements and curriculum,*
(b) *any appropriate modifications to the application of the National Curriculum,*
(c) *any appropriate exclusions from the application of the National Curriculum, in detail, and the provision which it is proposed to substitute for any such exclusions in order to maintain a balanced and broadly based curriculum; and*
(d) *where residential accommodation is appropriate, that fact*].

Monitoring

[*Here specify the arrangements to be made for—*

(a) *regularly monitoring progress in meeting the objectives specified in this Part,*
(b) *establishing targets in furtherance of those objectives,*
(c) *regularly monitoring the targets referred to in (b),*
(d) *regularly monitoring the appropriateness of any modifications to the application of the National Curriculum, and*
(e) *regularly monitoring the appropriateness of any provision substituted for exclusions from the application of the National Curriculum.*

Here also specify any special arrangements for reviewing this statement.]

PART 4: PLACEMENT

[*Here specify—*

(a) *the type of school which the authority consider appropriate for the child and the name of the school for which the parent has expressed a preference or, where the authority are required to specify the name of a school, the name of the school which they consider would be appropriate for the child and should be specified, or*
(b) *the provision for his education otherwise than at a school which the authority consider appropriate.]*

PART 5: NON-EDUCATIONAL NEEDS

[*Here specify the non-educational needs of the child for which the authority consider provision is appropriate if the child is to properly benefit from the special educational provision specified in Part 3.*]

PART 6: NON-EDUCATIONAL PROVISION

[*Here specify any non-educational provision which the authority propose to make available or which they are satisfied will be made available by a district health authority, a social services authority or some other body, including the arrangements for its provision. Also specify the objectives of the provision, and the arrangements for monitoring progress in meeting those objectives.*]

The local authority must arrange the provision specified in a statement under section 324 unless the child's parents have made suitable arrangements. The authority:

1. shall arrange that the special educational provision specified in the statement is made for the child; and
2. may arrange that any non-educational provision specified in the statement is made for him in such manner as they consider appropriate. If the name of a maintained, grant-maintained or grant-maintained special school is specified in the statement, the governing body of the school shall admit the child to the school.[3]

Once the LEA have decided that they are required to determine some of the special educational provision that should be made for the child because it is necessary, they must make a statement setting out all his special educational needs

[3] s. 324(5)(b).

as assessed. Once a need has been specified, the special educational provision for that need has to be specified: *R. v. The Secretary of State for Education, ex p. E.*[4] The LEA must make the statement in respect of the whole child, so that all the child's needs and learning difficulties are addressed.

Interpretation of the statement

In relation to Part 2 of the statement the Court of Appeal in *ex p. E* [5]approved the approach of Nolan J. namely that Part 2 of a statement was the equivalent to a medical diagnosis, and Part 3 of the statement, the special educational provision, was the equivalent of a medical prescription. The prescription has to match the needs diagnosed, and provision has to match each and every need.

The 1996 Act contains no change to that approach. However, Dr Neville Harris in his book *Law of Schools* suggests that in *R. v. Salford Education Authority, ex p. L,*[6] the Court of Appeal sought to limit the extent of or detract from the judgment of the Court of Appeal in *ex p. E* (above). This is an incorrect reading of the case of *ex p. L*, because that case was about whether or not the local appeal committee's reasons were unlawful, or whether the decision of the local appeal committee was unreasonable. The Court of Appeal agreed with the judge below that the matter of the form and contents of the statement were for the Secretary of State on appeal under section 8 of the 1981 Act. The Tribunal has now replaced this role of the Secretary of State. However, any remarks of the Court of Appeal in the case of *ex p. L* are clearly dicta, whereas the *ratio* of *ex p. E* included Nolan J.'s medical comparison. The Code of Practice itself in any event follows the Court of Appeal in *ex. p. E.*[7] Schiemann J. in *R. v. Cumbria County Council, exp. P*[8] followed this approach as does the Tribunal.[9]

Duty of professionals giving advice

This matter was extensively argued in the educational negligence cases. In the Court of Appeal these three cases are reported as *E (a minor) v. Dorset County Council.*[10] In dealing with the duties of professionals, particularly psychologists, and also those giving medical advice under the regulations as well as qualified teachers, Evans L.J.[11] analysed the duty of those professionals normally employed by local authorities who give such advice. When these persons are asked for their advice they owe to the authority a duty to exercise a reasonable degree of professional skill and care. Likewise, when the advice is negligent the child may suffer actionable damage. There is no reason why damages can not be recovered. Evans L.J. went on to say: "in the present case, on the other hand, the doctor or

---

[4] [1992] 1 F.L.R. 377.
[5] See n. 4 above.
[6] [1994] E.L.R. 16.
[7] Code of Practice, para 4:28.
[8] [1996] E.L.R. 337.
[9] See Digest of Tribunals decisions, [1996] F.L.R. 266.
[10] [1994] W.L.R. 853.
[11] See at p. 883.

specialist is engaged not merely to report but to advise in the best interest of the child. The advice is a form of treatment." The cases were appealed to the House of Lords together with two Children Act cases.

The cases are reported as *X (minors) (Appellant) v. Bedfordshire County Council (Respondents) and Others.*[12] The House of Lords agreed with the Court of Appeal on the issue of negligence, the leading judgment being given by Lord Browne-Wilkinson V.-C. Dorset and Hampshire conducted a considerable attack on the medical approach to statements of special educational needs, both in relation to the judgment in the Court of Appeal below and the judgment of the Court of Appeal in the earlier case *R. v. The Secretary of State for Education and Science, ex p. E.* However, in applying the test of negligence and accepting the approach of the Court of Appeal below, the House of Lords clearly rejected the attack on the medical approach to statements. It held that psychologists and teachers were under a duty of care, and that such advice was a form of treatment. Lord Browne-Wilkinson V.-C. stated that "educational psychologists and other members of the staff of the defendant authority owed a duty to use reasonable professional skill and care in the assessment and determination of the Plaintiff's educational needs." The Court of Appeal's approach to statements in *R. v. The Secretary of State for Education and Science, ex p. E*[13] has therefore been affirmed by another Court of Appeal and by the House of Lords. It is interesting to note that the minor, E, in both cases was the same child.

Specification of appropriate provision

Once a statement is made in final form, the authority, unless the child's parents have made suitable arrangements, shall arrange the special educational provision specified when the statement is made for the child. Clearly this means it shall arrange this as soon as is reasonably practical. If authority is needed for this, the judgment of Balcombe L.J. in *ex p. E* provides it. However, not only must the authority specify all the provision required to meet the needs, it must also be satisfied that the provision is actually available to meet the child's needs. In *R. v. The Secretary of State, ex p. W,*[14] Harrison J. quashed a decision of the Secretary of State for Education under section 8 of the 1981 Act, because the Secretary of State had not satisfied himself that the provision was actually available in the school specified in the statement to meet the child's needs. The provision must be actual and not theoretical.

The provision must be appropriate provision in the sense that it has to be reasonably effective to meet the child's needs. While a local education authority is under no obligation to provide a Utopian system or to educate a child to his or her maximum potential (*per* Slade L.J. in *R. v. Surrey Education Committee, ex p. H*[15] the provision must be effective. In *South Glamorgan v. Long,*[16] Carnwarth J. points out that local education authorities, and the Tribunal had a discretion to provide above the minimum required by statute. Further, there is a discretion to

[12] [1995] 3 W.L.R. 152.
[13] [1992] F.L.R. 377.
[14] Unreported, May 29, 1994.
[15] (1995) 83 L.G.R. 219.
[16] Unreported, December 1995.

provide non-educational provision, and if the child will not benefit from the provision made by the local education authority in the statement without an element of non-educational provision it is difficult to see how an authority can reasonably exercise its discretion by refusing to make such provision. Additionally, such a refusal would be contrary to the intention of the statute.[17]

The procedure for making a statement

On completion of an assessment, the authority by regulation 14(1)(b) is required to serve a copy of the proposed statement on the child's parents together with a written notice under paragraph 2 of Schedule 27 of the Act. The written notice required under paragraph 2(b) explains the arrangements under paragraphs 3 and 4 of Schedule 27. It must serve details of prescribed information—see regulations 12 and 13 of the Special Educational Needs Regulations. The prescribed information particularly addresses the parental rights to express a preference for a school under Schedule 27. A copy of the proposed statement is not required to specify matters under section 324(4), which means a school or institution. This is deliberately the policy of statute in order that the parents may genuinely choose a school. By Schedule 27 paragraphs 3 and 4, the parents have the right to express a preference for a choice of school, and secondly, the right to make representations about the proposed statement. These paragraphs continue and expand the parental rights first provided for in Section 7 of the 1981 Act which allows the parents to require meetings in relation to the contents of the statement, and if necessary with the actual person who gave advice or somebody appointed in his or her stead.

Paragraph 3 of Schedule 27 provides for the authority to make arrangements to enable the parents to express a preference as to a maintained or grant-maintained school, whether a special school or not, and to give reasons for the preference. The preference must be expressed within 15 days. Where a preference is expressed for such a school, the authority shall specify the name of that school unless:

1. the school is unsuitable to the child's age, ability or aptitude or its educational needs; or
2. the attendance of the child at the school would be incompatible with the provision of efficient education for the children with whom it would be educated or the efficient use of resources.

By paragraph 3(4) the local education authority, before specifying the name of any maintained or grant–maintained or grant–maintained special school in a statement, must consult the governing body of the school, and if the school is maintained by another local education authority, consult that authority.

Once the school is specified on this statement the governing body must admit the child. Unless the school is full it is difficult to see, other than in exceptional cases, an example of which is where a child may previously have been excluded, that the school can raise any objections other than those raised in paragraph 3 of Schedule 27.

[17] *Padfield v. Minister of Agriculture* [1965] A.C. 977.

In case no. 95/6 Tribunal Digest of Decisions[18] where no issue was raised on efficient use of resources and the child might have developed problems if she did not go to a grant–maintained school the Tribunal nominated that school. So far as the reasons given by statute which allow a local authority to refuse to name a school, namely that the school is unsuitable for the child or for his special needs, or the child's education will be so disrupted as to be incompatible with provision of efficient education for other children in the school, these will be matters of fact. However, the issue of efficient use of resources is likely to be of relevance. Clearly, the word "resources" includes the physical resources of the school, its teaching expertise, as well as financial considerations. This approach has been adopted by the Tribunal, in practice, in case 95/6. The Tribunal looked at the schools as a suitable provision before concluding that the LEA was not correct on a resource basis.[19]

Representations

The right to make representations is continued from the 1981 Act in Schedule 27, paragraph 4. The parent on whom a copy of the proposed statement has been served may:

1. make representations or further representations to the local authority about the contents of the statement; or
2. require the authority to arrange a meeting between him or officer of the authority at which the statement can be discussed.

When the meeting is arranged and the parent disagrees with any part of the assessment in question, he or she may require the authority to arrange a meeting or meetings such as the authority consider will enable the parent to discuss the relevant advice from an appropriate person. An appropriate person means the person who gave the advice, or another person who in the opinion of the authority is an appropriate person to discuss it with the parents. There are 15 days to make representations or to request a meeting. If further meetings are requested under paragraph 3(2), a further period of 15 days begins after the date fixed for the meeting. The importance of these meetings cannot be ignored. Under the 1981 Education Act, the statutory process of meetings resolved a number of cases. It is not clear how the increased rights of appeal are affecting these rights to make representations, but it would be much to be regretted if parents and local authorities regarded these meetings as irrelevant.

Making a statement

The authority does not make a statement until it has considered the representations, if any are made, and the period allowed for in paragraph 4 of Schedule 27 for the making of representations or requiring meetings has expired. The statement may be in the form originally proposed, save as to the issue of school,

---

18 [1996] E.L.R. 119.
19 *ibid*, p. 117.

or in a modified form in the light of the representations.[20] Clearly, therefore where the parent does not make any representations or make any choice of school, the local authority will make a statement and nominate the school or institution it considers appropriate.

Choice of school

Where parents do not express a preference for a school which is a maintained or grant–maintained school, whether a special school or not, the duty under Section 316 to secure a mainstream education does not apply. If they apply for a special school then it must be nominated, subject to the statutory criteria.

If the parents make representations in favour of a non-maintained school, the Code of Practice suggests that an officer of the LEA should discuss with them why they believe that school should be named.[21] By section 348, there is power for the local education authority to pay the fees including board and lodging, if the child is sent to a non-maintained school if that school is named in the statement or if the local authority considers it to be in the child's interests that the provision be made for him at a school that is not a maintained school. Clearly, in cases where children cannot be assisted in the state sector or within the local area, these powers apply.

If the authority as a result of a parental preference as expressed or as a result of its own views, names a maintained, grant-maintained or grant-maintained special school, the governing body of the school must admit the child to the school.[22] The statement should either specify the special school or institution appropriate for the child, or if an independent school is required, whether in the United Kingdom or elsewhere, it should be specified.[23] If the authority is satisfied that special educational provision should be provided otherwise than in a school, having consulted the child's parents, it is empowered under section 319 so that provision shall be nominated in the statement.

The parents have the right of appeal against the contents of the statement given to them by section 326 of the Act. This section will be considered in more detail in the chapter on appeals. By section 328, the Act provides for reviews of statements of educational needs.

Annual reviews, amending statement and ceasing to maintain statements

Reviews of statements, amendment of statements and the decision to cease to maintain a statement are topics which ought to be considered together. In practice, they will be interlinked. The 1993 Act substantially changes the provisions dealing with reviews, and decisions to cease to maintain statements. Only in relation to amendments does the law remain effectively the same, although it is to be expected

[20] Sched. 27, para. 5(2).
[21] Para. 4:48.
[22] s. 324(5)(b).
[23] s. 324(5)(b).

that the changes in the provisions governing reviews will result in more frequent consideration of amendments.

The annual review

The local education authority must review a statement within 12 months of making a statement or of the previous review; and also on the making of the assessment under section 323 for a child who already has a statement (section 328(5)). Reviews of statements are governed by regulations 15, 16 and 17 of the Education (Special Educational Needs) Regulations 1994.[24] Regulation 15 deals with reviews of statements where the child is not yet aged 14 and attends school.

Regulation 16 deals with reviews of statements where a child aged 14 attends school. Regulation 17 deals with the other cases of children who do not attend school.

The introduction of detailed procedures which are mandatory, for the purposes of annual reviews, is a considerable reform. Also new is the division of a review into three categories.

LEAs have the power to review a statement at any time during the year. The Code of Practice recommends that LEAs should aim to secure the agreement of the school and the child's parents before exercising the power of review, and then conduct the review at a time that is appropriate for all parties. However, they are under a mandatory duty to review all statements on an annual basis.

The Code of Practice suggests that the timing of annual reviews should reflect the circumstances of the child and the action which may flow from the review. For example, it is appropriate to conduct an annual review before a child moves to secondary school and not afterwards. The timing of the review should also reflect the circumstances and organisation of the school.

Obviously, if a school is attempting to conduct annual reviews on all statemented children at the same time, problems will undoubtedly follow.

The purpose of an annual review

The purpose of an annual review is to check on the effective working of the statement. The authority is required by regulations 15(2) (in the case of children not aged 14), 16(2) (in the case of school children aged 14) and 17(2) (where a child does not attend school) to obtain a written report from the head teacher of the child's school where the child is at school, and from the authority itself where the child does not attend school. It must serve a copy of the report (which must be supplied within two months of the date given) to the child's parents.

Advice required

The head teacher in the case of children at school is required to obtain advice from:

1. the child's parents;

[24] S.I. 1994 No. 1047.

2. any person whose advice the authority considers appropriate for the purpose of arriving at a satisfactory report and whom it specifies in the notice, and any person whose advice the head teacher considers appropriate for the purpose of arriving at a satisfactory report (Regulations 15(3) and 16(3)). In the case of children not at school, the authority is required to seek advice on matters referred to in Regulation 15(4)(e), namely from any person whom the authority considers appropriate (in the case of children who have attained the age of 14 who are not at school), from the child's parent or from any other person considered appropriate.

The advice required shall be written advice as to:

1. the child's progress for meeting the objectives specified in the statement;
2. the child's progress towards attaining any targets established in furtherance of the objectives specified in the statement;
3. where the school is not established in a hospital and is a maintained school, grant–maintained or grant–maintained special school, the application of the provisions of the National Curriculum to the child;
4. where the school is not established in a hospital and is a maintained school, grant–maintained or grant–maintained special school, the application of any provision substituted for the National Curriculum in order to maintain a broadly balanced curriculum;
5. where appropriate, and in any case where a transition plan exists, any matters which are appropriate subjects of such a plan;
6. whether the statement is considered to be appropriate;
7. whether the authority should cease to maintain the statement.

The provisions of Regulation 15(4) apply in the same manner to children aged 14. Regulation 17(2) with the appropriate modifications, applies to those who do not attend school.

Requirements of the annual review

The purpose of the annual review is to focus on what the child has achieved, as well as any difficulties which need to be resolved. The first annual review after the child's fourteenth birthday is particularly significant in preparing for his or her transition to the further education sector and adult life. The requirements of these annual reviews are therefore directed to this future transition.

In essence, therefore, the object of an annual review is to see whether the statement is working effectively, and if it is not, what should be done and whether the statement should be changed and provision either deleted, altered or amended. In some cases it is to consider whether there is a reason to cease to maintain a statement.

Attendance to discuss review

The Regulations provide new and important rights for parents in relation to the annual review. The head teacher is required to invite the following persons to attend a meeting in relation to the annual review before the report made by the head teacher is submitted:

1. the representative of the authority specified in the notice;
2. the child's parents;
3. a member or members of the staff of the school who teach the child or who are otherwise responsible for the provision of education of the child whose attendance the head teacher considers appropriate;
4. any other person whose attendance the head teacher considers appropriate; and
5. any person whose attendance the authority considers appropriate and who are specified in the notice (see Regulation 15(5)).

These provisions are slightly amended in the case of young persons aged 14 or over, where the authority[25] shall invite the following persons to attend:

1. the child's parents;
2. a member or members of the staff of the school who teach the child, who are otherwise responsible for the provision of education for the child, whose attendance the head teacher considers appropriate and whom he has asked the authority to invite;
3. the representative of the social services authority;
4. a representative or person providing career services by section 45 of the Trade Union and Employment Rights Acts 1993;
5. any person whose attendance the head teacher considers appropriate and whom he has asked the authority to invite; and
6. any person whose attendance the authority considers appropriate.

Regulation 17, for young persons not at school, provides for the attendance of the child's parents where a young person is over 14, a representative of the social services authority, together with a careers services advisor under section 45 of the Trade Union and Employment Rights Act 1993, and any other person whose attendance the authority considers appropriate.

The reason for the difference in the regulations is the fact that the future for those who are to go into further education or employment training needs to be considered in the case of pupils with special needs who are about to leave school. The first important decision is whether they need to remain in school until they reach the age of 19, or whether they should leave at 16. If they need to leave at 16 because the local education authority has not appropriate provision, then the agreements with the Further and Higher Education Funding Council apply, and must be explored in detail.

In the cases of children with more severe problems, and young adults, the differences in Regulation 17 reflect the individual circumstances of children and

[25] By Reg. 16(3).

young adults who are not at school. Obviously, detailed planning for their future is needed, but the Regulations reflect the much more flexible approach that is needed in these cases.

It is obviously important that parents attend such meetings. If there are disagreements with the likely view of the school, parents should attend such meetings having, if possible, obtained independent professional advice such as psychologists' reports, medical reports, or other relevant reports and advice on the child or young person. Of course if agreement can be reached in advance and enquiries made by the parents, this would be the most appropriate course.

In practice, however, the following issues are most likely to concern parents (these are examples only and do not represent an exhaustive list of possibilities).

1. Should the statement be amended because there is a need for more or less help, or simply different help, to deal with problems that have emerged as a result of an increase in age of the child and different demands of the curriculum?
2. Is the authority planning adequately for further education? Has it looked properly at the local Further and Higher Education Funding Council's provision in the area?
3. Is there good reason to cease to maintain the statement?

Annual review for children at school

The Code of Practice gives guidance on this issue in Chapter 6, particularly at paragraph 6:16(2), (6) to (9). As set out above, the LEA must convene the meeting, giving the head teacher at least two months' notice of the date on which the report must be submitted, and inform the head teacher who should contribute to the review.

In relation to children with special needs, if there are medical or social problems, the LEA ought to consider whether the representatives of the health services or social services or both should attend the meeting. Where under the Regulations the head teacher requests information from district health authorities and social services authorities, they are required by section 322(1) of the Education Act 1996 to respond to the head teacher's request unless the exceptions apply.

Parental attendance at annual review

When the evidence is received, comments on the evidence, together with an account of the review meeting, form the basis of the review report. Parental attendance at such meetings is advisable. These meetings can produce surprises. The Code of Practice provides in Chapter 6 paragraph 6:6(15) that, where possible, pupils should be actively involved in the report process and, if appropriate, contribute to the review meeting. They should be encouraged to give their views of their progress during the previous year, discuss difficulties and share their hopes and aspirations.

The Code of Practice recognises the right of parents to bring a friend, adviser or relative or their named person (the person the LEA identifies as an independent person) or somebody from a voluntary organisation or parent partnership scheme to the meeting.

The Code of Practice requires the LEA and the school to make every effort to inform parents of their rights and responsibilities and to encourage them to attend the meeting.[26]

Language

Where the child or family does not have English (or Welsh) as a first language, the timescale and planning for the annual review should take into account the following requirements:

1. Translation of the relevant documents into the family's mother tongue.
2. Ensuring that interpreters are available to the child and family both in the preparatory stages to the review meeting and the review meeting itself.
3. Ensuring that professionals from the child's community have similar interpretations and translational facilities in order that they may contribute as fully as possible to the review process. Indeed, where possible, a bilingual support teacher and/or teacher with English (or Welsh) as a second language is available to the child and family.

The same principles apply where the child or their family have communication problems because of physical impairment. Each issue should be approached on the basis of the disability, and the appropriate facilities made available.

Care orders

Where a child with a statement is subject to a care order, the local authority designated by the order has parental responsibility for that child. This obviously creates difficulties as to the extent of contributions to be made by the child's parents, the child's carers, residential social workers or foster parents. This should be determined by the authority in consultation with the local social services department. Such matters only apply where there is a care order.

Where care orders or education supervision orders are in force, or the local authority looks after the child, the local authority social services departments should include information on the arrangements for the education of a child within its care.

The meeting

The review meeting is normally expected, under the Code of Practice, to take place in the child's school and to be chaired by the head teacher or the teacher who has responsibility for the school-based elements and to whom the review has been

[26] Chap. 6 para. 6:17.

delegated. Chapter 6 of the Code, paragaph 6:22, suggests some 10 questions which should be asked at the meeting. These are sensible questions and are good guidance.

Children otherwise than at school (regulation 17)

Where children are educated otherwise than at school (as discussed above) the regulations are effectively the same and are adapted to deal with that situation. The venue is more likely to be the LEA's offices, or a hospital, and will normally be chaired by a representative of the local education authority itself. In cases where there are severe medical and associated problems, the views from health services and social services will obviously be crucial. Equally, where children have been excluded from school it is important that the review takes place to produce a considered detailed plan for the child's future.

The result of the annual review

The annual review should record satisfactory progress, or that the statement should be given a further chance to work. If this is the case, obviously no changes in the statement are necessary. If, however, the annual review shows that the child is not making adequate progress or has developed further problems or, alternatively, has made progress, the following matters are some of those that should be considered:

1. Have significant new needs emerged or been discovered which are not recorded on the statement?
2. Have the child's needs changed so that some of the statement is inaccurate? Are the changes due to an improvement in the child, or a change in needs, in any event?
3. Should the provision be amended to meet the child's changes in needs?
4. Should the child change schools, either at the normal point of transfer (i.e. junior to primary), or can the child's needs be more appropriately met in a different school; for example, with a more disabled child, should they now be integrated, or should a programme of reintegration or integration be commenced?

If the basic model used by the Court of Appeal in *R. v. The Secretary of State for Education and Science, ex p. E*[27] is followed, namely at the annual review, one should look at the needs on the statement, then see if they are correctly expressed. If the provision is appropriate, few problems will be encountered.

Finally, the meeting may record that a statement is no longer necessary.

[27] [1992] F.L.R. 377.

Amending the statement

Proposals to amend the statement would normally come from the annual review process. If the LEA proposes to amend a statement, whether to change the name of the school or make any other amendment, they must write to the child's parents informing them of the proposal and of their right to make representations within 15 days of the receipt of the proposal. They should always explain the reason for the proposal and ensure the parents have copies of any evidence which prompted the proposal.[28]

The LEA must consider the representations made by the parents before deciding whether and how to amend. If they conclude that an amendment should be made, they must make the amendment within eight weeks of sending the letter of proposal to the parents. They must also write to the parents informing them of the decision to amend and the reasons for it, enclosing a copy of the amended statement and any relevant advice. Equally, they must inform the parents of the right of appeal. If they decide not to amend, they should write to the parents explaining why, again within eight weeks of the letter setting out the original proposal.[29]

What is an amendment?

The provisions relating to amendments of statements of special educational needs remain effectively unchanged (with some alterations as to the time limits) from the 1981 Act. There has been no Court decision on what constitutes an amendment.

In practice, this issue is likely to become more important, since there is now a new right of appeal. However, the key factor is likely to be evidence, because if the local authority makes an amendment which is not justified or which did not follow from a proper reassessment of the child's needs, a parent will normally be able to obtain proper professional evidence to show that the amendment has been made in an unwarranted and unprofessional manner, without proper professional advice, and that the child has a different need. An amendment is any change which does not require a full reassessment. Such a definition is likely to be theoretical, as an amendment which required a reassessment is likely to result in a successful parent appeal.

Issues involving a change of school

The Code of Practice devotes some consideration to this point at paragraphs 6:30 to 6:33 . This is due to the existence of new appeal rights, and rights given to parents who request the LEA to name a school or substitute the name of a maintained school or special school or grant–maintained, or grant–maintained special school for the name of the school in Part 4 of the statement.

It is, however, important that an annual review gives detailed and proper thought, as well as careful advance planning, to the transition either into a special

[28] Paras. 9 and 10 of Sched. 27 to the Education Act 1996.
[29] Para. 10(5) of Sched. 27.

school, if that is what is needed, or to integration into an ordinary school, or to transfer from primary to secondary school. Arrangements for a child's placement should be finalised in advance, and the Code of Practice recommends that this should be by the beginning of the child's last term before transfer. It is important for placements to be finalised as early as possible in order for any advance arrangements to be made, and to ensure that parents feel confident and secure about the arrangements in question. It is in the child's interest to plan such transitions properly. Cases may arise when a provision breaks down and urgent action has to be taken.

Annual reviews from 14 to 19

Some pupils with statements of special needs remain at school after the age of 16, some do not. The local education authority remains responsible for pupils until they are 19.[30] Others with statements will, however, leave school at 16 and move, for example, to a college within the further education sector or, in cases of more severely disabled pupils, to social services provision. Whatever the intended destination of the young person, the annual review has great significance as he or she approaches the age of 16.

In practical terms the significance of the annual review is also increased due to the changes brought in by the Further and Higher Education Act 1992. If a young person leaves school and goes into the further education sector, a statement will automatically lapse as the young person no longer falls within the definition of a child with special needs for whom the local education authority is responsible under section 312.

The Further and Higher Education Funding Council has duties under section 4 of the 1992 Act to young persons with special needs. In appropriate cases, this will include a placement at a specialist educational establishment, which may or may not include a school outside that sector.

However, it is the primary responsibility of the local education authority, when a young person has a statement, to continue that statement until the age of 19, if they require a school education. They cannot divest themselves of their responsibility for a young person simply because they have, for example, placed him at a school outside the local educational system, and that school ends at 16, if he requires attendance at a further school with an A-level facility: *R. v. Dorset C.C. and others, ex p. Goddard.*[31]

The LEA may have concentrated its resources in sixth form colleges not sixth form schools. It is therefore quite possible that, where a child has to transfer school at 16, or to transfer to the local further education college. Considerable work may be necessary to establish the existence of adequate provision and an adequate opportunity to succeed in further education. Regulation 15(4) requires such issues to be considered, but in addition, seeks to plan for the future.

[30] s. 312(5).
[31] [1995] E.L.R. 109.

Disabled persons

Under section 5 of the Disabled Persons (Consultation, Services and Representation) Act 1986 (as amended), the LEA must seek a determination as to whether a young person is a disabled person under the Act and whether they require services from the local authority when leaving school.

For this reason, the LEA must also ensure that other providers, such as social services, are aware of the annual review and that they attend the review so that any parallel assessments under the Disabled Persons (Consultation, Services and Representation) Act 1986, the NHS and Community Care Act 1990 or the Chronically Sick and Disabled Persons Act 1970 can be considered. Where children have been in the care of the local authority or accommodated by the local authority, Children Act duties continue beyond the age of 18, and Children Act assessments are equally appropriate. Duties under the NHS Community Care Act 1990, and the Chronically Sick and Disabled Persons Act 1970 commence at 18 years old.

The review meeting

The LEA must invite the careers service to be represented at the review meeting, to enable all options for further education, careers and occupational training to be given serious consideration. The careers service will also be able to identify any specific targets which should be set as part of the annual review, and ensure that independence, training, personal and social skills and other aspects of the wider curriculum are fully addressed during the young person's last years at school.

The LEA should then review the report and the transition plan after the meeting and circulate it to the young person's parents, head teachers, those from whom advice was sought, or those attending the meeting, and any others that the LEA consider appropriate. In particular, the LEA should consider passing the review report and transition plan to the Further Education Funding Council, particularly in cases where a decision needs to be taken about specialist college provision outside the further education sector.

The Code of Practice[32] lists some 16 questions to be considered at the meeting. The essential object of the review is to produce a proper transition plan at the appropriate time for the young person. The appropriate time to move from school will obviously depend on the person, the disability or problem and its nature.

The transition plan should be a detailed plan based on all the available evidence, including the previous annual review, and should deal with the strengths and weaknesses of the young person.

Practitioners should be familiar with the following legislation, which is important in the case of all young persons with special needs:

- the Chronically Sick and Disabled Persons Act 1970;
- the Employment and Training Act 1973, as amended by the Trade Union Reform and Employment Rights Act 1993;

[32] Chap. 6, para. 6:46.

- the Disabled Persons (Consultation, Services and Representation) Act 1986;
- the Children Act 1989;
- the National Health Service and Community Care Act 1990;
- the Further and Higher Education Act 1992.

Under the Children Act 1989 and the NHS and Community Care Act 1990, social services departments are required to arrange a multidisciplinary assessment and to provide care plans for children and adults with significant disabilities. These may include the provision of further educational facilities. These reviews are therefore extremely important.

The Further and Higher Education Funding Council has published a yearly circular, currently 95/07, on its responsibility in these issues, and has agreed with local authorities an assessment procedure.

The circular approves the terms of the agreement between the LEAs and the FEFC, in that in practice the LEA will conduct assessments on behalf of the FEFC.

It is important that the young person be involved in the assessment and review. Paragraphs 6:59 and 6:60 of the Code of Practice deal with a number of issues personal to the young person themselves which should be considered. What is important is that the review produces a proper detailed plan for the future which is practical, personally tailored, and realistic.

The conclusion of all reviews

Following the conclusion of a review meeting, the head teacher submits his report to:

1. the child's parents;
2. the persons from whom advice was sought;
3. the persons who are invited to attend the meeting;
4. any other person whom the authority considers appropriate;
5. any other person whom the head teacher considers appropriate (Regulation 15). For those over 16 and not at school, the provisions in the Regulations are effectively the same, but adapted to particular circumstances—see Regulations 16(8) and 17(8) . The report must be completed within a week.

On receipt of the report, the authority is required to review the statement in the light of the report.[33] It is at this point that the decision about the young person's future is made. Following the making of a decision the authority is required, within one week, to serve copies of recommendations and any transition plan or the result of the review to the persons who attended the meeting and to whom the head teacher has submitted his report.

[33] Regs. 15(12), 16(9) and 17(9).

Ceasing to maintain a statement

A decision to cease to maintain a statement can come about as a result of a reassessment, but this is highly unlikely to happen, because the authority must consider the statement necessary in order to conduct a reassessment. Therefore it is likely that, for practical purposes, it will result from a review.

As a matter of law, a statement remains in force until an LEA ceases to maintain it, or the child is no longer the responsibility of the LEA,[34] where the child leaves school or goes into further education. Alternatively, if the child moves to another area and will become the responsibility of another authority and will not lapse.

The LEA may cease to maintain a statement only if it believes that it is no longer necessary to maintain it. The Code of Practice points out that there should be no assumption that, once the LEA has made a statement, it should maintain the statement until it is no longer responsible for the young person.[35] Statements should only be maintained where necessary; section 324(1) of the Education Act 1996 makes this clear. However, the Code of Practice sensibly points out that a decision to cease to maintain a statement should be made only after careful consideration by the LEA of all the circumstances of the case and after close consultation with the parents. The Code of Practice directs the LEA to consider the results of recent annual reviews and to consider whether the objectives of the statement have been achieved, and whether the child's needs can be met in future without the need for continuing LEA oversight.

The Code goes on to say that the LEA should always therefore consider, notwithstanding the achievement of some, or even all, of the objectives in the statement, whether the child's progress will be impeded or reversed if the special educational provision specified in the statement or in a modified form still required in the statement was not made. If so, a statement will still be "really needed".

In general, the Code of Practice provides very sensible guidance on this issue. Statements are not made unless children have a problem which justifies a statement. Severe and complex learning difficulties are not normally instantly cured. It is true that different considerations will apply to some emotional and behaviourial problems, but if they are not severe enough to merit a statement, they may well continue to justify the oversight of the LEA, at the very least.

For most children who are the subject of a statement, there is an inherent condition which is at the root of statement and the provision. That condition can, or course, be alleviated or minimised, but in few cases will it be cured. A dyslexic child cannot be cured, for example, although teaching and experience can teach the child to avoid the problem, and other skills are used in order to maximise potential. The fact, therefore, that a child achieves and makes progress does not mean that in the absence of provision of the type provided in a statement a child will progress. Indeed, in many cases, the child's condition remains and there is a requirement for support in order to continue progress. In the absence of that support, progress will often not be made, and regression will take place.

The right of appeal granted when such a decision is made, which will be considered in the later chapter on appeals, is an important reform. If an LEA decide

---

[34] Under s. 312.
[35] See para. 6:37.

to cease to maintain a statement, the statute does not preserve the statement pending appeal.[36] However, if the decision is in breach of statutory duty or unreasonable, a judicial review remains available pending the outcome of statutory appeal.

[36] *R. v. Oxfordshire C.C., exp. Roast*, unreported, CO/1995/95, September 1995.

Chapter 5
Tribunal Practice and Procedure

The right of appeal

The right of appeal to an independent Tribunal was one of the principal changes introduced by Part III of the Education Act 1993, and was eagerly awaited. This Chapter deals with the basic rules of procedure and with issues and concerns arising out of the Special Educational Needs Tribunal practice, which at the time of writing has been up and running since September 1994.

The appeals system under section 8 of the Education Act 1981 was twofold, consisting first of an appeal to a local appeal committee, set up and administered by the LEA, which had the power to make recommendations, but not orders, to the LEA and thereafter a further right of appeal to the Secretary of State. This was generally considered to be at best lengthy and cumbersome, and at worst, an unfair system. The ethos behind the SEN Tribunal was a desire to create a system which would be:

> "quick, simple, impartial and independent; a system in which informality is the key word and which at the same time gives parents complete confidence that their children's needs would be properly met and fully considered".[1]

The jurisdiction of the Special Educational Needs Tribunal is set out in sections 326 and 329 of the Education Act 1996 and Schedule 27 and encompasses LEA decisions:

- not to undertake an assessment pursuant to section 323 E.A. 1996, of a child's special educational needs;
- not to make a statement of special educational needs, under section 324 E.A. 1996;
- in relation to the contents of a statement of special educational needs and against amended statements;
- which include failure to name a school/the school named in part iv of the statement;
- to cease to maintain statements, (para. 11 of Schedule 27).

[1] *Hansard*, H.L. Vol. 543, col. 567 *per* Baroness Blatch.

A right of appeal arises solely in relation to the above issues. Other common areas of concern which are not subject to an appeal to the Tribunal, but are capable of judicial review or complaint to the Secretary of State include:

- delay in undertaking an assessment, failure to comply with the statutory time limits set out in the Education (Special Educational Needs) Regulations 1995[2];
- arrangements for delivering the specified provision made by the LEA, or failure to deliver the specified provision;
- non-educational needs and provision which are not within the jurisdiction of the SENT, unless it is contended that the need for *e.g.* occupational therapy or physiotherapy is an educational need. Speech therapy will almost always be considered an educational need. The ultimate responsibility for provision will lie with the LEA.[3]

In relation to delay and failure to make the provision specified in the statement, judicial review is likely to continue to be the appropriate remedy.

The Special Educational Needs Tribunal Regulations 1995[4] set out the Tribunal rules of procedure. These regulations are contained in appendix 3 of this volume, and are divided into five parts. The first part includes interpretations[5] and composition of the panel and the Tribunal.[6] Lay members must have knowledge and experience of children with special educational needs, or local government.

Lodging an appeal

The parents bring the appeal, which must be received by the Tribunal no later than the first working day after the expiry of two months from the date upon which the parents were notified by the LEA that they had a right of appeal.[7] The appeal must be made by way of a notice which states the name and address of the parent making the appeal, the name of the child, the fact that the notice is a notice of appeal, the name of the respondent LEA, the date upon which the parents were notified of the disputed decision, and the grounds of appeal, (Regulation 7(1)(a)). Regulation 7 (1)(b) specifies that the notice must be accompanied by a copy of the disputed decision and, where appropriate, a copy of the child's statement of special educational needs. At this stage the parents may inform the Tribunal of the name of any representative to whom the correspondence is to be addressed. The notice of appeal is to be signed by the parents and it is important to note that the parents bring the appeal themselves—not on behalf of the child as next friend. This has important repercussions, which are set out in Chapter 6, for parents seeking to challenge SENT decisions.

---

2 S.I. 1995 No. 3113.

3 See *R.v. Lacashire County Council, ex p. CN* [1989] 2 F.L.R. 279 and para. 4:35 of the Code of Practice.

4 S.I. 1995 No. 3113.

5 Reg. 2.

6 Regs. 3 and 5.

7 Reg. 7(3).

Time can be extended in "exceptional circumstances".[8] The regulations are worded in a similar fashion to the Industrial Tribunal Regulations. Currently we are aware of refusals to lodge notices of appeal, due to, for example, failure to sign a notice or to attach all the previous documents. It is important to note the SENT are applying the Regulations strictly. At the time of writing leave to seek a judicial review of the President's refusal to file a notice of appeal out of time, has been given by Sedley J. This will result in consideration of what constitutes 'exceptional circumstances'. In addition leave has been obtained in a number of cases which the SENT have settled.

As considered below, there are considerable restrictions upon amending grounds of appeal once lodged and, without taking a scatter-gun approach, it has been found to be helpful to identify grounds as fully and clearly as possible at an early stage. Of course it is recognised that many parents will lodge an appeal themselves and only seek legal advice at a later stage, and consideration should be given to lodging supplementary grounds of appeal or to expanding grounds of appeal in a Response to the LEA's reply. The latter course of action is likely to be more straightforward.

In addition, whilst only a copy of the statement of special educational needs and notification of the decision are mandatory, consideration should be given to attaching to the notice of appeal :

–any draft statement or earlier statements, as well as relevant correspondence,
–expert reports which do not form part of the appendices to the statement.

Tribunal's jurisdiction

Upon receiving any notice of appeal the Tribunal is required to consider whether it has jurisdiction to deal with the matter.[9] If the Secretary to the Tribunal is of the opinion that the appeal is outside the Tribunal's jurisdiction, the parent is notified of that fact and the appeal will not be registered unless the parent notifies the Tribunal Secretary that he/she wishes to proceed with the appeal. Aside from the examples given above an example of where the Tribunal would not have jurisdiction would be where a final statement had been issued prior to September 1, 1994.[10]

Having received an appeal, the Secretary of the Tribunal acknowledges its receipt and notifies the parents of the SENT address and the fact that advice can be obtained from the SENT office.[11] The Tribunal then sends to the LEA a copy of the Notice of Appeal and attached papers, notification of the SENT address and a notice setting out time limits within which the LEA must reply and the consequences of failing to do so.[12]

---

[8] Reg. 41.
[9] Reg. 17(2).
[10] See SENT, *Digest of Decisions*: 95/1; [1996]E.L.R. 117.
[11] Reg. 16(1)(ab).
[12] Reg. 16(1)(c).

The LEA's reply

By regulation 12(3), the LEA must reply within 20 working days of the date upon which a notice of appeal was received from the SENT. That reply must:

- acknowledge service;
- state whether the authority intends to oppose the appeal, and if it does, the grounds upon which it relies;
- state the name of the authority's representative and address for service (Regulation 12).

The first issue the authority may wish to consider is whether an appeal is within the SENT'S jurisdiction of the SENT and/or is misconceived. If they conclude it is not within the jurisdiction, an application may be made to strike out on the grounds set out in regulation 36. That application must be made by service of a notice setting out the grounds of the application upon the Secretary of the Tribunal, who then sends a copy of the notice to the parent. The basis of such an application would be either that there is no jurisdiction or that the appeal is frivolous or vexatious.

Preliminary issues

Any preliminary issue can be determined, either at an interlocutory hearing as a preliminary point prior to the substantive hearing, or at the start of the substantive hearing. Whilst it is accepted that public funds should not be dissipated contesting substantive proceedings which are misconceived, there is a danger that pointless preliminary issues will be taken by local authorities which disadvantage the unrepresented parent and/or increase the costs of all parties.

As an illustration of this point, one LEA applied to strike out an appeal lodged against the contents of parts II and III of a final statement and which contended that the child's special educational needs could only be met in an independent specialist school. During the course of the statutory assessment the child had been placed at what was accepted to be an appropriate independent specialist school by her parents, where she continued to attend. The LEA applied to strike out the appeal as being misconceived, the grounds for that application being that, as appropriate arrangements had been made for the child's education pursuant to section 168(5) of the Education Act 1993, the LEA was obliged to maintain the statement of special educational needs, but was relieved of its responsibility to make provision for the child's special educational needs. By some convoluted logic the LEA contended that in those circumstances an appeal against a statement of special educational needs did not lie to the SENT.

At the hearing of the issue as a preliminary point, the LEA amended its application, acknowledging that an appeal must be allowed against parts II and III of the statement, but that the appeal in relation to the appropriate school to be nominated in part IV of the child's statement should be struck out. The authority sought to rely on a decision of Tumer J. in *R. v. Kent County Council, ex p. W.*[13] Unsurprisingly the LEA's application was dismissed. However, the Tribunal did not feel the LEA's application fell within regulation 33(1)(a) and rejected the appellant's application for costs.

This would appear to be a good, though hopefully rare example, of an LEA raising issues, albeit based on a fundamental misunderstanding of the statutory framework, with which the unrepresented parent would be ill-equipped to deal. To date all preliminary issues have been raised by the LEA, or rarely on jurisdiction by the Tribunal.

In the absence of any such application the LEA must lodge its reply within the time limit and would be advised to ensure its grounds of opposition are clear and comprehensive, as, again, rights of amendment are limited[14] to exceptional cases with the permission of either the President prior to the Tribunal hearing, or the Tribunal at the substantive hearing itself. In addition, that permission may be given on whatever terms the President or the Tribunal think fit, including the payment of costs and expenses.[15]

If the LEA fails to reply within the time limit, notifies the Tribunal in writing of its intention not to oppose the appeal, or withdraws its opposition to the appeal, the Tribunal may determine the appeal on the basis of the appeal notice either by considering the papers solely, or at a hearing at which the authority is not represented.[16] Any appeal considered by the SENT will be determined on its merits, not simply on the absence of opposition from the LEA.

Opposition to an appeal

Interestingly, regulations 15(3) and 27(2) allow the authority to oppose an appeal to which it has filed a reply without being represented at the hearing, and at least five days before a substantive hearing to file additional representations.

Part III of the regulations: "Preparation For A Hearing" allows the Secretary of the Tribunal, at any stage, but in practice generally when it is clear that the LEA intends to oppose an appeal, to enquire of each party whether they wish to attend the hearing, if they intend being represented and bringing any witnesses and whether either party wishes the hearing to be in public.[17] In addition, regulation 17(b) allows a further enquiry to a parent only as to whether the parent wishes any person other than a witness or representative to attend a hearing. Curiously the parent has this right only when the hearing is held in private; we are unaware of any rationale behind this particular regulation.

---

13 [1995] E.L.R. 362.
14 Reg. 13(1) and (2).
15 Reg. 13(2).
16 Reg. 14.
17 Reg. 17(a), (iv).

Directions of the tribunal

Regulations 18–24 provide for a number of interlocutory orders to be made. Regulation 18(1) allows the President at any time to give directions, of his own motion, requiring either further particulars or a supplementary statement to be provided by a party,[18] or requiring either party to make available to the Tribunal any document or other material[19] and providing for a right of discovery or inspection,[20] comparable to County Court rules.

The above directions may also be made upon the application of a party in writing. Any such application may be subject to an objection by the other party, which must be considered by the President and if appropriate determined by way of oral hearing.[21] Where a direction has been made upon which a party has not had an opportunity to object, that party may apply to set aside the direction by notifying the Secretary to the Tribunal. The other party has a right to make representations and to have them considered by the President.

Where parties fail to comply with directions, the Tribunal may either dismiss the appeal, determine the appeal on the papers, or hold a hearing without notifying the defaulting party.[22] Any direction must include a statement of the consequences of failing to comply.[23] In addition, section 336(5) of E.A. 1996 allows, in relation to a summary conviction, for failure to comply to be fined on Scale 3.

Power is also provided to the President enabling witness summonses to be issued; however, such witness summonses can only be issued upon the application by a party, and not of the President's own motion.[24] Any individual can be required to attend a hearing and/or to produce documents or other material within his control, but only in so far as he/she could be compelled to do so in a court of law.[25] The President is required to consider the issue of protection of personal, financial or confidential information. Five working days' notice is required of the date of hearing, although that requirement can be waived if the witness agrees to do so and the expenses of attending are payable. [26]

Experience of SENT practice thus far suggests that interlocutory applications are still not frequent. However, where documents such as professional assessments are held by the LEA, or information may be on a school file, *e.g.* regarding disciplinary action, such applications may be useful.

[18] Reg. 20.
[19] Reg. 21(1).
[20] Reg. 21(2).
[21] Reg. 18(4).
[22] Regs. 24(1) and (2).
[23] Reg. 19 (5)(a).
[24] Reg. 19(3).
[25] Reg. 23(a).
[26] Reg. 23(c)(d).

The hearing date

Unless any decision has been taken to determine the appeal without a hearing,[27] the Secretary to the Tribunal arranges a hearing date and venue, giving the parties normally not less than 10 days' notice. In doing so the Secretary is required to "fix a time and date having consulted the parties".[28] Both parents and LEAs have expressed considerable concern over dates for substantive hearings being fixed at very short notice causing genuine problems with witnesses, particularly expert educational psychologists, and venues being selected which are neither in the locale of parties nor particularly convenient—*e.g.*, a north Gloucestershire appeal being determined in Reading. There have been a range of problems with venues which were inappropriate for hearings—*e.g.*, hastily prepared hotel bedrooms being used for hearings.

The notice of hearing must include information for the parties as to witnesses attending, documents and rights of representation, together with a statement setting out the consequences of non-attendance for either party.[29]

Regulation 24(4) allows the Tribunal to change the substantive hearing date not less than five working days prior to the original hearing date, to any date after that date, and to adjourn a hearing.

Pre-trial review

Currently, no form of pre-trial review is provided for in the Regulations. However, we understand that some consideration is being given to the most efficient way of identifying issues in advance of the substantive hearing. Current practice is for the Chair of the Tribunal to indicate to the parties at the start of the hearing the issues upon which the Tribunal wishes to be addressed.[30] This does not preclude parties from addressing any additional issues. Representatives and parties would welcome an indication of those issues in advance of the hearing, to assist in more effective presentation of their case.

As in most legal forums, it is often only at the door of the Tribunal that parties begin to seriously look for ways of resolving or limiting the issues to be tried, and this has led to substantial amounts of time on the hearing day being spent agreeing, for example, amendments to parts II and III of a statement of special educational needs, which could and should have been resolved in advance. It is considered impractical to hold a formal pre-trial review in each case, due to difficulties with Tribunal administration; however, some form of mediation may be considered as an option to be offered to parties prior to the substantive hearing dates, and may be introduced in the future.

---

27 Reg. 25.
28 Reg. 26(1).
29 Reg. 24(3).
30 Reg. 28.

The hearing

As indicated above, certain forms of practice are now fairly well developed within the Tribunal. Regulation 27 allows the Tribunal a wide discretion in determining the form of proceedings, the order in which the parties are heard and the issues addressed. The Tribunal is required to "seek to avoid formality in its proceedings".[31] This has been found in practice to be of considerable assistance in enabling issues to be determined in a non-adversarial manner; however, it has led in some cases to a somewhat chaotic result, with evidence being given in a fragmented form and with no formal opportunity for questioning witnesses. Parties have come away with the impression that although the hearing was "fair", it was difficult for them to put their case across coherently. Unrepresented parents and representatives of National Charities have in particular found the procedure difficult. The procedure adopted can vary from tribunal to tribunal and area to area, *e.g.* a common indication given in London SENTs is that lengthy cross-examination is rarely helpful and is to be discouraged. Outside London this indication appears not to be given. Consideration of some decisions and experience has shown that some Tribunals have identified few of the issues, or in some cases, the wrong issues. While the authors do not suggest that this happens in a high proportion of cases, it is certainly happening too often to be ignored.[31a]

Whilst the Chair of the Tribunal is required to take an interventionist role on occasions, it may be necessary for parties' representatives to take a robust approach to presentation of their evidence and the making of the essential points.

Witnesses

Parties are limited to calling two witnesses,[32] (in the parents' case, this is in addition to themselves). It is useful to note that there is no limit on the written statements which can be filed with the Tribunal, and careful consideration should be given as to which witnesses are called and which are best able to corroborate oral evidence by way of written statements. However, regulation 29(2) allows the Tribunal to require the personal attendance of the maker of any written statement at any stage of the proceedings. The Tribunal also has an additional power to require the maker of any written statement to give that evidence by way of affidavit, or to require oral evidence to be given on oath or by affirmation.[33] Express provision is made for parties to question witnesses and to address the Tribunal.

Evidence

The information which can be placed before the Tribunal is not constrained by any rules of evidence. The Tribunal may consider evidence of any facts which appear to

---

[31] Reg. 28(2).

[31a] On issue of adjournments see *R. v. Cheshire County Council and Special Educational Needs Tribunal ex p. Cherrian* (unreported) Sedley J. CO/88/96.

[32] Reg. 29(1).

[33] Reg. 19(4).

them to be relevant, notwithstanding that the evidence would not be admissible in a court of law.[34] It is important to bear in mind that the issues to be determined concern the education of a particularly vulnerable group of children, and that will determine the approach taken by the Tribunal.

In addition the Tribunal may, if it is in the interests of justice and reasonable to do so, allow either party to rely on grounds not stated in either the notice of appeal or LEA reply, and to present evidence which was not available at the time of the LEA's decision. Regulation 8(3) provides that evidence will only be admitted in exceptional circumstances after the time limit for filing a Parental Response to an LEA's Reply in opposition to an appeal in respect of a parent. Similar restrictions apply to the LEA from the date of filing its Reply.[35] This on the face of it conflicts with the President's practise direction that the child's needs should be determined as at the date of the hearing. The practise direction was itself approved by Carnwarth J. in *South Glamorgan v. Long*.[36] It is considered that the approach of the Presidents direction is the correct approach. It reflects the rapid rate of children's development and their changing needs. For example, an LEA may decide not to undertake a statutory assessment of a child, whom they are satisfied is at stage 3 in the Code of Practice. By the time of the substantive hearing, the child may have made demonstrable progress, in response to the provision being made from within the school, supporting the LEA's decision. Conversely, however, she/he may exhibit greater retardations or emotional or behavioural problems as a consequence of her/his special educational needs being inadequately addressed.

The President's direction of March 15, 1995 makes it clear that the Tribunal's role is not to consider the correctness of the LEA decision, at the time it was taken, but the special educational needs of the child at the date of the hearing. This approach is particularly relevant, as it is taking a substantial amount of time for appeals to be heard. For example, a notice of appeal filed at the beginning of February 1995 and which involved no interlocutory applications or delay on the part of either the parties was not heard until the middle of September 1995. The Tribunal's caseload has greatly exceeded that anticipated and this timescale is likely to be the norm.

The Tribunal decision

Whilst regulation 30(2) allows for the Tribunal decision to be given orally at the end of the hearing, in practice decisions are always reserved and given to the parties in writing as required by regulation 30(2), including a short statement of reasons signed by the Chair. The decision may be that of a majority,[37] but the record of the decision must not include any reference to any majority decision.[38] The decision should also address any application that has been made to the Tribunal in respect of

[34] Reg. 29(3).
[35] Reg. 13(3).
[36] CO/3073/95, presently unreported, but due to be updated in the 1996 *Education Law Reports*.
[37] Reg. 30(1).
[38] Reg. 30(3).

costs. The duty to give a short statement of reasons was considered by Latham J. in *S.v. SENT.*[39] The reasons must address the vital issues in the case.

School Placement (independent schools)

Section 347 of the Act provides for the approval by the Secretary of State of independent schools suitable for the placement of children with special educational needs under a Statement. However, there are a number of specialist schools that do not seek section 347 approval, or parents choose schools that can make a specialist provision that are not registered under section 347. On an informal basis, the President of the Tribunal agreed with the Secretary of State, a process whereby the Secretary of State gives approval to a particular independent school which is not registered, without prejudice to the Tribunal's decision in any appeal. The object of such enabling consent is to avoid the situation whereby the Tribunal has to adjourn, having decided that the parents case for a specialist placement is correct, to see whether the Secretary will or will not approve such a school.

Section 347(5) provides:

> "No person shall so exercise his functions under this Part that a child with special educational needs is educated in an independent school unless—
>
> (a) the school is for the time being approved by the Secretary of State as suitable for the admission of children for whom statements are maintained under section 324, or
>
> (b) the Secretary of State consents to the child being educated there".

Therefore even if the Local Authority, prior to an appeal, agrees that a child should be educated in such a school, consent is required.

The issue as to the meaning of section 347(5) was considered *obiter* by Brooke J. in *The Council and City of Sunderland v. Plumpton and Child "C".*[40]

Brooke J. pointed out that the Tribunal in Part III of the Education Act 1993 was known as "*the Tribunal*" and as such, it could not be a person within the meaning of section 347(5).[41] In the light of this construction, it appears arguable that whilst the enabling system is useful it is not essential. It shows that the independent school is an appropriate school in the view of the Secretary of State, and the consent is of evidential significance. It would therefore be beneficial for the purposes of presenting the case to the Tribunal and to all concerned in the conduct of the case, but may not be a mandatory prerequisite. This point is likely to be the subject of fuller judicial consideration.

---

[39] *S. v. SENT* [1995] 1 W.L.R. 1627.
[40] CO/3383/95, Wednesday February 14, 1996.
[41] See the transcript, pp. 194-20E.

Limits of Tribunal's Powers

A further issue arising out of the case of *The City of Sunderland v. Plumpton and Child* "C",[42] is that Brooke J. held that the Tribunal had no power to amend a Statement, to nominate a school in the maintained sector which was not approved by the Secretary of State for admitting the child concerned and at which the Secretary of State did not consent under section 347 to the child being educated. There is a limitation on the powers of the Tribunal to nominate a school within the maintained sector, namely that the school must be approved in a proper statutory form by the Secretary of State.

[42] *supra.*

Chapter 6
Appeals against Special Educational Needs Tribunal decisions

There are three possible means of reviewing Tribunal decisions:

1. an application for review under regulation 31 of the Special Educational Needs Tribunal Regulations 1995: Education, England and Wales (S.I. 1995 No. 3113);
2. appeal to the High Court under R.S.C. Ord. 55;
3. appeals to the High Court by case stated, R.S.C. Ord. 56, only during the course of proceedings.[1]

In addition, judicial review will still be available, but only in unusual or exceptional cases. In *R. v. The Special Educational Needs Appeal Tribunal, ex. p. South Glamorgan,*[2] the Court of Appeal reversed the decision of Turner J. to grant leave to move for judicial review, on the basis that Parliament intended that the primary remedy against a decision of a Tribunal to be an appeal on a point of law. In an unusual or exceptional case, judicial review would still remain available on the normal principles; however, such cases should be rare.

An area in which judicial review remains valid is where decisions are taken by the Tribunal staff or secretariat. Whilst section 11 of the 1992 Tribunal and Inquiries Act creates an appeal against decision of the Tribunal by a *party to proceedings*, where the Tribunal staff have refused to register appeals, judical review is the remedy. Leave has been granted on this point in a number of cases.

Additionally judicial review remains a main remedy where a Local Authority has delayed under the Regulations in assessing a child. This issue is not subject to a right of appeal. It is also available where the Local Authority fails to implement a Statement. Unfortunately, these situations remain frequent. However, considerable problems arise where the Local Authority has decided to cease to maintain a Statement or amend a Statement reducing the special educational provision contained in the Statement. There is no power given to the Tribunal to grant interim relief. The Act itself in Schedule 27 does not preserve the Statement where an Authority decides to cease to maintain it pending any appeal.[2a] If however

[1] *Allton-Evans v. Leicestershire County Council*, (unreported) August 19, 1996, Carnwarth J. CO/1749/96.
[2] *The Times*, December 3, 1995.
[2a] *R. v. Oxfordshire County Council ex p. R*, Mr J. Dyson, (unreported) CO/1995/95.

grounds arise to show that the Authority is acting either irrationally, or in breach of statutory duty, grounds for judicial review still remain. However, such a case needs to be a very strong case. Cases have arisen where the Authority are not maintaining the present Statement and have amended the Statement, obviously in such cases grounds arise for judicial review solely on the basis of breach of statutory duty. There have been a few cases which have settled in which leave has been granted, where the Authority's evidence in support of an amendment has been non-existent. Settlements have been reached in such cases by agreement to retain the provision pending appeal.[2b] Where however the argument was simply that the provision should be preserved pending an appeal, the Court of Appeal in *Re M (a minor)*,[2c] pointed out that in the absence of arguments which sustained a case on the basis of irrationality, judicial review was not available. Therefore, any application for judicial review must address issues which are in effect outside of the issues before the Tribunal on appeal.

Review of the Tribunal's decision

Regulation 31 of the Procedure Rules allows a party to apply or the Tribunal of its own motion to review any decision that is made. There are three grounds for review of a decision:

1. that the decision was wrongly made as a result of an error on the part of the Tribunal staff;
2. a party who is entitled to be heard at a hearing but failed to appear or be represented had good and sufficient reason for failing to appear;
3. there was an obvious error in the decision of the tribunal which decided the case;
4. the interests of justice require it.

On a review the parties will have an opportunity to be heard before the same Tribunal which decided the original case, or where this is not practicable they will be heard by a Tribunal appointed by the President. A reviewing Tribunal has powers to set aside or vary the relevant decision made by the original Tribunal. If, having been reviewed, the decision is set aside, the Tribunal has the power to substitute such decision as it thinks fit or to order a rehearing before either the same or different constituted Tribunal. Applications for a review may be refused by the President or by the Chairman of the Tribunal which decided the case if, in either of their opinions, it has no reasonable prospect of success. In any event any application for a review must be made not later than 10 working days after the date on which the Tribunal decision was sent to the parties. The application should be in writing stating the grounds in full.

Where the Tribunal proposes to review its decision of its own motion it must serve notice of that proposal on the parties within the same period. Any decisions made by the President may also be reviewed—for example, where the President rules that a Tribunal can go ahead without the presence of the applicant parent. Again a review of a President's decision is made by application of a party to the

[2b] *R. v. London Borough of Havering ex p. H* (unreported) Mr J. Popplewell, May 8, 1996.
[2c] [1996] E.L.R. 135.

Secretary of a Tribunal or of its own motion.[3]

There are two grounds for such a review:

1. a decision by the President was wrongly made as a result of an error on the part of the Tribunal staff;
2. there was an obvious error in his decision; or
3. the interests of justice require it.

Such a review will be determined by the President, and again the President when reviewing has powers to set aside or vary any decision he has made. The same rules on the nature of the applications and the time limits apply as in a review of the Tribunal's decision under regulation 31.

Reviewing power

Several general points should be noted with regard to this reviewing power. First, these rules substantially mirror the 1993 rules governing industrial tribunals.[4] Powers to review Tribunal decisions are increasingly seen as important additional powers enabling Tribunals and parties to reconsider decisions. However, it is clear from the prescribed grounds that the review is very narrow. Secondly, the speed necessary for requesting a review limits its usefulness. The 10-day time limit under the Special Educational Needs Tribunal regulations is four days shorter than the 14-day limit in the Industrial Tribunal regulations. There is also a difference due to the fact that applicants in an industrial tribunal are more often supported by legal advisers or by their trade unions. In education appeals such expertise is often not available. The Tribunal does now in its decision letter outline rights to appeal to the High Court on the point of law and the 28-day time limit. The notification letter does not describe how a party may ask for a review under regulation 31.

The third general point is that the power under regulation 31 is restricted to the review of decisions. "Decision" under the Special Educational Needs Tribunal regulations is not defined, unlike the situation under the 1993 Industrial Tribunal regulations, where a decision is defined as including a declaration, an order, including a striking out order, a recommendation or an award and a jurisdiction or determination of entitlement to bring or contest proceedings. The 1993 industrial Tribunal regulations specifically exclude from the definition "decision", any other interlocutory order or any other decision or interlocutory matter. Given that "decision" is not defined in the 1994 Special Educational Needs Tribunal regulations, it may be taken as inclusive and all-embracing of any decision made by the Tribunal, through the President, a Tribunal or a Chairman under the rules.

An application for a review can only be made within a set period of 10 days; there is no power to extend time. The only practical recourse, if that time period has expired, is therefore to appeal pursuant to Ord. 55.

Uses of review

In relation to the uses of a review, there are now two judgments dealing with this issue—at present both unreported but to be reported in the 1996 *Education Law Reports*.

[3] Reg. 32.
[4] Constitution and Rules of procedure Regulations 1993 (S.I. 1993 No. 2687).

In the first judgment, *C and S v. the SEN Tribunal*,[5] Latham J. pointed out that the power to review was an extremely limited power, and that advisers should therefore be aware that the appeal should be lodged within 28 days. He stated that even unqualified but experienced advisers would be treated in the same manner as solicitors. He pointed out that the rule restricted the grounds of review, which are considered below. He was clearly warning the profession that appeals need to be pursued promptly, and that reviews should normally apply only in exceptional cases. This is consistent with the approach of the industrial tribunals.

However, in *South Glamorgan County Council v. V L*,[6] Carnwarth J. stated that as the Tribunal's rules provided for "summary" reasons, the existence of that duty did not exclude a request for the elaboration of reasons, if one of the parties wished such an elaboration:

> "It seems much more sensible for elaboration of the reasons to be asked for and given at that stage [the stage of review] when the matter is fresh in everyone's mind, than to await the determination of the Court [on an appeal] some months later."

Carnwarth J. went further than suggesting that a review was appropriate where the parties were dissatisfied with the reasons, and that the reasons themselves, although brief, were apparently inadequate:

> "If the matter goes further than a defect of reasons, and one of the parties thinks that the decision has been reached (on a radically flawed basis of fact) it would seem an obvious case for a review under regulation 32. Interests of justice would require the Tribunal to look into the matter and if it found the point justified, to review the decision."

In so stating, Carnwarth J. had decided that an appeal on a point of law did not include an appeal on a point of error of fact. Therefore the power to apply for a review was appropriate where the Tribunal had made a mistake of fact as it was not subject to an appeal under the provisions of section 11 of the Tribunal and Inquiries Act 1992.

There is some conflict between the views of Latham J. in *C and S* and Carnwarth J. in *South Glamorgan v. L*, in that Latham J. was of the view that inadequate reasons would not be a matter for a review, particularly bearing in mind the time limits, while Carnwarth J. was of the opposite view.

The practitioner would be well advised to apply for legal aid if appropriate to appeal, but to put in a short application for a review if they are within the 10-day period. If they are not within the 10-day period, the situation does not arise because a review is not possible outside that period. In practise the Tribunal appears to reject applications for a review even if made on the basis of error of fact. The regulation is of little practical use at present.

The 1996 Education Law Reports at p. 278 include the President's Practice Direction on reviews. This may clarify the position. Reviews are appropriate for:

1) Error of law from a minor proceedural mishap,

---

[5] Unreported.
[6] CO/3073/95 unreported, February 21, 1995.

2) where the tribunal contributes to a misunderstanding or mistake of law,
3) mistake as to jurisdiction,
4) fresh evidence not available at the time of the hearing.

Procedural slip or error

In *British Midland Airways Limited v. Lewis*,[7] it was held, under the Industrial Tribunal regulations, that where a procedural slip or an error of law is discovered shortly after the hearing, an application for review is more appropriate than an appeal to the Employment Appeal Tribunal. There is no reason, however, that the two procedures should be considered as mutually exclusive. It is worth noting that in the Order 55 or 56 rules on appeals to the High Court, there are no provisions whereby a litigant must exhaust their potential remedies before appealing to the High Court.

Review on particular grounds

The interests of justice rule[8] is the widest ground available and mirrors a similar rule within the Industrial Tribunals review rules. The only cases under the new Act were considered above. In *Flint v. Eastern Electricity Board*,[9] Phillips J. described this ground as "a residual category of case designed to confer a wide discretion on Industrial Tribunals." However, in the same judgment the discretion was described as undoubtedly wide but not boundless, and should be exercised judicially and with regard not just to the interests of the parties but also to the interests of the other party and to the public interest requirement that there should as far as possible be finality in Industrial Tribunal litigation.

Most interestingly for purposes of the Special Educational Needs Tribunals, there has been a category of cases whereby the Tribunal's decision has been undermined by events occurring shortly thereafter. In *Yorkshire Engineering and Welding Company Limited v. Bernam*,[10] this ground was used to apply for a review on the ground of subsequent developments. Given the very short timescale for requesting a review, it is quite possible that this ground of this category of case may be too restricted to be of use. Nevertheless, where a change of circumstances occurs or fresh evidence arises immediately after a Tribunal decision, such to give rise to radical changes in the needs of a pupil or young person, it may be that a request for review is an appropriate strategy to adopt.

A final point to note is that legal aid is not available on application for review of a Tribunal decision. This restriction may have a practical application when considering which appeal procedure to adopt, since asking witnesses to reappear at another hearing may be too expensive for parents of limited means. Accordingly a High Court appeal, if relevant or suitable, may be the only practical approach available.

[7] [1978] I.C.R. 782, E.A.T.
[8] Regulation 32(1)(c).
[9] [1975] I.C.R. 395 at 401.
[10] [1973] IRLR 316; [1974] I.C.R. 77, NIRC.

Appeal from SEN Tribunal to the High Court

An appeal from the SEN Tribunal lies on a point of law to the High Court either by direct appeal or by requiring the Tribunal to state and sign a case for the opinion of the High Court. This appeal process arises by virtue of paragraph 118(3)(d), Schedule 37 of the Education Act 1996, which amends section 11(1) and para. 15 of part 1 of Schedule 1 of the Tribunals and Inquiries Act 1992 to bring the SEN Tribunal under the direct supervision of the Council of Tribunals.

As far as is material to SEN Tribunal appeals, section 11(1) of the Tribunals Act as amended, states:

> "... if any party to proceedings to any Tribunal specified in paragraph... 15..(e) of schedule 1 is dissatisfied in point of law with the decision of the Tribunal he may, according as Rules of Court may provide either appeal from the Tribunal to the High Court or require the Tribunal to state and sign a case for the opinion of the High Court."

In order to initiate an appeal from the SEN Tribunal to the High Court, an applicant must be a party to the proceedings before the Tribunal and must also be dissatisfied on point of law with the decision of the Tribunal. An appeal may be lodged under R.S.C. Ord. 55 or Ord. 56. The Tribunals Act provides that R.S.C. Ord. 94, rr. 8 and 9 provide the relevant procedures for appeals.

Appeal on point of law or by way of case stated

The Tribunal is a recently created statutory body. In many respects its situation is essentially different from other tribunals, for example the duty is to the child, yet it is the parent who appeals. Inadequate or the wrong provision will damage a child in some cases. Practise and procedure is developing and is not yet established law.

It is worth noting that these procedures for appeal on a point of law, or by way of case stated as envisaged by the Tribunals and Inquiries Act are, on the face of section 11, alternative and not cumulative, and therefore the appropriate approach is either an appeal on a point of law *or* by way of case stated by the Tribunal. In some cases this may well be a preferable route therefore. It is not unusual for unassisted parents to instruct solicitors after the 28-day time limitation has expired.

Within proceedings either the Appellant or the Tribunal may take action to state a case.[11] There are four points of issue that need considering under appeals to the High Court:

1. who is a party to the proceedings;
2. what is a point of law,
3. what is a definition of decision; and

[11] Ord. 95, r. 9(1).

4. what is the correct route to take, Ord. 55 or Ord. 56. Time plays an important part in this decision.

In the case of *S v. The Special Educational Needs Tribunal and the City of Westminster*[12] Latham J. considered three of these four points. The case was affirmed on the issue of parties in the Court of Appeal.[13] In that case the applicant was a child seeking to appeal against a decision, the effect of which was that the school named in the child's amended statement of special educational needs was an ordinary maintained school as proposed by the local education authority, the second named respondent, and not a recognised independent special school as contended for by the applicant's mother. The consequence of the dispute between the second respondent and the mother was that the applicant, at the time of the appeal 13 years of age, had not attended any school for a year. In his judgment Latham J. ruled on two preliminary issues. First, was the child appellant a person entitled to appeal against the decision in question? Second, should the appeal, whoever was entitled to bring it, continue to be brought before the Court under R.S.C. Ord. 55, as had been done in this case, or should it be by way of case stated pursuant to R.S.C. Ord. 56?

Who is a party to proceedings before the SEN Tribunal?

In construing the statutory structure set up under the Education Act 1993 and now consolidated in the Education Act 1996, which constituted the new Special Educational Needs Tribunals, Latham J. determined that the Tribunal's jurisdiction can only by invoked by an appeal brought by a parent. This is by virtue of the fact that section 326 of the Education Act 1996, and indeed the other appeal provisions, provide that the parent of any child under assessment by virtue of section 323, or with a statement by virtue of section 324, may appeal to a Tribunal when a statement is first made, when an amendment is made and if and when the local education authority has determined to cease to maintain it or where pursuant to sections 328 and 329 of the Act the parent of a child may appeal to a Tribunal against a refusal by a local education authority to make an assessment or a further statutory assessment in respect of a child for whom a statement is maintained. A child, for the purposes of the relevant part of the 1996 Act, includes, pursuant to section 312(5), any person who has not attained the age of 19 years and is a registered pupil at a school.

This definition of a child is different from most other statutory interpretations of child. In fact a child becomes an adult at the age of 18. Therefore under the 1996 Education Act and the Tribunal regulations, an adult affected by any of the relevant decisions of the local education authority who was a registered pupil at a school would not be able to invoke the jurisdiction of the Tribunal himself, but would only be able to do so through his parents. This construction of the statutory framework led to a decision that only the parents or the local education authority may appeal a decision to the High Court, *S v. SENT*[14] The Court of Appeal confirmed this

[12] [1995] 1 W.L.R. 1627.
[13] *The Times*, December 18, 1996.
[14] [1995] 1 W.L.R. 1627, *The Times*, December 18, 1995.

judgment on the basis of the 1993 Education Act Part III, and the terms of section 11 of the Tribunals and Inquiries Act.

There is no definition in the 1993 or 1996 Acts as to who are to be considered parties to any appeal heard by a Tribunal. It was held therefore that looking at the overall structures of the appeals both in terms of the provisions of the Act and the regulation, there can be only two parties to such an appeal: first the parents and secondly the local education authority. In his judgment Latham J. relied heavily on the fact that regulation 7 of the SEN Tribunal regulations 1994 provides that an appeal is constituted by a notice of appeal signed by the parent and the name of the authority which made the disputed decision and regulation 8 which makes provision for a reply by the education authority and regulation 9 which provides a withdrawal of appeal by the parent.

However, neither the High Court nor the Court of Appeal considered the definition of a parent in the 1993 Act, which is the same as in the Children Act, and which appears in section 114 of the 1944 Education Act. Additionally, by debarring a person of legal age or capacity from an appeal, there is a possible breach of the European Convention of Human Rights.[15] It is surprising that no issue was raised on the issue of the definition of parent in section 114 of the 1944 Act, as amended by the Children Act. It is in fact possible that this definition does not exclude the child as a party to an appeal, if of sufficient age and capacity.

The main practical effect of this judgment on this point is to debar applications for legal aid in the name of the child to appeal direct in appeals such as this. The parent of limited means who is not eligible for legal aid is in a particular precarious position, whether they wish to appeal a Tribunal decision themselves or more worryingly where they are put in a position of being a respondent to an appeal brought by a local education authority. A parent in this situation may be put in the unsavoury position of not being able to afford to respond to a local education authority's challenge to a Tribunal decision which had gone in the parent's favour.

Intervention by an interested party

This problem for the non-legally-aided parent may be overcome by use of R.S.C. Ord. 15, r. 6 dealing with misjoinder and non-joinder of parties. Under this rule a person who is not a party but who is an interested party may be added as a defendant or equally a respondent against the wishes of the plaintiff or applicant, either on the application of the defendant/respondent or on his own intervention, or in rare cases by the Court of its own motion. The Court has an entirely discretionary jurisdiction under this rule, however, a child whose future educational interest is the substantive issue in an appeal to the High Court should satisfy the rule requiring that the would-be intervener should have some interest which is directly related or connected with the subject matter of the action. The law as to this avenue is presently unclear. It is presently only a possible route.

[15] Arts. 1,16,14; Art 2 of Protocol 1 to the European Convention of Human Rights. Also Arts. 6, 7 and 10 of the Universal Declaration of Human Rights 1948, and Arts. 14 and 16 of the International Covenant on Civil and Political Rights 1966.

Rights at appeal of the child

The Court has an inherent jurisdiction enabling it to do justice in particular cases to allow a person not a party to intervene in proceedings where the effect of such proceedings has been or is likely to cause such a person serious hardship, difficulty or damage. This rule may be used to good effect to prevent the future educational provision of a child being determined on appeal to the High Court in his or her parents' absence due to financial constraints. It is important to note that the appeal rights are expressed to be used by the parents, but the Act creates a statutory duty to the child, not to the parent. The child therefore enforces a breach of duty. In *South Glamorgan County Council v. L*[16] the Court of Appeal, in related earlier judicial review proceedings had allowed the appeal of the Tribunal to reverse the order of Turner J. who had granted leave to proceed by judicial review, against the decision of the Tribunal. On appeal, the Court of Appeal granted the education authority appellant leave to proceed out of time against the decision of the Special Educational Needs Appeal Tribunal, but ordered the child to be represented on the facts of that particular case only.

Before the High Court on appeal under Ord. 55, the child was represented, and the mother did not appear. In giving judgment in favour of the child Carnwarth J. drew attention to the provisions of Ord. 15 r. 6 in such circumstances where a parent was unable to appear in an appeal as a respondent. The child was an obvious interested party under the rule. He approved the actions of the Legal Aid Authority in granting legal aid in that case to the child in those circumstances, and stated "It would be most unfortunate if, the Authority having sought as a matter of principle to challenge the decision of the Tribunal, [the child] was deprived of legal representation to defend his interest."

The Judge referred to the situation being possibly different in a converse situation, because of the fact that a parent was a party as decided ultimately in the Court of Appeal in *S v. The SEN Tribunal.*[17] However, if a parent commences an appeal but cannot continue it, clearly the principles of Ord. 15, r. 6 may apply in such circumstances and a child could intervene.

Ord. 55 appeal on a point of law or Ord. 56: Case stated?

The major issue in these cases is the issue of time. Although time can be extended under Ord. 15, r. 5, clearly a reason has to be shown for the exercise of the Court's discretion. Under Ord. 55 an appeal on a point of law, the time provided for is solely 28 days. An extension can be applied for, but obviously it is best if an application is made within time.

Under the provisions of Ord. 56 concerning an appeal by way of case stated, no actual time is specified for the request to state a case and time only commences from the decision of the Tribunal either to agree to state a case or to refuse such a request.[18] However this route is only available within the proceedings, prior to a

[16] CO/3073/95, December 21, 1995, (above), (as yet unreported).
[17] *The Times*, December 18, 1995.
[18] Ord. 56, rr. 8(3) and 10(4).

final decision. However, the law in this area is again not clear, Carnwarth J. in *R. v. SENT, ex p. Brophy,*[19] stated *obiter* that case stated was only available subject to a final decision, and not as an appeal after a decision. This was despite the fact that the Tribunal had in fact accepted case stated was available. This point has now been confirmed in *Allton-Evans v. Leicestershire County Council.*[20]

Appeals to the High Court under R.S.C. Ord. 55

Section 11(1) of the Tribunals and Inquiries Act 1992, to which reference has already been made above, establishes that for the purposes of the Act itself, an appeal from the Special Educational Needs Tribunal can be made either to the High Court by way of Ord. 55 or Ord. 56. In interpreting the relevant rules Latham J. stated, in *S v. The Special Educational Needs Tribunal*[21] :

> "it is clear that an appeal under Order 55 is appropriate in relation to a decision of the Tribunal but that the Tribunal may of its own motion or at the request of either party state the case on any question of law arising in the course of the proceedings."

This judgment might be taken to imply that when there is a decision made by a Tribunal, the proper course is to appeal to the High Court by way of Ord. 55. Case stated therefore would be more appropriate, where some question of law arises in the course of the proceedings. In fact the Judge was considering a case where the Appeal was under Ord. 55 and as to whether Ord. 56 had a role.

An example of a case in which the Tribunal agreed to state a case has arisen in an earlier appeal lodged with the Tribunal in autumn of 1994; the decision is reported in the first edition of the president of the Tribunal's *Digest of Decisions.*[22] In this case on May 13, 1994 the LEA wrote to the parents refusing to make a statement, but issuing a note in lieu. The parents protested and in a letter dated August 1, 1994 the LEA agreed to amend the note in lieu but repeated that they did not consider a statement justified. The parents submitted further evidence to the LEA, which replied on October 6, 1994 saying that having reconsidered the papers, it was still of a view that it should not make a statement. The parents lodged an appeal to the Tribunal on October 6. The Tribunal decided that the LEA had ended its formal assessment procedure on May 13 and its later letters did not represent new decisions against which an appeal would lie to the Tribunal.

Accordingly on a preliminary hearing as to the status of a statement issued before September 1, 1994, the Tribunal's view was that it had no jurisdiction to hear an

[19] CO/3363/95, unreported, May 8, 1996.
[20] August 19, 1996, Carnworth J., CO/1749/96.
[21] [1995] 1 W.L.R. 1127 at 1653 DGF.
[22] 95/1 [1996] E.L.R 117.

appeal. This case was brought to the notice of legal advisers well after the 28-day expiry time limitation for appeals to the High Court. An appeal by way of case stated was lodged on the basis that the Tribunal failed to apply the law correctly, given the evidence in front of them as to when in law the formal assessment procedure has been completed. The Tribunal stated a case but in fact the case settled.

Latham J. in *S v. Westminster and the Special Educational Needs Tribunal*,[23] in an appeal made under Ord. 55 accepted a Tribunal could be requested to state a case, or could do so by its own motion. Carnwarth J. in *R. v. SENT, ex p. Brophy* and *Allton-Evans v. Leicester County Council*[24] are the only guidance on this issue.

Procedure on appeal to the High Court from the SEN Tribunal: R.S.C. Ord. 55

Time

First, if an application is not made in time, the appeal must be lodged together with a summons to extend time, and supporting affidavit. An application to extend time can be heard by a single judge, of the Queen's Bench Division.

The principles upon which the Courts are prepared to extend time require that there is jurisdiction to extend time, under Ord. 3, r. 5. If there is a good reason the Court will normally exercise its discretion and extend time. However, in appeals on a point of law the Courts will bear in mind the fact that the decision challenged is that of a statutory Tribunal. In such cases the reasonable requirements of public administration have a significance which is absent in ordinary *inter partes* litigation.

The leading case on this issue, *Regalbourne Limited v. East Lindsey District Council*,[25] is inaccurately reported in the [1993] *Crown Office Digest* 277 and a transcript is therefore essential and is referred to in this chapter.

In that case, the Court of Appeal considered an application to appeal out of time in decisions relating to properties in the area of East Lindsey District Council as regards their valuation for community charge. Such valuations can be appealed on a yearly basis; this was clearly a relevant factor in the decision of the Court of Appeal, namely that even if prejudice was suffered, it was only for one year.

Kennedy L.J. in his judgment made it clear that a reasonable explanation had to be offered by those acting for the appellant as to the reason why the application was to be made out of time.

An appeal could only be revived or extended if the Court would extend time, but it would be slow to do so. The reason was that the Court was being asked to

[23] See n. 21, above.
[24] May 8, 1996, CO/3363/95 and August 19, 1996, CO/1749/96.
[25] [1995] C.A.

intervene to deprive a party of his or her existing right. Errors or ignorance by lawyers would not be a good reason, at least on their own.

However, in the most important section of the judgment Sir Thomas Bingham M.R. at p. 13B–G pointed out that prejudice was of less significance than normal, but not of no significance at all. The most important part of his judgment is at p. 13C where he stated, "There is in this context a different statutory framework and the Court must do its best to give effect to the intention of Parliament in the particular context before it." The Court of Appeal in this case plainly had regard to the statutory framework, which meant that this decision was reviewed annually, a unique position. It stated that a reasonable explanation should be given, and that prejudice was of less significance but not of no significance or minor significance. Most importantly it drew attention to the statutory framework, which in cases of children with special needs, in the absence of any further right of appeal and the contention of continuing prejudice to the child, must be extremely important.

The authors have quoted this judgment at length. In the unreported case of *Van de Velde v. The SEN Tribunal*[26] Popperwell J. refused to extend time, and set out an analysis of the principles on which time could be extended. At p. 4B-D, the judge was wrong in law, as he referred to delay being of only "marginal significance", citing on his judgment from the *Regalbourne* case. This was not said by the Court of Appeal in that case, and he further failed to have regard to the fact that the statutory regime was of considerable importance. Leave to appeal was subsequently granted by Schiemann L.J.

An application to move out of time can be made by agreement with the other side or by showing that not only is there an acceptable explanation, but also that the delay will not unduly prejudice the respondent. Ignorance of time limits, however, is not an acceptable excuse, and prejudicial delay without good reason is likely to lead to a refusal of the Court to exercise its discretion. Even where there is a good reason, substantial delay or significant prejudice may still lead to a refusal to extend time. On hearing the appeal the Court has powers to make any order the Tribunal could make and can make any further orders as the case requires, or remit the matter back to the Tribunal for rehearing a determination with its own opinion.[27]

Procedure on appeal

The appeal will be heard by a single judge of the Queen's Bench Division. The appeal must be brought by originating motion stating grounds and the decision appealed against, including why it is contended that the decision is wrong. The appeal is limited to a point of law by Ord. 55, r. 1(4) whereby the statutory provisions in Tribunals Act are invoked.

The Tribunal records proceedings. If the parties require a note of evidence, an application must be made to order the Tribunal to produce such, as Ord. 55, r. 7 which applies to the High Court also applies to the Tribunal and gives the Court power to receive further evidence on questions of fact and to direct the manner in which such evidence is to be given.

By r. 7(4) the appellant is under a duty to apply for a note to the person presiding

[26] reported briefly in 1996 *Crown Office Digest*.
[27] R.S.C. Ord. 55, R. 7(5).

at the proceedings for a signed copy of any note made by him or of the proceedings and to furnish that copy for the use of the Court. In default of such note the Court may hear and determine the appeal on any other evidence or statement of what occurred in proceedings as appears to the Court to be sufficient.

In *South Glamorgan County Council v. Long*, Carnwarth J. in dealing with the issue of obtaining the notes for the Tribunal stated: "in my view it should not normally be necessary to seek the notes of proceedings. In case of doubt, directions from the Court should be sought."

Evidence

In normal cases, the notice of motion will be accompanied by an affidavit, exhibiting the documents before the Tribunal and giving evidence as to the facts. The respondent too has power to file evidence; see *S v. The Special Educational Needs Tribunal.*[28] It will therefore not normally be necessary to obtain the notes of evidence, save in an exceptional case.

The case of *Green v. Minister of Housing and Local Government*[29] concerned the provisions of the Tribunals Act and rights of appeal specifically limited to an appeal on a point of law. *Green* determined that in these circumstances the provisions of Ord. 55(3) could not be invoked to justify a rehearing of the primary facts on which the case itself depended. Nonetheless in his judgment[30] Widgery J., did not preclude the use of fresh evidence in fact when the Court is faced with an issue of law, for example on jurisdiction or a question of procedure.

Respondent

A normal respondent to the appeal will be the local education authority—*S v. The Special Educational Needs Tribunal.*[31] However, the Chairperson of the Tribunal is plainly a party to the appeal, but will not normally attend. If the Tribunal seeks to attend and be represented, it is entitled to appear and file evidence, *per* Latham J. in *S v. The SEN Tribunal.*[32]

By virtue of Ord. 55, r. 3(3), an appeal under Ord. 55 does not operate as a stay of proceedings unless the High Court or the Tribunal itself so orders. A stay can of course be sought under S.C. Ord. 55, r. 3(3) and an application should be made by motion on two days notice to the respondent. The President of the SEN Tribunal and all parties to the proceedings should be served. This would normally only be the local educational authority concerned.

28 [1995] 1 W.L.R. 1627.
29 [1967] 2 Q.B. 606.
30 At p. 615 G.
31 *ibid.*
32 *ibid.*

Appeals to the High Court by way of case stated: RSC Ord. 56

On an appeal by way of case stated within proceedings, the hearing will take place before a single judge of the Queen's Bench Division. By virtue of section 11(1) and (3) of the Tribunals Act, outlined above, any party to Tribunal proceedings may request a Tribunal to refer a question of law to the High Court for the determination by way of case stated. If the Tribunal refuses to do so it is necessary to apply to the Court for an order directing a Tribunal to state a case.[33] This application must be made by originating motion to be served on the Secretary of the Tribunal and every other party to the proceedings in question, *i.e.* the parent and the local education authority.

The notice of motion must state the grounds of the application and the question of law on which it is sought to have the case stated and any reasons given by the Tribunal for refusing to state a case. The notice must be entered for hearing and served within 14 days after receipt by the applicant of notice of the refusal of his request to state a case. A case stated must be signed by the Chairman or President and served on the party who has requested the application. Where the Tribunal or the President states a case of his own motion, he must serve a copy of the case on persons who appear to him to be appropriate and must notify every other party to the proceedings in question that the case has been served on the party named and the date specified.

It is for the person whose request or on whose application the case was stated, to begin proceedings by service of request, under Ord. 56, r. 7, and if refused, by originating motion. Notice of motion and a copy of the case must be served on the President or the Tribunal by whom the case was stated and every other person concerned in the proceedings in which the case in question arose.[34] The case must be lodged together with the motion which must set out the applicant's contentions on the point of law concerned and must be served and entered within 14 days of service on the applicant of the case.

Should the applicant fail to enter the motion within 14 days, any other party concerned in the proceedings may do so as though he were the applicant, within 14 days of receipt of the case. This route is likely to have little practical use in the majority of cases.

The effect of appeals to the High Court

The Tribunals Act clearly restricts appeal to the High Court on a point of law alone. Appeals by either route allow the High Court to give the SEN Tribunal proper guidance on the interpretation of the 1981 and 1996 Education Act and associated regulations, thereby preventing inconsistent rulings from different Tribunals. The main question then is what is a point of law?

---

[33] R.S.C. Ord. 56, r. 8(1).
[34] Ord. 56, r. 10(1)(2).

What is a point of law?

Jurisdictional matters

A detailed analysis of this issue was considered by Carnwarth J. in *South Glamorgan v. Long*.[35] In rejecting the appeal on the basis that it was truly an appeal on fact, in a comprehensive judgment he considered the jurisdiction of the High Court.

Jurisdictional questions may arise at the outset of the SEN Tribunal proceedings. For example, should the Tribunal appeal be struck out because the parents are already making suitable educational arrangements for their child? In *R. v. Shoreditch Assessment Committee, ex p. Morgan*[36] this issue was considered at p. 880; Farwell L.J. stated:

> "no Tribunal of inferior jurisdiction can by its own decision finally decide on the question of the existence or extent of such jurisdiction; such question is always subject to review by the High Court, which does not permit the inferior Tribunal either to use a jurisdiction which it does not possess, whether at all or to the extent claimed, or to refuse to exercise a jurisdiction which it has and ought to exercise."

The case of *Anisminic Limited v. Foreign Compensation Commission*[37] has determined that if a Tribunal exceeds its jurisdiction it makes an error of law. This therefore allows a High Court to quash such decisions through appeal and it means that judicial review is not necessary. The safest comparison is with appeals from Social Security Appeal Tribunals. By virtue of section 101 of the Social Security Act 1975, grounds for appeal from the Tribunals lie where "the decision of the Tribunal was erroneous in points of law". In R (A) 1/72, the test for determining whether an appeal will lie was established. It was held that a decision would be wrong in law if:

1. it contained a false proposition of law on its face;
2. it was supported by no evidence; or
3. the facts found were such that no person judicially and properly instructed as to the relevant law could have come to the determination in question. Further grounds were added in the case of CSB 29/81, which cited R (1) 14/75 whereby the grounds of breach of rules of natural justice and failure to state adequate reasons were established. Procedural Tribunal errors which are fundamental and cause prejudice all give rise to appeal as a point of law.

Failure to give reasons would clearly give rise to an appeal to the High Court on a point of law. The Tribunals Act as amended makes it clear that adequate reasons must be stated in the decisional letter from the Tribunal. The present practice and procedure of the Tribunal is for the Chairman's decision letter to be approved by the President, before being sent out. This is based on the Procedure Rules which

[35] See n. 16, above.
[36] [1910] 2 K.B. 859.
[37] [1969] 2 A.C. 147.

provide for brief reasons. This should ensure that adequate reasons are given in the decisions letter. Nonetheless a decision letter which did not give adequate reasons would give rise to an appeal on a point of law. However, such a decision under the rules can be brief: *S v. SEN Tribunal and Westminster*,[38] Latham J. Carnwarth J. took the opposite view to Latham J. stating that only if a failure to give reasons revealed an error of law would the Court quash the decision. However, this conflicts with the Court of Appeal in *R. v. Surrey, ex p. H*,[39] which applied to the 1981 Act Appeals, and *R. v. Immigration Appeal Tribunal, ex. p. Khan*.[40]

Fact based on no evidence

For a Tribunal to find the facts based on no evidence is an error of law and challengeable by appeal. A no-evidence rule comes into play when a Tribunal makes insupportable findings, as opposed to when it makes findings on conflicting evidence which might justify a conclusion either way. This extends the perverse decision principle under the *Wednesbury* unreasonable test. Thus appeal on a point of law is available in a case where no Tribunal could reasonably reach a conclusion reached on the evidence. Lord Denning M.R. clarified the scope of the no-evidence rule in a Housing Act case, *Ashbridge Investments Limited v. Minister of Housing and Local Government*[41]:

> "the Court: can interfere with the Minister's decision if he acted on no evidence or if he has come to a decision to which on the evidence he could not reasonably have made. Or if he has given the wrong interpretation to the words of the statute or if he has taken into consideration matters which he ought not to have taken into account or vice versa: or has otherwise gone wrong in law, it is identical with the position when the Court has power to intervene with the lower Tribunal which has erred on points of law."

Factual mistake

The law in this area has been in doubt for some years. There has been considerable interest in this area as an additional ground for judicial review or on appeal to the High Court. In two recent education cases this issue has been more clearly considered.

This head of error in law was described by Scarman L.J. as "misunderstanding or ignorance for an established and relevant fact", and by Lord Wilberforce as acting "upon an incorrect basis of fact" in *Secretary of State for Education and Science v. Thameside M.B.C.*[42] In the case of *Smith v. Inner London Education Authority*,[43] Lord Denning M.R. stated that the Court could intervene if a Minister plainly misdirects himself on a fact or in law. However, Wade expresses a view at pp. 317 and 318 of *Administrative Law* that the "wrong factual basis" doctrine has not

[38] See n. 28, above.
[39] [1984] 83 L.G.R. 213.
[40] [1983] 2 Q.B. 790.
[41] [1965] 1 W.L.R. 1320 at 1326.
[42] [1977] A.C. 1014 at 1030.
[43] [1978] 1 All E.R. 411.

become fully established as a new head of the *ultra vires* doctrine. The doctrine would be analogous to the no-evidence rule and the acting upon a misapprehension of law rule. In *South Glamorgan v. L*,[44] Carnwarth J. rejected the contention that mistakes of fact gave rise to an appeal on a point of law. This would amount to a fundamental change in the common law: *R. v. London Residuary Body, ex. ILEA.*[45] In *R. v. Secretary of State for Education, ex p. S*,[46] Sedley J. applied this case to reject the submission that there was jurisdiction on mistake of fact. It is, however, likely that a challenge to a Tribunal on the basis that it did not have the relevant material before it in correct form may be entertained as a point of law.

Nonetheless, in terms of the likely success of an appeal, the case law implies that specialised Tribunals are leniently judged. In *R. v. Preston Supplementary Benefits Appeal Tribunal, ex p. Moore*[47] Lord Denning stated:

> "the Courts should hesitate long before interfering by certiorari with the decisions of the appeal Tribunals. The Court should not enter into a meticulous discussion of the meaning of this Act or that word in the Act, they should leave the Tribunals to interpret in a broad and reasonable way according to the spirit and not the letter."

However with the advent of the 1992 Tribunals Act and the use of legally qualified Chairmen of Tribunals, the High Court may not be lenient where there are misdirections on facts or errors in law.

Questions of fact or questions of law

Case law shows that there are two competing doctrines in distinguishing questions of fact from question of law. It is likely that legal advisers will need to analyse closely when asked to consider papers on appeals to the High Court whether there is a point of law or whether they are dealing with issues relating to dispute over facts. The primary facts doctrine is based on a proposition that matters in fact of the primary facts of a particular case have to be established before the law can be applied. Whether the facts once established satisfy legal definition or requirement is a question of law. In *O'Kelly v. Trusthouse Forte Plc*,[48] Sir John Donaldson M.R. stated: "the appeal Tribunal has no jurisdiction to consider any question of mixed fact and law until it has purified or distilled the mixture and extracted a question of pure law."

Thus a question in respect of whether the gathering of reports is an "assessment", within the meaning of the Education Act 1996, the source of the report, and the nature of the reports, their age, the circulation of the reports and so forth are questions of fact. Once the facts are established, the question of whether they constitute an "assessment" within the meaning of the Act is a question of law.

In a Housing Act case, *Tanden v. Trustees of Spurgeon's Homes*,[49] the House of

[44] CO/30 73/95.
[45] *The Times*, July 24, 1987.
[46] [1995] E.L.R. 238.
[47] [1976] 1 W.L.R. 1047.
[48] [1984]Q.B. 90 at 123.
[49] [1992] A.C. 755.

Lords applied this principle in holding that whether it was reasonable to call a building a "house" was ultimately a question of law. This analysis would clearly allow an appeal on a point of law on every question of legal interpretation arising out of the primary facts in a case that had been established. The application of the legal definition or principle to ascertain facts is a point of law. Thus Sir Donaldson explained the limited function of the Court in the *O'Kelly* judgment[50] at p.123:

> "... it must be satisfied there must have been a misdirection on a question of law before it can intervene. Unless the direction on law has been expressed it can only be so satisfied if, in its opinion, no reasonable tribunal, properly directing itself on the relevant question of law, could have reached the conclusion under appeal."

The House of Lords have not fully clarified the distinctions between fact and law on appeals. Nevertheless, in the leading tax case of *Edwards v. Bairstow*,[51] Lord Radcliffe, referring to the situation where an application of the law to the primary facts does not support the determination, said at p. 36:

> "[The court] has no option but to assume that there has been some misconception of the law and that this has been responsible for the determination. So there too has been an error in point of law. I do not think it much matters whether this state of affairs is described as one in which there is no evidence to support the determination or as one which the evidence is inconsistent with and contradictory of the determination, or as one in which the true and only reasonable conclusion contradicts the determination. Rightly understood each phrase propounds the same test."

This principle clearly aligns with the doctrine of reasonableness and likewise with the doctrine of review for no evidence. In *Administrative Law*, Wade states that effectively the Courts have been balancing the need to have broad powers to review unjustifiable decisions, while allowing administrative Tribunals a margin of error.

---

[50] See n. 48 above.
[51] [1956] A.C. 14.

Chapter 7
Post 16 Education and Transfer to Further Education

The Education Act 1981 did not deal with post-16 further education. This was due to the fact that the local education authority maintained post-16 education, if it was provided in a College of Further Education or sixth form college, as well as within school sixth forms. The Further and Higher Education Act 1992 placed post-19 and some post-16 further education outside the control of local educational authorities. It introduced a number of necessary changes to the legislation. Whilst it did not create a similar appeal system to the 1981 or the 1996 system. It did create statutory rights, where few had existed before. The Code of Practice in dealing with annual reviews, in Chapter 6, is a considerable improvement on the earlier position. However, despite these improvements there remains a substantial imbalance as between the rights of young persons who retain a statement, and remain at a school until the age of 19, and those who transfer into the Further Education Sector.

For those young people with Statements who remain in school after the age of 16, LEAs remain under a duty to provide for them in accordance with their Statements. This means that the LEA is still required to fund the specified provision. Some local education authorities retain few sixth forms. Furthermore for those for more severe disabilities, special schools may not provide beyond the age of 16. The further education sector may develop greater expertise than the local education authority in dealing with special educational needs in some areas, as a result of the statutory reforms.

The fact that a young person has reached the age of 16 is not an adequate reason for declining statutory responsibility for their education or withdrawing a statement. In *R. v. Dorset Education Authority and the FEFC exp. Goddard*,[1] Auld J. held parents could compel an LEA to retain a statement until the age of 19 as the statute required. Further, attempts to restrict statements to the age of 16, or to contend that they simply stopped at 16, were in breach of the legislation. As the duty under section 165 of the Education Act 1993 (now section 321 of the Education Act 1996) continued to the age of 19, the local authority could not divest itself of such a duty, save in lawful circumstances.

The 1992 Act established new Further Education Funding Councils (FEFCs) with effect from April 1, 1993. These took over the statutory responsibility for provision of full-time education for those aged 16–18 within colleges, and for those over compulsory school age but in full-time education over the age of 19 up to 25.

[1] [1995] E.L.R 109.

General duties and powers of the Further Education Funding Councils

Section 1 of the 1992 Act establishes new Further Education Funding Councils: one for England and one for Wales. Regional Advisory Committees have also been set up under the Act. Section 2 places a duty on each Funding Council to secure the provision of sufficient facilities for full-time education suitable to the requirements of all 16- to 18-year-olds in their area. This duty replaces the former duty of the local education authority. It must be discharged in such a way that the facilities are provided at such places that are of such character and are so equipped as to be sufficient to meet the reasonable needs of all persons to whom the duty extends. This is a general target duty, the equivalent to section 8 of the Education Act 1944, imposed upon local education authorities. The Council must take account of the different abilities and aptitudes of young people and must make effective use of resources and avoid disproportionate expenditure. It must also take into account any education provided by schools, including special schools and colleges.

Section 3 places a duty on the funding council to provide adequate facilities for the part-time education of persons of any age over compulsory school age, and the full-time education for those who have attained the age of 19 years. This duty, however, only applies where the education falls into certain categories, which are set out in Schedule 2 of the Act. The following courses, in summary, are included in the Schedule:

1. certain vocational qualifications and qualifications such as GCSEs and A-levels;
2. basic literacy;
3. basic principles of numeracy;
4. access to courses of various kinds;
5. English for students where English is not the language spoken at home;
6. courses to teach independent living and communication skills to persons who have learning difficulties, which prepare them for entry to another course included in one of the above categories.

These are all courses which generally teach basic literacy, numeracy or lead to obtaining formal qualifications such as GCSEs, higher qualifications, or to professional vocational work skills courses.

The local education authority retains responsibility for non-Schedule-2 education, but this form of education is likely to be very much less important at ages 16 to 19 for students with learning difficulties. The LEA's duty in this respect is important in relation to their provision of day centres for young adults with learning difficulties, particularly post-19.

The LEA's functions in respect of youth service are not affected by amendments to section 1 of the 1944 Act which are made by the 1992 Act. They still have a duty to provide adequate facilities, including the youth service. Section 53 of the 1944 Act imposes a duty on LEAs to secure adequate facilities for recreation, social and physical training. On the recreational side they therefore retain this important function, together with non comitant duties in relation to community care.

The essential duties for young people with learning difficulties

It is necessary to read sections 3 and 4 of the 1992 Further and Higher Education Act together. Section 3 provides as follows:

> "**3.**—(1) It shall be the duty of each council to secure the provision for the population of their area of adequate facilities for education to which this subsection applies, that is—
>
> (a) part-time suitable to the requirements of persons of any age over compulsory school age, and
> (b) full-time education suitable to the requirements of persons who have attained the age of nineteen years,
>
> where the education is provided by means of a course of a description mentioned in Schedule 2 to this Act.
> (2) A council shall discharge that duty so as—
>
> (a) to secure that facilities are provided at such places, are of such character and are so equipped as to meet the reasonable need for education to which subsection (1) above applies, and
> (b) to take account of the different abilities and aptitudes of persons among that population.
>
> (3) A council may secure the provision of facilities for education to which subsection (1) above applies where they are not under a duty to do so.
> (4) A council shall discharge their functions under this section so as to make the most effective use of their resources and, in particular, to avoid provision which might give rise to disproportionate expenditure.
> (5) In discharging those functions a council shall have regard to any education to which subsection (1) above applies provided by institutions outside the further education sector or higher education sector.
> (6) The Secretary of State may by order amend Schedule 2 to this Act."

Section 3 of the Act is therefore very similar in its structure to section 8 of the Education Act 1994. It is a target duty, imposed upon the council to organise the F.E. sector. A young person will go to a college which is maintained and funded by the council. It is the college that will implement and arrange provision for the young person. The duty is specific in relation to those with learning difficulties, and that duty is imposed by section 4.

Section 4 is as follows:

> "**4.**—(1) In exercising their functions under sections 2 and 3 of this Act, each council shall (subject to the provisions of those sections) do so in accordance with subsections (2) to (4) below.

(2) Each council shall have regard to the requirements of persons having learning difficulties.

(3) A council shall, if they are satisfied in the case of any person among the populations of their area who has a learning difficulty and is over compulsory school age but has not attained the age of twenty-five years, that:-

(a) the facilities available in institutions within the further education sector or the higher education sector are not adequate for him, and
(b) it is in his best interests to do so,

secure provision for him at an institution outside those sectors.

(4) A council shall, if they are satisfied that they cannot secure such provision for a provision for a person as they are required to secure under subsection (3) above unless they also secure the provision of boarding accommodation for him, secure the provision of boarding accommodation for him.

(5) In exercising their functions under sections 2 and 3 of this Act in the case of any person who has a learning difficulty and is over compulsory school age, a council may—

(a) if they are satisfied that the facilities available in institutions within the further education section or the higher education sector are not adequate for him, at an institution outside those sectors, and
(b) secure the provision of boarding accommodation for him.

(6) Subject to subsection (7) below, for the purposes of this section a person has a 'learning difficulty' if:-

(a) he has a significantly greater difficulty in learning than the majority of persons of his age, or
(b) he has a disability which either prevents or hinders him from making use of facilities of a kind generally provided by institutions within the further educations sector for persons of his age.

(7) a person is not to be taken as having a learning difficulty solely because the language (or form of the language) in which he is, or will, be taught is different from a language (or form of a language) which has at any time been spoken in his home."

For young persons with learning difficulties the Further and Higher Education Funding Council's duties are as follows:

1. They are required to have regard to the requirements of persons with learning difficulties, as defined by s. 4(b).
2. Section 4(3) means that the duty extends from the ages of 16 to 25.

Extent of duty and definition of learning difficulty

The definition of learning difficulty, therefore, is exactly the same as that under the 1981 Act and section 321 of the Education Act 1996. This is a very wide definition indeed; it basically covers all forms of disability, including mild ones. The extent of this definition has been considered under the 1981 Act in *R. v. Hampshire Education Authority, ex p. J,*[2] where Taylor J. made it quite clear that this is a very wide and extensive definition, covering effectively all possible learning difficulties. This is good authority in relation to the 1992 Act.

The extent of the duty in section 4 is therefore extremely wide and is owed to all those who would have fallen within the 1981 or 1996 Acts, whether or not they have statements of special educational needs. The definition in section 1 of the 1981 Act and in the 1996 Act covers all young persons with learning difficulties, not just children who are the subject of a statement; see *R. v. Hampshire.*[3]

This definition, also applies to young persons disabled due to disease, or who have been disabled as a result of accidents.

The council under section 4(2) shall have regard to requirements of persons who have learning difficulties. The duties under section 3 must be discharged so as to:

1. secure that the facilities provided at such places are of such character and so equipped as to meet the reasonable needs of education to which subsection (1) applies;
2. take account of the different abilities and aptitudes of persons among their population.

This is the general duty. Equally they have a discretion to secure these facilities where they are not under a duty to do so, section 3(3). However, the duty considered above can be best described as a target duty, equivalent to section 8 of the 1944 Act, which gives no individual rights save the right to be educated, enforceable in judicial review proceedings for young persons to secure the education which would normally be given. In *E. v. Dorset County Council and Others,*[4] where Sir Thomas Bingham M.R. and Evans L.J. considered the extent of the right of an individual to enforce the duty to educate. The considerations in Chapter 1 in relation to local authorities apply equally to the F.E.F.C. duty.

Adequacy of local facilities

Section 4, whilst lacking a mechanism such as the assessment procedure given by statute by the 1981 and 1996 Education Acts, does impose a more stringent obligation in section 4(3): a council shall, if they are satisfied in the case of any person among the population of their area who has a learning difficulty and is under the age of 25 years,

1. that the facilities available in institutions within the further education sector or the higher education sector are not adequate for him; and
2. that if it is in his best interest to do so,

secure provision for him at an institution outside those sectors. This obligation applies to a restricted class of persons, but not just to previously statemented pupils.

---

[2] (1985) 84 L.G.R. 547.
[3] *exp. J, supra.*
[4] [1994] 3 W.L.R. 853.

By section 4(4), therefore, they are obliged, if they are satisfied that they cannot secure provisions under section 4(3) unless they arrange boarding accommodation for him, to secure boarding accommodation for the young person.

By section 4(5) the council exercising functions under sections 2 and 3 in the case of any person who has a learning difficulty who is over compulsory school age may, if they are satisfied that the facilities available in institutions within the further and higher education sector or the higher educations sector are not adequate for him,

1. secure provision for him at an institution outside the sectors;
2. secure the provision of boarding accommodation for him.

There is therefore a power and a duty. What, then, does section 4(3) actually mean? The reasoning is as follows:

1. The council *must* be satisfied that the facilities available in institutions within the further or higher education sector are not adequate for the young person.
2. If it is in his best interests to do so, then the council *must* secure provision including accommodation, if necessary outside that sector. This, therefore, is a mandatory duty on the basis that the council is satisfied local facilities are not adequate and the council must act in the best interests of the young person.

This of course stresses the considerable importance of a proper assessment, and of presenting a properly prepared detailed case to the council on behalf of the young person.

Section 4(5) provides that the "council may . . . ", and is therefore a discretionary power. It extends to the provision of boarding accommodation as well. However, the conditions of the exercise of the discretion match section 3(a); namely, that they must be satisfied that the facilities are inadequate. The only material difference, therefore, between subsections (3) and (5) amounts to the fact that the subsection (3) test of whether it is "in the best interest" of the young person does not apply. In either case the council must be factually satisfied of the inadequacy of the facilities. This second discretionary power will have a practical effect where it is not necessarily "in the best interest" of the young person. This power is very relevant where there are two sides, one arguing that he be best kept at home, and the other saying that he would be better off receiving fuller support amounting to proper provision. If the council is faced with reasonable arguments of this nature evenly balanced, then obviously the provisions of section 4(5) apply. In practice, this would effectively be the difference between the two statutory provisions. The views of the young person in such a situation would, if capable of expression, be the most relevant factor.

For young persons with learning difficulties, these powers are very important. If the FEFC does not have provision for certain types of problems, then they cannot be satisfied as a matter of law that they have adequate facilities within the relevant sector. Section 4 requires a funding council to provide adequate facilities. If it does not, the effect is that it will have to pay for it elsewhere. It is to be hoped that DFE Circular 1/93 is applied in practice. This states that adequate facilities will be provided within the local area in as many cases as possible. However, obviously the council would find it cheaper, where specialised provision is needed, or for rarer forms of problems, to pay for adequate provision, as do local education authorities.

Section 4 does not require as a part of statutory policy (unlike the 1981 Act and to a lesser extent 1996 Act) education in the ordinary institution. The overall effect is to require adequate provision to be provided for, if it is not available locally.

It is important to realise that the duty under section 4 is not restricted to the young persons with statements of special educational needs.

Even after the long period of time since the implementation of the Education Act 1981, many children with severe special educational needs have not been made the subject of a statement. Equally, children or young persons with special educational needs can be given considerable help without being the subject of a statement of special educational needs. On a practical basis, a statement of special educational needs, together with an assessment under the Disabled Persons (Services, Consultation and Representation) Act 1986, ss. 3 and 5, or the use of the review assistance of the LEA, will be of considerable assistance where the duty under section 4 to make special educational provision either in the local area or outside the local area arises. The statement is not a prerequisite of any such help, neither is it a sole key to out-of-area specialist education.

In practice, the long-term effect of the legislation may well be to include virtually all children with a requirement for out-of-area special provision, or who have such a prospect in the category of statemented children.

The majority of students will be catered for in the local college under this duty. The duty is not placed directly on the college, it is a duty which is imposed on the council. Arguably a college would be acting unlawfully were it to accept a young person, without making adequate provision for that young person. There would at least be a legitimate expectation as to appropriate provision in such circumstances. Whilst the Act would expect specialised placement under section 4 where the local college provision is not adequate; however, the expectation is that the local colleges will be able to make provision that the council will fund and plan for it within the local area.

Planning between local authorities and the FEFCs for assessment: the importance of annual reviews post-14

By section 328(5)(b), annual reviews must be carried out on an annual basis and the Regulations provide for the system. The purpose of all annual reviews is to integrate a variety of perspectives on the child or young person's progress, to ensure that he or she is achieving the desired progress and, if necessary, to amend the statement to reflect newly identified needs and provisions. The object of the annual review at 14 is to produce a transition plan, which will draw together information from a range of individuals within and beyond the school, in order to plan carefully and accurately for the young person's transition into further educational and adult life.

The involvement of social services in the first annual review after the young person's fourteenth birthday is required under sections 5 and 6 of the Disabled Persons (Services, Consultation and Representation) Act 1986, and the Code of

Practice, to which local education authorities must have regard under section 313(2) of the 1996 Education Act. They are required to consult the careers service, the child health services, and any other professionals such as educational psychologists, speech therapists or occupational therapists, other psychologists, or doctors who may have a useful contribution to make.

Review procedure

The basic procedure is that the LEA initiates the review in writing to require the teacher of the school to submit a review report by the specified date. The LEA must give at least two months notice of the date by which the report is required. As with normal annual reviews, a review report is prepared; the head teacher acts as co-ordinator and must seek written advice from people specified by the LEA. The head teacher must be informed by the LEA whom he or she should invite to contribute to the review and attend the meeting. Those invited must include the child's parents, or, if the child is accommodated by the local authority, his or her carer, and relevant teacher. The latter may be the school's special educational needs co-ordinator (SENCO), but the choice rests with the head teacher. Where appropriate the head teacher may tell representatives of the district health authority or social services department or other professionals closely involved that they are invited to contribute to the review summary and to attend the meeting.

The head teacher has the power to invite such representatives and professionals as he or she sees fit, even if not asked to do so by the LEA. The Code of Practice[5] suggests in such cases that the head teacher should indicate the priority attached to their attendance. Where a young person is placed outside the area of the LEA responsible for a statement, a representative of the responsible LEA and of relevant professionals such as educational psychologists should wherever possible attend the meeting.

In preparing for the review meeting, the head teacher must request written reports from the child's teachers, parents and all relevant professionals. He then summarises the evidence received and circulates a copy of that review summary to all those hoping to attend the meeting at least two weeks before the date of the meeting. Additional comments should be invited.

In annual reviews at the age of 14, the LEA must ensure that other providers such as social services are aware of the annual review and the procedures to be followed. They should always invite social services to attend, so that any parallel assessment or work under the Disabled Persons Act 1986, the NHS and Community Care Act 1990, the Chronically Sick and Disabled Persons Act, or the Children Act 1989 can be considered in the review.

The LEA must invite the regional committee of the FEFC to be represented at the review meeting, to ensure that any information which may be required by the FEFC in determining admission arrangements to a local college or to an independent college outside the sector is collected. Also, the young person and his or her family must be fully informed about the full range of options.

---

[5] Code of Practice, para. 6:42–6:62.

Formulating the transition plan

It is particularly important that the LEA should invite the careers service to be represented at the review meeting, to enable all options for careers and vocational training to be given serious consideration. The careers service will also be able to identify any specific targets which should be set as part of the annual review to ensure that independent training, personal or social skills or aspects of a wider curriculum are fully addressed in the young person's last years at school.

The Code of Practice[6] states that the plan should address the following questions.

1. What are the young person's curriculum needs during transition?
2. How can the curriculum help him or her to place his or her role in the community, and make use of leisure and recreational facilities, assume new roles in the family, develop new educational and vocational skills?
3. How can professionals develop close working relationships with colleagues and other agencies to ensure effective and coherent plans for the young person in transition?
4. Which new professionals need to be involved in planning for transition (*e.g.* occupational therapists, careers service, other therapists)?
5. Does the young person have any special health or welfare needs which require planning and support from health and social services, now or in the future?
6. Are the assessment arrangements for transition clear, relevant and shared between all the agencies concerned?
7. How can information best be transferred from the children to adult services to ensure a smooth transition?
8. Does the young person require particular technological aids? The arrangements for a transition should include appropriate training and arrangements for securing technological support.
9. What do the parents expect of their son or daughter?
10. What can the family contribute in terms of helping their child to develop personal and social skills, an adult lifestyle, and the acquisition of new skills?
11. Will the parents experience new care needs and require practical help in terms of aids, adaptations or general support during these years?
12. What information does the young person need in order to make informed choices?
13. What local arrangements exist to provide advocacy and advice or other relevant support services?
14. How can young persons be encouraged to contribute to their own plans and make positive decisions about the future?
15. If the young person is away from home, or attending a residential school outside their area, are there special issues relating to their return when they leave school, which require specific planning?

The transition plan which results from the 14-year review is to be built upon. The next annual review, and later annual reviews, should focus on all the aspects of

[6] Code of Practice, para. 6:45–6.47.

the young person. Social services departments, health authorities and the careers service should be invited to be actively involved.

The need for specialised placement

In such reviews, issues as to whether the powers under the National Health and Community Care Act 1996 and the Chronically Sick and Disabled Persons Act 1970, help in the home and with adaptations in the home, should be actively considered and raised with social services. Obviously, for those who are to be in community care, and who will require either considerable and constant attendance at home, or placement outside of the home, the reviews are crucial. It is at this point where consideration must be given carefully as to whether individual care plans may be needed.

Where the annual reviews reveal a need for an FEFC specialised placement, the FEFC has agreed a procedure with the local authorities. The agreed policy is published so far almost annually in circular currently 95/07 and provides a system of assessment, for those with learning difficulties. In order to substitute for the Education Act 1996 assessment act system, the FEFC has agreed with the local authority associations, that the LEA will:

1. assess the educational needs of young people with learning difficulties and disabilities; and
2. support their effective transition to further education where that is appropriate.

The agreement is reproduced in the full text of the current circular issued by the FEFC The object of the assessment is to produce a thorough consideration of a student's needs so that the council can make an appropriate decision as to whether education provision at a specialist college outside the local sector is required.

The agreement provides for the local authority to make available to the FEFC advice on the educational needs of a student, and supporting assessments which are carried out by the LEA under the 1996 Act. It is expected to identify the provision required and the support which is not available which requires a specialist provision. It is also expected to recommend to the FEFC a placement which will meet a student's needs at an institution outside the local sector. The FEFC will then receive the recommendation and make a decision as to placement.

Clearly, for the duty to place outside area to apply, the LEA must have no appropriate local provision itself, assuming the young person is still within the jurisdiction of the LEA, and the *Goddard* case[7] clearly establishes that the LEA must retain responsibility where it has adequate provision. Equally, the circular gives rise to a legitimate expectation by the young person, and a breach of procedure would entitle the young person to seek judicial review. In disputed cases the FEFC is now in some cases offering an appeal. This appeal is based on the old 1981 Act Advisory Appeal Committees. Procedures are informal, and the

[7] See n. 1, above.

Committee issues an advisory decision. The final decision is made by the F.E.F.C., not the Advisory Committee.

However, the powers of the authority do not include powers to fund a provision maintained by a local education authority. Section 5(4) of the 1992 Act provides that the FEFC cannot support financially a local education authority, the governing body of a grant-maintained school, or a person maintaining or carrying on a city technology college or a city college for the technology of the arts, thereby preventing a council from paying a local authority for specialised provision at any public sector school. It can, however, fund a placement at a private sector school which has a post-16 role or provision.

Chapter 8
Negligence and Children with Special Educational Needs

Professional liability

The law concerning the duty of care of professionals in assessing children with special needs was clarified by the House of Lords in *X (a minor) v. Bedfordshire County Council*,[1] for the first time defining the liability of professionals in this area.

The private sector

Psychologists in private practice, independent schools, teachers acting privately as specialist teachers and advisory teachers in the independent sector, are all providing a service. They work under fairly clearly defined legal duties, which are relatively easy to discern due to the law of contract. The law in negligence concerning those in the independent sector could have been described as less obvious, but as they provide a contractual service, analogies could be drawn from others providing similar services such as private medical services. There was little doubt that they were subject to liability.

For those involved in statutory assessments, statute provided guidance as to the task in the assessment, but not as to professional liability.

However, apart from the more obvious type of case involving claims for school fees, there was little litigation in this area.

The public sector

For those working in the public sector the situation was different. Psychologists, specialist advisory teachers working with local education authorities, those staff working within school in the equivalent role, together with education officers, who interpreted advice, were thought by some to be subject to the same liability as those working in the private sector. There was, as in the independent sector, no clear law on this issue, and opinion was divided as to whether those working in the state sector were liable in negligence other than for physical injury due to breach of duty. As with all local authority employees, there is no question of contract therefore within the constraints of public policy the law of negligence governs their position.

[1] [1995] 3 W.L.R. 152.

The House of Lords' cases

The debate in this field was resolved by the House of Lords, which also considered the position of social workers and specialists, doctors and psychologists advising in Children Act cases, in a series of five cases—two Children Act cases and three Education Act cases.

The issues of liability and negligence, for those who work with children with difficulties, and who assess their needs, produces considerable controversy. At first instance in the High Court Otton J. struck out the two lead cases, *E (a minor) v. Dorset* and *Christmas v. Hampshire County Council*, on the basis that no such claim was sustainable. The cases are unreported. The two Children Act cases, although heard in the High Court after the judgment of Otton J., went to the Court of Appeal first, and by a majority of two to one, on the issue of common law and negligence, the Court of Appeal dismissed the cases largely on the basis of the reasoning of Otton J.: *M (a minor) v. Newham L.B.C.*[2] When the Education Act cases came to the Court of Appeal they were joined by a third case, *Keating v. Bromley*. All three cases succeeded unanimously on the issue of common law negligence.[3]

In the House of Lords the defendant LEA's appeals failed. The opinion of the House of Lords upheld the striking out of all three claims in so far as they are based on breach of statutory duty. Whilst accepting that the careless performance of statutory duty, which led to inadequate or inappropriate provision being made for a child with special educational needs could cause damage, for the following reasons, the House of Lords concluded it would not be appropriate to conclude that any such breach of statutory duty could give rise to a private law cause of action:

1. The involvement of the parents through the statutory mechanisms of the Education Act 1981 and now the Education Act 1996 Part IV. In addition, the existance of the statutory appeals structure.
2. The risk of hopeless, possibly vexatious cases being brought. Lord Browne-Wilkinson went on to say as follows:

> *"If there were no other remedy open this is a price which might have to be paid in the interests of justice. But, in almost every case which could give rise to a claim for negligent exercise of the statutory discretions, it is probable that, as in the present case, there would be an alternative remedy by way of a claim against the Authority on the grounds of its vicarious liability for the negligent advice on the basis of which it exercises its discretion . . ."*

3. The structure of the statutory framework which contains detailed safeguards for securing the performance of the Authority's statutory purpose together with a subsequent appellant structure. This structure has now been reinforced by the creation of the Special Educational Needs Tribunal, with its power to make orders binding upon Authorities.[4]

---

[2] [1994] 2 W.L.R. 554.
[3] *E (a minor) v. Dorset County Council* [1994] 3 W.L.R. 853.
[4] Lord Browne-Wilkinson *X v. Bedfordshire County Council* [1995] 3 W.L.R. 152 *per* Lord Browne-Wilkinson 189–191.

However, the House of Lords indicated that educational psychologists were liable in negligence, and by parity of reasoning so are education officers who implement their advice. They extended this category to head teachers of schools, who were responsible for children failing or under-performing, and teachers who gave specialist advice. The implications of the House of Lords' opinion, particularly in the *Christmas* case, where there was evidence of failure by a head teacher or a specialist teacher, is wider than the actual claims made in all three cases before the House of Lords.

The Court of Appeal based its reasoning on a medical comparison and the comparison with private schools. The medical comparison had previously been adopted in cases of statement of special educational needs, *i.e.* Parts II and III of a statement providing a diagnosis and perscription of a child's special educational needs.[5] It is interesting that it was considered likely that if the standard of education provided in a private school was not reasonably fit for its purpose—a contractual test—that an action was available. Although perhaps tangential to the issue of professional negligence, it does raise the issue of redress for failure to provide education in the public sector, an area where no law presently exists on the issue of defective education.

The issue of professional negligence

On the issue of professional negligence, the opinion of the House of Lords was delivered in detail by Lord Browne-Wilkinson. In the case of *Christmas v. Hampshire County Council*, the views of their Lordships on the duties of teachers were a considerable expansion in the area of liability. At pp. 198D–199B Lord Browne-Wilkinson pointed out that "the education of the pupil is the very purpose for which the child goes to the school. The head teacher, being responsible for the school, himself comes under a duty of care to exercise the reasonable skills of the head master in relation to such educational needs." The *Dorset* and *Christmas* cases were both based on traditional negligence claims, the foundation of which was the existence of special educational needs rooted in a discernible physical origin or an identifiable and recognised illness thus encompassing both teaching staff and educational psychology services. In the *Dorset* case, it was made clear that dyslexia or specific learning difficulties and their origins were based on psychological defects in the brain. Therefore there was no difference in the role of specialists in this area from those offering treatment at a hospital, or a doctor's surgery to remedy a medical problem, whether inherent or accidental.

For example where a person presents to hospital staff as a result of brain damage at birth or a road accident, it is immaterial that the condition arises either from problems the person was born with, or problems experienced as a result of accident or injury. The hospital staff hold themselves out as experienced in remediating the condition so far as it is possible to do so on the basis of the current knowledge and facilities available to the profession.

The House of Lords have certainly left open the issue as to whether educational needs which are linked with other issues which do not arise from psychiatric illness, physical origin, or some later accident or injury can found an action in negligence.

[5] *R. v. Secretary of State, ex p. "E"* [1992] F.L.R. 377.

However, for those assessing learning difficulties, the cases where it will be difficult to show an origin of this type will be rare or possibly non-existent, and the law is relatively clear.

Neither reported judgments considered whether it is possible that a claim can be extended for education that is so bad that it is not fit for its purpose in contractual terms. For those who work in the public sector a claim that education has been negligently delivered remains a theoretical possibility. However, by equating the professionals in this field with those in the health service, the House of Lords has afforded them considerable protection.

The position in negligence (applicable to those working for the public sector or in the independent sector).

The law in this field is the same for all those providing professional services education, whether in the public sector or in the independent sector. This extends to educational psychologists, education officers (a category that would include those who work for FEFCs, and for that matter within universities) teachers who provide specialist advice, whether with specialist qualifications or simply by the exercise of their experience, and head teachers. The liability of a head teacher arises on the basis that he is responsible for the school, and he himself comes under a duty to exercise the reasonable skills of a head master in relation to such educational needs:

> "If it comes to the attention of the head master that a pupil is under-performing, he does owe a duty to take such steps as a reasonable teacher would consider appropriate to try to deal with such under-performance. To hold that, in such circumstances, the head teacher could properly ignore the matter and make no attempt to deal with it would fly in the face, not only of society's expectations of what a school will provide, but also of the fine traditions of the teaching profession itself," *per* Lord Browne-Wilkinson in the House of Lords *X (Minor) v. Bedfordshire and others.*[6]

Clearly therefore if the school does not identify the child with special needs, where the matter does not come to the head teacher's attention, if the failure to identify the child as under-performing and failing is due to negligence in the organisation of the school, or the negligence of a class teacher or a number of teachers, then the head teacher will not escape liability.

This reasoning of course has considerable implications, particularly for teachers, and education officers, but even more so for psychologists. It is advisable for all those who come in from outside, particularly from a local authority, or those in the independent sector who are advising on the child in a school, to carefully check the facts brought to their attention and the true position.

[6] [1995] 3 W.L.R. 152, pp. 198D–199B.

Vicarious liability

The judgment in the House of Lords was based on the principle of vicarious liability in the public sector and the independent sector. Psychologists, education officers, all in the teaching profession, are normally employed, and it will be their employers who will be the subject of an action. For those in the independent sector, particularly for educational psychologists operating their own service or part of such a service, and specialist teachers in the same position, there is a plain need to ensure that insurance cover is available, and has been taken out. Teaching and administrative staff in the private sector are governed by the same principle of vicarious liability, and it will be their employers against whom an action is brought.

The duty of care: psychologists and related staff.

The imposition of a common law duty of care in the present field was stated, *per* Lord Browne-Wilkinson as follows:

> "Psychologists (including educational psychologists) hold themselves out as having special skills and they are, in my judgment, like any other professional bound to possess such skills and to exercise them carefully. Of course, the test in *Bolam v. The Friern Hospital Management Committee* will apply to them."[7]

This test means that psychologists are only bound to exercise the ordinary skill of a competent psychologist, and if they can show that they acted in accordance with the accepted views of some reputable psychologist at the relevant time, they will have discharged the duty of care, even if some psychologists would have taken a different view. It was pointed out by the Lords that the advice on the treatment of dyslexia had advanced considerably in recent years, and this may be an important factor in liability. Therefore so long as psychologists work in accordance with an acceptable body of opinion in the profession, they will normally be exempt from liability.

However, it is to be noted that in a leading medical negligence case in this issue, *Sidaway v. Board of Governors of the Bethlem Royal Hospital and the Maudsley Hospital*[8] the House of Lords expressly reserved the issue as to whether a reputable body of opinion could be regarded by the courts as unreasonable. There have been cases where a failure to make adequate provision for educational needs was due to administrative decisions or lack of funds, despite the fact that the statutory duty is that the law requires provision to be reasonably appropriate, irrespective of cost. This would mean a body of opinion which related solely to cost at the expense of any effective but not Utopian provision would not be reasonable, even if respectable. A decision by a psychologist which is related to costs may be in conflict with his or her own duty. The fact that there is a supporting body of opinion may not be sufficient to justify the decision.

---

[7] [1957]1 W.L.R. 582.
[8] [1985] A.C. 871.

Psychologists exercise a higher degree of professional skill for the purposes of legal liability than teachers.

However, the question of whether the provision of a psychology service is simply a different aspect of authorities' performance of statutory function therefore precluding the existence of a duty of care, was left open.

The duty of care: teachers

The House of Lords considered the following question in the case of teachers:

> "The question therefore is whether the Head Master of any school whether private or public or a teaching adviser, is under a duty to his pupils to exercise care and skill in advising on their educational needs?"

It is accepted that a school and teachers at the school are under a duty to safeguard the physical wellbeing of a pupil—see *Van Oppen v. Clerk to the Charity Trustees*.[9] The House of Lords extended this principle to cover the advice given to and remediation of those pupils with special educational needs. In the passage already quoted, the House of Lords held that a head teacher does exercise a duty of care. In the case of an advisory teacher brought in to advise on the educational needs of the specific pupil, such a teacher knows that his advice will be communicated to the pupil's parents, or should proceed on the basis that they will rely on such advice. Therefore in giving such advice such a teacher owes a duty to the child to exercise the care and skill of a reasonable advisory teacher. The teaching profession therefore falls within the same category as psychologists.

The standard of care for teachers

The head teacher and an advisory teacher are only bound to exercise the skill and care of a reasonable head teacher and advisory teacher. The test in the *Bolam* case[10] which applies to an educational psychologist will apply to the teaching profession: namely, whether the advice and views might have been entertained and given by reasonable members of the teaching profession. Clearly such teachers are not under any duty to exercise a higher degree of skill such as that of an educational psychologist. If the views they hold represent a reasonable view held on the date by a responsible body of educational thinking, in the same way as psychologist would escape liability, so will teachers, even if they are actually wrong.

On a practical basis, liability is likely to be proved in cases which involve maladministration—for example doing nothing—when the needs of the child are known at least to a degree and are provided for inadequately, either by ignoring clear evidence as to greater extent of the needs, by failing to act, or by deliberately taking the decision not to act. In such cases, professionals will not escape liability simply because they might have had another view available, where no such view was ever consulted or applied.

[9] [1990] 1 W.L.R. 235.
[10] See n. 6, above.

It is possible that, in the long run, the independent sector, because of its constituency, could face many claims.

The position in contract

Private sector staff

The law of contract has no application in the public sector, those working within the public sector not being subject to liability and contract. For those working in the private sector, however, matters are different. For those working within schools, particularly head teachers and advisory teachers, the House of Lords equated the position within the independent sector and within the state sector as being exactly the same. It is a useful guide to the duty and contract. A school and all independent psychologists and advisors will most certainly be expected to provide advice in this area that is reasonably fit for its purpose. Where there is specialist provision, the provision also must be reasonably fit for its purpose, and delivered by those who are competently qualified either by experience or qualification to deliver such provision, in a manner that is efficient and fit for its purpose.

The main implication for the independent sector for those in teaching, is that it would be wise and expedient to have views of the school checked by a competent independent professional, normally an educational psychologist. This would in any event mirror the public sector, which is under such a statutory duty, and would be an appropriate move by those working in the independent sector.

Private sector educational psychologists and advisory or specialist teachers

The position of the independent educational psychologist and independent advisory or specialist teacher will be governed by the contract that they will have with the parent. In practice such contracts are often governed by the absence of anything in writing, or alternatively the absence of anything relevant to the task in hand. Clearly, as a result of the House of Lords judgment, it can be said that psychologists exercise a higher degree of professional care and skill than the teaching profession and are to be treated as skilled professionals, with a degree of skill and ability which is equated to that of the medical profession. The law will imply into a contract a term that all psychologists will exercise a reasonable degree of care and skill, to the appropriate standard.

Secondly, the advice given must be fit for its purpose. This is a term of the contract well established as a matter of law and is in fact trite law. Experience in dealing with children with special needs has shown, however, that reports of independent psychologists sometimes do not provide advice that is fit for the purpose, as they do not deal with all the issues.

If the referral is from a school, it is highly likely that the school will want more than a simple diagnosis of the child's needs and that they will also want advice on the provision to meet those needs. In the same way if a parent consults a psychologist, they will expect not only a diagnosis but advice on provision. Clearly the law will imply such terms into such a situation; the advice needs to be fit for the purpose which governs the consultation between the psychologist and the child's parents. For the psychologist, a failure to advise on provision adequately will be capable of sustaining a claim in contract and they will be expected to provide their advice competently to a high degree of care and skill. That means that, for example, where a child is entitled to a statement, as some are within the state sector, then the psychologist may be in breach of a contract or negligent in failing to advise the parent to seek an assessment by statute for a statement. The report must deal therefore with the basis of the advice sought by the parent on behalf of the child or young person.

Chapter 9
Legal Aid and Education Law

The Advice and Assistance Scheme (Green Form)

The eligibility rates quoted are as at April 8, 1996 and Key Card No. 28 applies. Please note these eligibility rates do vary; the Legal Aid Handbook lists current eligibility tables.

To receive advice and assistance, the applicant must meet both a capital qualification and an income qualification. The following are the present financial details. They will change during the production of this edition.

Disposable Capital

The limits are as follows:
No dependants: £1,000;
one dependant: £1,335.00;
two dependants: £1,535.00.
£100.00 is allowed for each additional dependant.

Disposable Income

1. The applicant will not be eligible if disposable income is in excess of £75.00 per week.
2. The applicant will automatically qualify on *income* grounds if in receipt of the following benefits:

- income support;
- family credit;
- disability working allowance.

Note – Although the above benefits will automatically meet the disposable income criteria, the applicant may not fulfil the disposable capital requirements.

Weekly dependants' allowances

Partner: £27.30
Dependants:

Under 11 years: £16.45;
11–15 years: £24.10;
16–17 years: £28.85;
18 and over: £37.90.

Financial limits on work to be undertaken

The advice and assistance scheme is limited to a solicitor undertaking up to two hours' work. The rates claimable for the work done vary according to whether the fee-earner works in a firm which holds a franchise in a particular area and whether the fee-earner is based in London or outside London.

The rates quoted below are for work undertaken since April 1, 1996. The rates for fee-earners in the London area appear in brackets.

	Franchises	Non-Franchises
Preparation	£45.50 (£48.25)	£44.00 (£46.50)
Travel and waiting	£25.50 (£25.50)	£24.50 (£24.50)
Routine letters and telephone calls	£3.55 (£3.70)	£3.40 (£3.55)
Costs limits:		
Petition preparation (divorce)	£136.50 (£144.75)	£132.00 (£139.50)
Other cases	£91.00 (£96.50)	£88.00 (£93.00)

Scope of advice and assistance

The advice and assistance scheme is aimed at providing general assistance, writing letters, negotiating and the preparation of written cases for Tribunal. The Legal Advice and Assistance (Scope) Regulations 1989 set out what is excluded from the scheme. In the case of education law, all areas would be covered by the present advice and assistance scheme.

It should be noted that the Green Form Scheme does not cover the taking of any step in proceedings. Additionally, it will not cover representation of a client at a hearing before the Special Educational Needs Tribunal or at an exclusion appeal hearing.[1]

[1] See n. 2, below. "Special cases" for Mackenzie friend.

Extension of advice and assistance scheme

It will often be necessary for the legal adviser to consider extending the limits of the advice and assistance scheme. In the case of education law matters, it is not usual for a fee-earner to be in the position of having devolved powers under the franchise. This may apply in certain limited cases, such as where personal injury arises. Given that devolved powers will not usually apply, the solicitor will need to obtain prior authority from the local area office before exceeding the prescribed limits.

Application is made to the area office on Form GF3. This requires a costing of work already undertaken and an outline costing of work to be done.

In considering an extension, the area office will need to be assured that the problem is one covered by the advice and assistance scheme, and is not an area where it would be more appropriate to seek full legal aid or ABWOR. Additionally, the area office will seek clarification of whether alternative sources of finance may be available, *e.g.* legal insurance.

Once these criteria have been met, the reasonableness of the extension in a particular case will be considered. This will include the prospects of success, whether the money or benefit justifies the expenditure, and whether it is reasonable for the client to deal with some of the steps him/herself, having regard to all circumstances of the case.

Extension of the Green Form Scheme can also be of considerable use in obtaining counsel's opinion. Prior authority will again need to be sought from the area office, which will look particularly at whether the matter appears to be beyond the expertise of a reasonably competent solicitor. In education matters, it should be possible to show that the specialisation of the area requires counsel's opinion.

In certain exceptional cases it is possible to extend the advice and assistance scheme to cover the obtaining of expert reports such as speech therapy reports, medical reports, etc. Any such application will be subject to the reasonableness test applied by the area office. It should also be borne in mind that when an application is being made for an extension for experts' reports, it is often the case that legal proceedings are being considered and it may therefore be more appropriate to make a full legal aid application.

Special cases

Mackenzie Advisers

In limited circumstances, extension of advice and assistance can be obtained to allow the legal adviser to attend with a client at a Tribunal hearing or Court proceedings. This is based on the interpretation of the definition of advice and assistance under the Legal Aid Act 1988, as set out in *MacKenzie v. MacKenzie*.[2]

It must be borne in mind that there can be no representation of the client at the Tribunal or Court hearing. The client must be fully aware that the legal adviser is present to help him/her informally without actually being able to represent the case.

[2] 1971, p.33.

To obtain extension to cover a MacKenzie Adviser, the area office will require evidence to show:

1. that full legal aid could not be granted for proceedings;
2. that the client requires the service of a MacKenzie Adviser due to the difficulty of the case, the importance of the matter to the client and/or the inability of the client to act on his or her own without legal help.

This can be very useful for parents attending at Special Needs Tribunals or at exclusion appeals. Both are formidable situations, when the informal guidance of a legal representative may be invaluable.

Age limits

The advice and assistance scheme is limited to those over school leaving age (at present, 16 years old). However, a child can receive help under the scheme if the application is made by the parent/guardian on the child's behalf. In that case, the parent/guardian's financial means will be relevant when assessing eligibility.

Where a legal adviser wishes to take instructions directly from the child, this can be done by obtaining a prior authority from the area office. A Form GF5 would need to be completed. Prior authority will be granted if:

1. there is good reason why a parent or guardian is not applying, *e.g.* conflict of interest *or* the child needs separate representation; *and*
2. the child is old enough to give instructions and to understand the nature of the advice and assistance.

The solicitor may consider it is just and equitable not to aggregate the child's means with those liable to maintain him/her in the above circumstances.

In very limited circumstances, a child can be advised without obtaining prior authority from the area office. This would usually apply to advising a child at the police station or where a child is entitled, in his or her own right, to begin, prosecute or defend proceedings without a next friend or guardian *ad litem*.

It should be remembered that young people over school leaving age, who are in receipt of income support, or who are in vocational training, may qualify for Green Form advice and assistance.

Civil legal aid

Civil legal aid is subject to both a financial means test and a merits test.

Financial eligibility

The Legal Aid Handbook has an assessment guide and eligibility tables. When an application is made for legal aid, a financial assessment is undertaken by the Legal Aid Assessment Office, part of the Benefits Agency. The Civil Legal Aid (Assessment of Resources) Regulations 1989 allow an element of discretion in the assessment, so that an entirely accurate means assessment can only be obtained by submitting a legal aid application. The following are therefore only guidelines.

Capital limits

Lower capital limit: £3,000.00.

Upper capital limit: £6,750.00 (£8,560.00 for personal injury).

Income limits

Lower income limit: £2,498.00 per year.

Upper income limit: £7,403.00 per year (£8,158.00 for personal injury).

Note – all applicants in receipt of income support are eligible for civil legal aid regardless of capital.

Yearly dependants' allowances

Partner: £1,423.00

Dependants:
under 11 years: £858.00;
11–15 years: £1,257.00;
16–17 years: £1,504.00;
18 and over: £1,976.00.

Contributions System

Since April 1993, a new system of legal aid contributions has been introduced. Instead of contributions from income being paid over a 12-month period, legal aid contributions are now payable for the lifetime of the certificate. Disposable income is assessed on an annual basis but is used to calculate an on-going monthly contribution liability. An applicant liable to contributions will be made an offer of legal aid. On acceptance of the offer, the applicant must pay any contribution from capital immediately together with the first monthly income contribution. Thereafter, contributions in respect of income must be made every month.

As a rough guide, on-going monthly contributions of 1/36th of income in excess of £2,498.00 per annum must be paid during the lifetime of the certificate. Contributions from capital would involve that in excess of £3,000.00.

As stated previously, guidance to assessing financial eligibility should be sought from the Legal Aid Handbook 1996/7.[3] For further help, contact the Customer Service Section of the Legal Aid Assessment Office.[4] Remember, this is only a rough guide.

[3] See pp. 523–529.

[4] 01772 898061 or 01172 898064.

Assessing the client's financial eligibility for civil legal aid

Step one: Identify clients in receipt of income support

Applicants properly in receipt of income support are eligible for free civil legal aid. If the client is not in receipt of income support, move on to step two. Other types of benefit, such as family credit, do not give automatic entitlement.

Step two: Work out capital

Add together all the capital of the client (and partner, if appropriate).

Capital includes:

- land and buildings other than the client's home and including interests in timeshares; market value of client's home in excess of £100,000;
- money in the bank, building society, Post Office, premium bonds, National Savings Certificates, etc;
- investments, stocks and shares;
- money that can be borrowed against the surrender value of insurance policies;
- money value of valuable items, for example, boat, caravan, antiques, jewellery (but not wedding or engagement rings nor usually the client's car);
- money owing to the client;
- money due from an estate or trust fund;
- money that can be borrowed against business assets.

Do not include any savings, valuable items or property the ownership of which is the specific subject of the court case; for example, a holiday cottage would normally count, but not if it was under attack as part of a disputed divorce settlement.

Do not include:

- loans or grants from the social fund;
- the client's home and its contents, for example (unless exceptionally valuable) furniture and household effects;
- personal clothing;
- personal tools and equipment of trade.

Step three: Does the disposable capital qualify the client for legal aid?

- If under £3,000 – no contribution from capital.
- If between £3,000 and £6,750 (personal injury £8,560) – civil legal aid subject to a capital contribution.

Over these limits, the client will not get civil legal aid unless the area office considers the probable costs would exceed the contribution payable.

Step four: Work out the size of the client's likely capital contribution

Deduct £3,000 from the client's total disposable capital to give their capital contribution.

Step five: Work out weekly income

Add together the client's weekly gross income (*i.e.* before tax) and that of his/her partner if appropriate.

Income includes:

- weekly earnings or profits from business;
- maintenance payments;
- pensions;
- all welfare benefits except housing benefit, attendance allowance, disability living allowance and constant attendance allowance;
- income from savings and investments;
- dividends from shares;
- moneys received from friends and relatives;
- student grants and loans.

Step six: Work out deductible allowances and expenses

Deduct the following from *weekly* income:

- income tax, national insurance contributions, pension scheme contributions; trade union membership;
- council tax;
- maintenance payments made;

- fares to and from work;
- childcare expenses incurred because of work;
- housing costs:
  - — rent (less any housing benefit), water rates and mortgage repayments (interest and capital); includes mortgage debt in excess of £100,000 proportionately;
  - — £5.08 weekly for necessary repairs and house insurance (where payable by the client owner-occupier);
  - — endowment policy premiums (if paid in connection with a mortgage);
  - — actual costs of accommodation, if the client is neither a tenant nor owner-occupier;
  - — if food is included, deduct from the rent £16.81 a week (£26.42 if living with someone as husband and wife); if heat is provided, deduct from rent £4.80 a week;
  - — ground rent and any other applicable charges; and service charges which have to be paid as part of a lease or tenancy agreement;
- fixed amounts for each dependant relative (adult and child) living with the client.

The *weekly* amounts of allowances for dependants are:

- £27.36 for a partner;
- £16.50 for each child under 11;
- £24.17 for each child aged 11–15;
- £28.27 for each child aged 16–17;
- £38.00 for each child or dependant aged 18 or over.

Note that other deductions may be made by the Legal Aid Assessment Office, *e.g.* for membership of professional associations connected with employment, fines and judgments, school fees and payments of arrears of tax, mortgage, gas or electricity.

Step seven: Work out yearly disposable income

Subtract client's deductions from their weekly income to give their weekly disposable income. Multiply by 52 to give their yearly disposable income.

Step eight: Does the yearly disposable income qualify the client for civil legal aid?

If under £2,498 – no contribution from income.

If between £2,498 and £7,403 (£8,158 in personal injury claims) – civil legal aid subject to a contribution from income.

Step nine: Work out amount of contribution from income

Deduct £2,498 from client's yearly disposable income then divide by 36 to give their monthly contribution.

Step 10: Work out total initial contribution

Add together the client's monthly contribution and capital contribution to give their "total initial contribution".

Emergency legal aid

It is often necessary in education matters to make an application for emergency legal aid, which will be granted if the case is urgent. In particular, if judicial review proceedings are imminent, an emergency application for legal aid should be made.

An application for emergency legal aid can be made by telephone, but more usually by submission of legal aid forms including CLA 3. It is obvious that a full assessment cannot be made, either of means or of merit. The emergency grant will therefore only last until the full assessment has been completed by the Legal Aid Board and a proper decision taken.

Merits test

The general principle as regards grant of Legal Aid is found under Part IV of the Legal Aid Act 1988. This sets out both financial eligibility and a test of reasonableness on two levels.

Schedule 2 to the 1988 Act also specifies the proceedings for which legal aid is available. Matters of education law and related areas would be covered by the scope of the Civil Legal Aid.

The merits test, as set out in section 15(2) Legal Aid Act 1988 has two parts. There is a legal merits test and a reasonableness test. See also *Legal Aid Handbook 1996/7*, pp. 62–76.

Legal merits test

This requires that the legal adviser puts forward sufficient information to show that, on the facts and the law which relates to those facts, there is a case or a defence which should be put before the Court for a decision. The likelihood of success will be considered by the area office, but is not of the essence in determination of the legal merits test.

This element of the merits test will be met if:

1. There is an issue of fact or law which should be submitted to the Court for a decision.
2. The solicitor would advise the applicant to take or defend proceedings privately, if the applicant had means which were adequate to meet the likely costs of the case.
3. The applicant can show that as a matter of law, he has reasonable

grounds for taking or defending proceedings. This is the success element of the test. The solicitor must be able to show that there is a case or defence which has a reasonable prospect of success assuming the facts are proved.

Reasonableness test

Even though the applicant may satisfy the criteria of the legal merits test, they must then go on to meet the requirements of the reasonableness test.[5]

As a basic guide, the reasonableness test will be fulfilled if a solicitor could say that, in all the circumstances, a fee-paying client of sufficient but not superabundant means, would be advised to take proceedings.

Legal aid is likely to be refused as unreasonable if the application reveals some illegal motive, or the conduct of the action is such as to be unacceptable to the Court. In addition, the local area office would take into account the cost effectiveness of the proceedings: that is, does the benefit to be achieved justify the cost.

In education matters, it is usual for the area office to accept that the benefit to the applicant will outweigh the costs of bringing the case. There is an acceptance by the Legal Aid Board that a loss of educational resources will significantly affect the applicant. However, this may not always be the case if the argument is, for instance, over provision of general assistant hours where the hours provided are marginally less than specified as required. Additionally, the new area of negligence will raise the issue of quantum as against the costs of a legal aid grant. It will therefore be necessary for the solicitor to bear this in mind when making a legal aid application and to ensure that sufficient evidence is shown on the legal aid forms or presented in documentation to the Legal Aid Board to justify the cost reasonableness test. See also *Legal Aid Handbook 1996/7*, pp. 65–72.

Children

It is possible for children to make application in their own right. This applies equally to those over 16 years old but in full-time education or undergoing vocational training. The means assessment is on the means of the children and not on the financial position of those liable to maintain them. A Form CLA 4F will need to be completed, and this raises questions of whether moneys are due to the child, *e.g.* from a trust fund or will.

In education and related Children Act and Community Care Act matters, it can be of considerable importance that Legal Aid can be granted to a child. The parent or guardian will appear on the certificate as the guardian *ad litem*/next friend.

It will still be necessary for the child applicant to fulfil the merits test applied by the Legal Aid area office.

---

[5] Legal Aid Act, s. 15(3).

Limitations on legal aid certificates

It is usual when a legal aid certificate is granted, for there to be a limitation in terms of steps that can be taken and also a financial limitation.

There is a general wording for limitations and this should be checked carefully prior to undertaking any steps. The same will apply to the costs limitation. Most certificates that are issued do not cover final hearing, and extension will need to be sought to cover this step. In judicial review proceedings, the Legal Aid Board will require counsel's advice to be submitted with the application for extension of legal aid where full judicial review hearing is due to take place. See "Notes for Guidance", *Legal Aid Handbook 1996/7*, p. 73.

Obtaining experts' reports

As education and related areas are complex matters, it is usually necessary to consider what expert reports might be needed. Application for prior authority to incur the costs of an expert should be made to the Legal Aid area office on Form CLA 31. It will be necessary to quote not only the estimated maximum cost figure, but also hourly rates for preparation and travel.

It is useful to build up a register of experts who have previously provided satisfactory evidential reports for various types of proceedings. Not every expert will have had the experience of preparing reports for legal cases. In particular, it needs to be borne in mind whether the expert can address the legal issues, be able to give evidence and to ensure that their advice is independent and objective.

Once the expert's expense has been incurred, application can be made for payment on account of costs. This is done on Form CLA 28.

In certain cases, firms with a franchise in such an area as personal injury may be able to instruct an expert without prior authority. This will necessarily depend upon the terms of the franchise they have been granted.

A client must be informed if an expert is instructed. This would be relevant to the issue of the "statutory charge".

Statutory charge

The statutory charge will arise in the following circumstances:

1. a judgment or settlement has resulted in an assisted person, wholly or in part, recovering or preserving property or money which does not come with any of the exemptions in regulation 94 of the Civil Legal Aid (General) Regulations 1989; and
2. there is a net deficiency on the assisted person's account to the Legal Aid Fund.

Until recently, the issue of the statutory charge has not raised particular difficulties in education and related matters, the reason being that damages or the receiving of money or property were not usually an issue. In certain cases, back-payments might arise for school fees or for specialist resources, but these were moneys already owed to institutions and could therefore be exempted from the statutory charge by the Board.

The recent negligence decisions will now give rise to claims in damages to which the statutory charge will apply. A solicitor who is dealing with a legal aid application should ensure that his client has the Legal Aid Board's latest leaflet on the statutory charge and that the principles of the statutory charge are fully explained to the client, both verbally and by letter.

In a considerable number of education law matters, costs will be met by the opponent—usually a local authority or statutory body. There is always an element that will not be covered by *inter partes* costs and which will need to be reclaimed from the Legal Aid Board. This is the element that will come out of any property or money not exempted by the Civil Legal Aid Regulations. The costs incurred under the Legal Aid Advice and Assistance Scheme will also be taken into account as being recoverable. If contributions have been payable, these will also be aggregated in working out what moneys are due. In certain circumstances, it may be that moneys are due back to the assisted person where contributions have been paid.

Costs

It is usual where a legally aided applicant has been successful in proceedings for a costs order to be made by the Court against the other side. It should be noted that this is not always the case in public law proceedings such as judicial review. If a matter is settled prior to full hearing, the Court may take the view that the public purse will pay whether costs are awarded against the respondent local authority or against the Legal Aid Board. This has ramifications for the solicitor of the assisted person. There is a considerable difference as to what rate the solicitor can charge on an *inter partes* basis as against the set remuneration rates allowed against the Legal Aid Board.

As regards the unsuccessful legally aided litigant, the Court may order payment of part of all the opponent's costs. The decision taken by the Court will depend on the legally aided applicant's means and conduct in connection with the dispute. It is often equal to the applicant's contributions under the Legal Aid Certificate.

As most education and related matters will be taken against local authorities, it is unlikely that a Court would make a costs order against a legally aided applicant; however, the possibility should be pointed out to the person in receipt of a grant of legal aid.

For what proceedings will a legal aid application be appropriate?

As has previously been stated, legal aid is not available for Special Educational Needs Tribunals or exclusion appeals. These will have to be dealt with, as far as possible, under the Advice and Assistance Scheme.

A full civil legal aid application may need to be made to cover taking steps in the following litigation:

1. applications for judicial review;

2. appeals from Special Educational Needs Tribunal;
3. negligence.

See "Notes for Guidance", *Legal Aid Handbook 1996/7*, pp. 73–74.

Judicial review

Prior to the 1993 Education Act and the setting up of the Special Educational Needs Tribunal, judicial review was the predominant method of challenging the decisions taken by education authorities and Secretary of State for Education. Since the alternative adjudication procedures under the 1993 Education Act, judicial review applications in education matters are now mainly limited to the following areas:

- breach of time limits under the 1993 Education Act and the Code of Practice;
- failure to provide resources specified in the Statement of Special Educational Needs;
- school transport.

Grounds for issuing an application for judicial review may also lie against the Special Educational Needs Tribunal for breach of procedure leading up to an appeal hearing. For instance, decisions not to register an appeal against a refusal to assess when the request for assessment is made by the school rather than the parent. It would be unlikely to lie against the decision of the Appeal Tribunal, as appeals can be made to the High Court on matters of law.

Applications for judicial review will usually need to be made by way of emergency application for full civil legal aid. Initial instructions and the letter before action always required for judicial review proceedings can be undertaken under the Green Form Scheme, if the client qualifies. Additionally, the legal aid application can be completed under the advice and assistance limits. See "Notes for Guidance", *Legal Aid Handbook 1996/7*, p. 73, specific to judicial review.

If judicial review proceedings are being considered, an emergency legal aid application will have to be made—judicial review proceedings have to be issued as soon as possible after the decision which they seek to challenge and, in any event, must be issued within three months of that decision.

There may be related decisions which can be subject to an application for judicial review. In particular, these might include Children Act assessments, assessments and resources provided under the Community Care Act, further education funding and other matters covered by related legislation.

The right to bring judicial review actions to challenge the decisions of the statutory bodies is that of the child, and legal aid will be granted to the child and assessed on the child's means. The parental/guardian's means will not be taken into account on any legal aid application made. This can be vital, as judicial review proceedings, being High Court proceedings, are extremely expensive and beyond the means of most parents.

A legal aid grant will not be given to the child if the challenge is to the procedures of the Special Educational Needs Tribunal. The right of appeal to the Tribunal is that of the parent, and any legal aid application will be based on the means of the parent/guardian. In certain cases, the parent may be entitled to legal aid in their own right, or on a contribution basis.

Appeal from Special Educational Needs Tribunal

This is separate from the possible lodging of judicial review proceedings and relates to appeals from decisions taken by the Tribunal following the Tribunal hearing. Under the 1993 Education Act and regulations governing the Special Educational Needs Tribunal, appeal against a Tribunal decision can only be on matters of law, not of fact.

The time limit for appealing against the decision of the Special Educational Needs Tribunal is 28 days. An Appeal must be lodged at the High Court within this period by way of case stated.

Any application for legal aid will necessarily again have to be on an emergency basis. Preparation for the legal aid application can be undertaken by way of the Advice and Assistance Scheme if the parents qualify. Legal aid for appeals against the Tribunal decisions will be based on the parent's/guardian's means.[6]

Negligence

This is an extremely recent development in education law. The possibility of bringing an action in negligence against the local education authorities has arisen following the ruling of the House of Lords in June 1995 in the cases of *X and Others (Minors)* v. *Bedfordshire County Council.*[7]

It was held that a Local Authority could be vicariously liable for a breach of duty of care committed by their employee. However, it must be bourne in mind that these were interlocutory applications. There has been no final determination of any of these cases.

In this instance, the legal aid application would be made by the child and assessed on the child's means. The child would have the right of action against the liable education authority.

It should be noted that compensation for maladministration in education matters has, for some time, been available by way of complaint to the Local Authority Ombudsman. Legal aid is not available to cover such complaints, although assistance can be given under the Green Form Scheme. It should be possible for a complainant to do much of the work to present the case to the Ombudsman.

[6] *S v. SENT* [1995] 1 W.L.R. 1627.
[7] [1995] 3 W.L.R. 153.

Appendix 1: Precedents

Precedent 1

IN THE SPECIAL EDUCATIONAL NEEDS TRIBUNAL CASE REFERENCE N:

(DOB:)

APPEAL AGAINST STATEMENT OF SPECIAL EDUCATIONAL NEEDS
ISSUED BY [ ] COUNTY COUNCIL
DATED 27TH SEPTEMBER 1995 AND RECEIVED 29TH SEPTEMBER 1995

REASONS FOR APPEAL

1) This is an appeal under Section 326 of the Education Act 1996 against a Statement of Special Educational Needs issued by [ ] County Council dated 27th November 1996. The Statement followed a reassessment of [ ] educational needs following a parental request made in June 1996.

2) Before detailed reasons for this appeal are given, Mr and Mrs [ ] wish to refer to the letter from the LEA dated 27th November 1996 in response to the parents representatives' letter of 25th November 1996. The LEA have known for a long time that in the parents view a change of school was necessary for [ ]. As the LEA refused to budge one inch on this, Mr and Mrs [ ] could see no purpose in having a meeting. They would, however, wish to see the LEA's response to their appeal in order to ascertain whether there can be any agreement on the wording in the Statement.

3) Part 2 – Special Educational Needs

Specifically in relation to Part 2 – Special Educational Needs, the following objections/comments are made which are the subject of this appeal:–

(a) [ ] has poor attention control and poor concentration skills.
(b) [ ] needs help to improve his social awareness and social skills with other people.
(c) The Statement specifies that [ ] "needs an individual programme

specifically designed to develop his language and communications skills within the learning environment" and reference is made in Item 2 of Provision "to the report by [ ] in terms of Speech Therapy" – more will be said about provision below, but in the meantime, [ ] needs not just "regular access" to Speech and Language Therapy but he requires intensive Speech and Language Therapy and additionally he requires specific help in connection with his visual, perceptual and dyspraxic difficulties as an integral part of the school day throughout the curriculum. It would be helpful for the Statement to identify the following specific difficulties with communication skills as reflected in [ ] report:–

(i) Delayed speech and language development.
(ii) Specific language disorder.
(iii) Dysarthria.
(iv) Dyspraxia (this has already been mentioned).
(v) Visual perception difficulties (this has already been mentioned).
(vi) Poor attention and listening skills (identified elsewhere in these Reasons for Appeal).

(d) The Statement acknowledges that "[ ] needs close liaison between his home and school" whilst this is acknowledged but despite the best efforts of both sides, Mr and Mrs [ ] have found it increasingly difficult to provide an effective liaison, [ ] behavioural difficulties at home are a severe problem.
(e) [ ] requires a 24 hour curriculum in the structured environment of a residential specialist school.
(f) The Statement acknowledges that [ ] needs a structured behavioural management programme and more will be said about the nature of this provision below, however, the reference to the involvement of Social Services is difficult to fathom as the Social Workers report attached to the Statement acknowledges that Social Services have failed to find an appropriate carer for [ ]. Due to the demands of [ ] siblings and the family structure, Mr and Mrs [ ] are unable to co-operate with the development of "a behavioural programme for use at home" as they believe it would be far preferable for a behavioural programme to be developed and managed across a 24 hour curriculum at school in an appropriate setting.

4) Part 3 - Special Educational Provision

In relation to Part 3 - Special Educational Provision, the following objections/ comments are made which are the subject of this appeal:–

First of all it should be noted that as [ ] states in her report "[ ] is experiencing difficulties in a large number of areas of both educational and social development, his needs are complex and varied ... "

(a) We will deal first with the issue of Speech Therapy. Reference is made to the report of [ ] at Item 2 of Provision in the Statement. This report is very specific in its recommendations in that [ ] requires intensive speech and language therapy with a carryover into all activities and areas of the curriculum, he requires specific help regarding his visual, perceptional and dyspraxic difficulties as an integral part of the school day, as a result, Mr and Mrs [ ] support [ ] professional opinion that [ ] current placement cannot provide the level of therapy and other input which he requires. The specific level of speech therapy must be set out in the Statement and the problems to be addressed in devising the programme should involve Makaton signing and include specific work on a child with particular difficulties.

(b) [ ] requires occupational therapy and a specific level of therapy should be set out in the Statement. He needs more than simply "being in an environment where he is able to benefit from the expertise of an occupational therapist in order to improve his gross and fine motor control skills".

(c) [ ] requires physiotherapy and the precise amount needs to be set out in the Statement.

(d) [ ] requires appropriate teaching provision to develop his concentration skills.

(e) [ ] requires to follow a structured social skills programme devised and monitored by a speech and language therapist.

(f) In relation to behavioural management programmes, it is Mr and Mrs [ ] view that this should be most efficiently and effectively organised in a school with a 24 hour curriculum.

(g) [ ] requires help to develop his skills in turn taking and play – this is to be monitored and devised by a speech and language therapist.

(h) The Statement does not set out details of any special technical or physical equipment or hardware such as computer or the like, and no consideration appears to have been given to this.

(i) [ ] requires in the words of [ ] "a clearly organised regime of day and evening activities of both an educational and leisure nature ... to allow him to develop a range of interests. Sports activities and energy consuming past times ... would be of benefit to [ ] in order to provide a legitimate outlet for his excuberance".

(j) The need for residential provision has not been properly considered by the Education Authority. [ ] has identified that this family is effectively "creaking at the seams", Mrs [ ] is on the "verge of exhaustion and despair" and there are terrific problems for the family unit, the welfare of [ ] siblings has not been considered either. This is an important area to which appropriate attention does not appear to have been paid by the Education Authority.

5) Part 4 - Appropriate School

Mr and Mrs [ ] do not consider that attendance at [ ] School which is a Local Authority maintained day special school for children with severe learning difficulties is appropriate. [ ] parents are practicing Catholics and it is their express wish that their son requires to be placed in a learning environment which has appropriate Catholic ethos commensurate with their religious beliefs. Mr and Mrs [ ] have identified [ ] School as being an appropriate placement for [ ]. It is a school approved by the Secretary of State for Education & Employment under Section 19 of the Education Act 1993. It provides a residential environment where [ ] would be able to have a chance of reaching his potential. The school is not far from the family home.

6) Parts 5 & 6 - Additional Non-Educational Needs & Provision

In relation to Parts 5 and 6, Occupational therapy and Physiotherapy are educational needs in [ ] case.

Precedent 2

COUNTY COUNCIL
(DOB:)

SUBMISSION ON BEHALF OF THE LOCAL EDUCATION AUTHORITY TO THE SPECIAL EDUCATIONAL NEEDS TRIBUNAL

(DOB:)

INTRODUCTION

1.1 [ ] is functioning at about the 2½ to 3 year old level at a chronological age of 9½ years.

1.2 In school, [ ] is a friendly, co-operative boy who has enjoyed progress in all areas of his education.

1.3 Mr and Mrs [ ] have found [ ] behaviour at home to be very difficult and have requested a move for [ ] to [ ] School which would allow him to remain on site 24 hours a day.

1.4 The Authority believes that [ ] current placement at [ ] school can provide for his special educational needs. [ ] School is a special school for children with severe learning difficulties.

1.5 Mr and Mrs [ ] are appealing for a change of placement for [ ] to an independent special school.

BACKGROUND INFORMATION AND CHRONOLOGY

2.1 On 6 April 1991, the Advisory Teacher for Early Years recommended that [ ] should undergo a formal assessment of his possible special educational needs (Appendix Al). This request was copied to Mr and Mrs [ ] and on 8 May 1991, the Local Education Authority agreed to the formal assessment (Appendix B1).

2.2 On 12 November 1991, a draft statement of special educational needs was issued for [ ] indicating that he should attend [ ] School from 8 January 1992 (Appendix C1-C4). The final statement for [ ] was issued on 10 January 1992 naming Colnbrook School (Appendix D1).

2.3 The first review of [ ] statement took place in October 1993. The review was issued on 25 November 1993 and referred to a change of provision. [ ] difficulties were assessed by his then school, [ ] School, and by an educational psychologist and it was decided that a referral to a school for children with a severe learning difficulty was the most appropriate course of action. [ ] transferred to [ ] School on 2 November 1993 (Appendix E1-E7).

2.4 The second review of statement was issued on 7 October 1994 and indicated that [ ] should continue at [ ] School (Appendix F1-F10).

2.5 On 14 March 1995, Mrs [ ] wrote to the Authority asking for a re-assessment of [ ] special educational needs given concerns about his behaviour at home (Appendix G1). The Local Education Authority arranged for a review to be carried out of [ ] involving, [ ], the school educational psychologist and the report is dated 1 July 1995 (Appendix H1-H2).

2.6 The third annual review of [ ] statement was issued to Mr and Mrs [ ] on 8 September 1995. This indicated that [ ] had continued to make progress but Mr and Mrs [ ], in response to the review, indicated they were unhappy with his placement and considered that [ ] would be able to provide a better environment for him (Appendix J1).

2.7 On 21 October 1995, the Local Education Authority wrote to Mrs [ ] indicating that given her request that [ ] become a weekly boarder at [ ], the Authority would be seeking Social Services' advice on any background which could support this request (Appendix K1). A response was received in a letter dated 4 November 1995 indicating that there were significant social reasons for the request for weekly boarding and confirmed that weekly boarding would allow [ ] a level of structure and consistency of approach that is not possible within the family (Appendix L1-L2).

2.8 Given the advice received, the Local Education Authority wrote to Mr and Mrs [ ] on 6 December 1995 indicating that their request was largely based on social reasons and they should contact the Social Services Department for guidance (Appendix M1).

REASONS FOR APPEAL

Mr and Mrs [ ] have appealed to the Special Educational Needs Tribunal for the reasons stated under 3.1 below and the Local Education Authority's response follows this:

3.1 Mr and Mrs [ ] have appealed on the basis of disagreeing with the contents of Part II and Part III of the statement prepared for their son,

3.2 The statement of special educational needs which has been prepared for [ ] confirmed that [ ] would need access to the following provision in order to maintain his educational progress:

(a) access to a curriculum which has been adjusted to meet the needs of a child who has severe learning difficulties.
(b) an individual programme designed to develop his language and communication skills within the learning environment.
(c) help to develop his gross motor and fine motor co-ordination skills.
(d) an individual programme to develop all his basic skills.
(e) a structured behavioural management programme.
(f) close liaison between his home and his school.

3.3 The Local Education Authority is confident that all these needs, as listed above, can be met and provided for by [ ] School. The School is maintained by the Authority to meet the needs of children similar to [ ] who have severe learning difficulties and ancillary needs. To this end, the school provides a differentiated curriculum for the pupils and very carefully monitors the provision to ensure the maintenance and improvement of the educational capabilities of pupils and their care. The school has skilled and experienced teachers and ancillary staff who provide for the emotional security of the children and ensure the very consistency of approach which has been identified as one of [ ] needs.

3.4 The school has been developed to provide an environment to meet a variety of learning difficulties and works very closely with the Health Authority to ensure that the highest level of physiotherapy and occupational therapy is available to children on site. Speech therapy is also provided at the school. The aim is to ensure a comprehensive and integrated approach to meeting children's needs at the school and therefore it will be able to meet [ ] needs.

3.5 Mr and Mrs [ ] in identifying [ ] School, have determined that [ ] needs a residential placement in order to ensure a continuity of the behavioural programme across a 24 hour period. Considerable effort has been made to involve Mr and Mrs [ ] in the very successful programme which has been developed for [ ] at [ ] School and which has resulted in him being a happy and contented boy whilst he is within the school premises. His attitude to strangers who visit the site and to adults on the school premises is one of politeness and a generous nature. The school have made a number of efforts to transfer the school's good practice to the home situation but without success. It is noted that Social Services are very involved with the family and have made a number of attempts in the past to ensure that the family receive guidance on the best way to handle [ ] at home.

CONCLUSION

4.1 The Local Education Authority has closely monitored [ ] progress since his statement was initially prepared in 1991, as shown by the detailed reviews that have taken place since that time and the most recent re-assessment of his needs. Mr and Mrs [ ] have commented during the reviews on how pleased they were with [ ] progress and by the care provided to him by the multi-disciplinary team available at [ ] School.

4.2 The holistic, multi-disciplinary approach which [ ] School follows will particularly meet [ ] needs. Therefore, although recognising the preference that Mr and Mrs [ ] have expressed for an independent school, it is the Local Education Authority's view that [ ] School can meet the very provision that is required for [ ] to ensure his progress in all aspects of his current needs. [ ] School will provide the security required for him and the learning environment which will maximise his potential.

4.3 The Local Education Authority has approached the Health Authority to discuss the levels of support which can be provided for [ ] School as part of a review of the delivery of these services. It is the Health Authority professionals who will advise the Education Authority on the specific medical needs of any pupil and how they will be met, but the Education Authority recognises its responsibility to ensure that adequate provision is made.

4.4 The Local Education Authority has a duty under the 1996 Education Act to ensure that the special educational needs of pupils are met and this requires the efficient use of resources. [ ] School is the most appropriate school for [ ] to attend and will meet his needs without the additional cost of out county provision. A placement for [ ] would cost the [ ] Local Education Authority approximately £17,000 compared with an approximate cost of £4,680 for a placement at [ ] School. The evidence suggests that the placement at an independent school is prompted by non-educational reasons and therefore the Authority would contend that Mr and Mrs [ ] approach Social Services to meet the cost of such a placement if it is supported by that Department.

Precedent 3

GREEN V. THE SPECIAL EDUCATION NEEDS TRIBUNAL AND NEWSHIRE COUNTY COUNCIL

QUEEN'S BENCH DIVISION

Notice of motion

Take notice that the High Court of Justice, Queen's Bench Division, at the Royal Courts of Justice, Strand, London WC2A 2LL, will be moved on the [ ] day of [ ] 1996, also soon thereafter as counsel can be heard, by counsel on behalf of the above named Theresa Green for an order that the decision of the tribunal dated

December 4, 1996 be set aside, and that a rehearing be ordered, and that the respondent pay the costs of this appeal or such further order as to costs as the court may see fit. And further take notice the grounds of this appeal are as follows:

(i) The tribunal failed to give any adequate reasons under the provisions of the Tribunals and Enquiries Act 1992, or alternatively under the provisions of rule 31 (2) of the Special Educational Needs Tribunal Regulations 1994 (S.I. 1994 No. 1910).

(ii) The tribunal erred in law in that it failed to take into account, and/or appreciate and/or consider adequately the expert evidence of the speech therapist for Theresa, Miss Blue, who had consulted with the expert speech therapist delivering provision at Theresa's school. She gave evidence as to Theresa's speech and language therapy needs. In particular the tribunal failed to make any finding or take into account her report and her oral evidence that Theresa required a language programme. This was set out in the final part of her report and Miss Blue gave evidence to that effect, this evidence being unchallenged. The conclusions she stated were accepted by the speech therapist at Theresa's school. Part 3 of the statement failed to make any provision for a language programme neither was any provision being given to Theresa for a language programme throughout the school day.

(iii) The tribunal erred in law in that it failed to make any findings in relation to Theresa's problems with stress and anxiety and as to whether they required provision in part 3 of the statement. At the invitation of the tribunal, the grounds of appeal were amended to make reference to the issue of a social skills programme to deal with stress and anxiety.

(iv) At the request of the tribunal, Mr Yellow, for the local authority and counsel for the appellant drafted agreed amendments to the statement, and also handed to the tribunal agreed additional issues for their determination on the basis of evidence that emerged at the hearing and the amended grounds of appeal. Although the tribunal had before it the said document because it adopted the agreed amendments in the order made by the tribunal, the tribunal failed to make any findings of fact, or consider the evidence in relation to the remaining issues.

(v) The tribunal failed to make any findings of fact in relation to the authority's evidence that Theresa had met a substantial number of the short term objectives in her statement. However, the authority accepted that Theresa had not met six of those objectives, nor did the authority adduce any evidence as to what was the effect of her failure to meet those objectives. On behalf of the parents Dr Grey on educational issues gave evidence that less than 10 of the short term objectives had been met, and that was not possible for the authority to achieve those short term objectives before Theresa left school and Miss Blue, whose evidence on this issue was unchallenged, gave evidence that the speech and language short term objectives had not been met in the main, and that they could not now be met before she left school. The tribunal failed to make any findings on these issues which were crucial to the case. Theresa had been given a statement at a late stage in her educational career, and became of statutory leaving date on the age at which she was expected to leave her present school within approximately four to five terms from the hearing. The issue as to whether these objectives could be achieved, was essential to the hearing. The issue as to the authority's acceptance that itself had failed to meet its objectives was an important fact on which the tribunal made no finding.

(vi) Further or in the alternative in the light of the fact that the authority's own case accepted that they had failed to meet six out of 20 short term objectives and that Theresa was due to leave school in the very near future, the decision of the tribunal that the Newshire School fulfilled the requirements of part 3 of the statement was not, justified by the evidence placed before it.

(vii) The tribunal failed to have regard to Theresa's view as required under section 1 of the Children Act 1989 and the Code of Practice.

Dated the [ ] day of [ ] 1997.
Signed by (Mr Laws) of V. Kind & Co.
Main Street
Newshire

Solicitors for the abovementioned Theresa Green

To the Secretary of Special Educational Needs Tribunal
71 Victoria Street
London SW1 0HW

Precedent 4

GREEN v. THE SPECIAL EDUCATIONAL NEEDS TRIBUNAL AND NEWSHIRE COUNTY COUNCIL

QUEEN'S BENCH DIVISION

Affidavit

I, John Jacques Laws, a Partner in the firm of V. Kind & Co. and a Solicitor of the Supreme Court make oath and say as follows:

1. I am a Partner in the firm of V. Kind & Co, and I have conduct of Theresa Green's case in this firm. I attended the appeal on her behalf, and on the fourth day of December 1996 we received a decision of the Special Educational Needs Tribunal. A copy of the decision was sent to Theresa's parents, Mr and Mrs Green, on the same day. On the sixth day of December following instructions from Mr and Mrs Green, legal aid applications forms were sent to the parents for signature. The legal aid

forms were received from Theresa's mother on December 13. A legal aid application was lodged on December 18.

2. As nothing had been heard from the Legal Aid Board in relation to the application for education, a reminder was sent to them on January 10. On January 11 a letter was received from the Legal Aid Board refusing legal aid on the basis there were no reasonable grounds. Although the application to the Legal Aid Board was phrased in terms of an application for Judicial Review, which is irrelevant to the issue as to whether the legal aid was granted or not the points made to the Legal Aid Board in order to assist the grant of legal aid were as follows:

   (a) No or no adequate reasons were given.
   (b) There were no findings made by the tribunal on the essential issues although the authority alleged 14 of the short term objectives had been established, the appellant's evidence was that less than 14 had been established, and that the absence of six objectives in any event was fatal to the authority's case.
   (c) No finding was made on the issue of the evidence on speech and language, which was that no progress had been made, and such provision was not being given to Theresa.
   (d) An issue in relation to the constitution of the tribunal was raised.
   (e) That the decision was unfair and unreasonable.

3. In the light of the refusal, assistance was sought from counsel, and the matter was re-submitted to the Legal Aid Board on the basis of an advice by counsel. As a result of the fact that the advice by counsel shed light on the situation legal aid was granted on January 24. The certificate dated January 22 was received in this office on 25th. Obviously the advice by counsel assisted in that it meant that an appeal did not have to be made to the Local Committee, and the Legal Aid Board were prepared to reconsider the matter and it granted it legal aid.
4. In the circumstances, I would respectfully submit that although the period of 28 days has been exceeded, the reason for the fact that the 28-day period was exceeded was a refusal of legal aid, which was erroneous in the circumstances. I therefore seek leave to extend time.
5. I now turn to the issues in the present case. There is now produced and shown to me a bundle of documents before the Appeal Tribunal marked "JJL.1". Further there is now produced and shown to me marked "JJL.2" true copies of my notes taken at the hearing. The hearing was listed for 2 o'clock on that day, and at approximately 5.30 p.m., when Mr Yellow for Newshire and counsel for Theresa drew the attention to the tribunal that the case was no where near finished, the tribunal indicated that it intended to proceed, but did not seek submissions on this point. Mr Theresa nor Mr Rich indicated that they were unable to stay although both indicated that their arrangements would be exceptionally disturbed for the evening. The case therefore continued. At the end of the hearing, Mr Yellow and Mr Rich remained, and settled a list of agree issues. The tribunal had requested assistance from Mr Yellow and Mr Rich, and they therefore a

formulation of the issues, on which the tribunal was required to decide relating to part 3 of the statement. Those issues were left in writing to the tribunal, and included an appropriate draft of the statement.

It is important to explain that the tribunal therefore had before it formulated by both sides not only in the issues upon which they were agreed, but a formulation of the disposal of the issues upon which they were not agreed. No finding of fact was made by the tribunal on any of the other issues.

6. The second matter before the tribunal gave evidence through one of it's experts, a specialist teacher, that Theresa had met 14 out of 16 of the short term objectives in her statement. The authority failed to give evidence as to the effect of this failure, bearing in mind that Theresa was due to take her GCSE's exams and I understand it leave her present school at the age of 16, four-and-a-half terms in the future.

7. Dr Grey who gave evidence on behalf of the parents, gave evidence that far less than 14 objectives had been achieved, less than 10 in fact. Miss Blue gave evidence, which is again not challenged in relation to language targets and the short term objectives especially as none had been achieved in the case because Theresa had made virtually no progress. She gave evidence that these objectives could not be achieved and therefore the statement could not be made effective before Theresa reached the age to take GCSE's and that therefore the provision and the statement was defective. There was no finding of fact in relation to these issues. The absence of evidence of the authority as to the effect of their own admission that six objectives had not been met, was specifically raised with the tribunal yet they made no findings of fact on this point. It is to be stressed that the evidence to the contrary was that the objectives could not be met and this was not countered by any evidence by the authority who were simply able to show that 16 objectives which were in dispute had been met.

8. In this context it is perhaps important that I stress that Theresa does not know her alphabet. This issue occupied a considerable element of evidence. It was of importance particularly to Theresa's parents. The failure to make any finding of fact on these points is in my respectful submission an important omission.

9. Additionally, evidence was given by Theresa's mother and father about Theresa's views. They gave evidence to the effect that Theresa was unhappy at the school and wished to move. Theresa's mother gave evidence to the fact that Theresa has now become school phobic and was refusing to go to school, and that her relationship with her specialist teacher had broken down. No findings of fact were made on these issues, notable in relation to Theresa's wishes. Further the authority had not sought Theresa's views in accordance with the Code of Practice as required by section 313 of the Education Act 1996.

10. The last issue which was before the tribunal was the issue to the accuracy

of the findings of the educational psychologist's tests in this case. All the scores provided by educational psychologists matched, including that provided by Newshire. Reports from Theresa's school, and the evidence given by her specialist teacher purported to show that she was able to do better than when tested by educational psychologists. However the parents produced her work books and gave evidence to the fact that Mrs Green actually helped Theresa with her homework and most of her homework was carried out by her mother. The book produced showed work done by Theresa alone without help which showed work done by a child at a very low level possibly operating the equivalent of well under the age of a 10-year-old child. Again no findings of fact were made on this issue. If the school had over estimated Theresa's abilities and her achievements, particularly as her mother had done her homework, this would have an important effect on the accuracy of the school's assessment of her work ability, and the accuracy of the findings of the educational psychologist, which were in agreement with test scores.

11. Following the final submissions made on behalf of both sides, we were invited to amend the grounds of appeal to reflect the issues that have emerged at the hearing, and orally the grounds of appeal were amended. There is no mention of these issues in the decision of the tribunal, nor are there any findings of fact on these amended grounds of appeal. The original grounds of appeal for example did not refer to the issues of stress and anxiety, and the fact that Theresa was becoming school phobic. This was a developing situation and had increased since the appeal was lodged. Neither did those groups of appeal refer to a language programme. The original grounds of appeal therefore required amendment. These issues were therefore well within the mind of the tribunal and to the forefront of the issues in the case.

12. In the premises, I respectfully seek the relief sought.

Sworn on [ ] day of [ ] 1997.

Precedent 5

Notice of Appeal to the Special Educational Needs Tribunal

Please use this form if you want to send a notice of appeal to the Special Educational Needs Tribunal. You must send in this form so that it arrives in the tribunal office no later than the first working day, two months after the LEA told you that you could appeal. If the end of the two month period is in August, you will have until 1 September to make your appeal.

- *Please fill in the boxes below. This form has to be photocopied, so please use black ink and capital letters.*
- *If there is not enough space for your answer, please continue on a separate sheet and attach it to this form.*

Section 1

Please give below the details of the child, for whom the appeal is being made:

Child's surname ....

Child's first names ....

Child's date of birth ....

Child's gender M/F ....

It will help us if you tick one of the boxes below. You do not have to, but the information will give the tribunal useful statistics. All information is kept in the strictest confidence. The tribunal is registered under the Data Protection Act.

Child's ethnic origin:

☐ Black African	☐ Bangladeshi	☐ Chinese
☐ Black Caribbean	☐ Indian	☐ White
☐ Black Other*	☐ Pakistani	☐ Other*

* If you have ticked other, please give details: ....

....

....

Section 2

Please give your details below. Parents can appeal jointly but if you live at different addresses we will only send papers to the address you give first.

Your name Mr ☐ Mrs ☐ Miss ☐ Ms ☐ Other ☐

Your surname ....

First names ....

Your relationship to the child, for example, father, mother, guardian, and so on ....

Your address ....

....

.... Postcode ....

Your telephone number, if any ....

Your name Mr ☐ Mrs ☐ Miss ☐ Ms ☐ Other ☐

Your surname ....

First names ....

Your relationship to the child, for example, father, mother, guardian, and so on ....

Your address ....

....

.... Postcode ....

Your telephone number, if any ....

Section 3

If it would help you for us to send tribunal papers to someone else instead of you, please give the following details:

Name: ....

Address ....

....

....

.... Postcode ....

Telephone number: ....

Section 4

Please give the name of the local education authority whose decision you are appealing against:

....

Please give the date you received the letter from the LEA telling you that you could appeal to the tribunal:

....

Please tick the boxes below that apply to your appeal.
Please include a separate sheet of paper explaining briefly why you disagree with the LEA.

I am appealing to the SEN tribunal because:

1 I have asked the LEA to assess, or re-assess my child, but they have refused. ☐

2 The LEA have assessed my child but refused to provide a statement. ☐

3 The LEA have provided a statement, but I disagree with part 2 or part 3 of it, or both parts. ☐

4 The LEA have provided a statement, but I disagree with the school they have named in part 4. ☐

5 The LEA have provided a statement, but they have not named a school in it. ☐

6 I have asked the LEA to change the school named in the statement, but they have refused. ☐

7 The LEA have decided not to maintain my child's statement. ☐

The school I would prefer my child to go to is: (Please give the name and address of the school if you have ticked the box in 4, 5 or 6.)

....

....

Section 5

If you live in Wales, do you want the hearing to be in Welsh?

☐ Yes ☐ No

Section 6

Please make sure you send the following documents with this appeal form. **We cannot register your appeal without them.**

- A copy of your child's statement of special educational needs (if he or she has one), **even if the LEA have refused to maintain it.**
- The other documents attached to the statement (appendices). **If they were not attached to the final statement, send the ones attached to the proposed (draft) statement.**
- A copy of the letter (notice) from the LEA which sets out the decision you are appealing against.
- If you have ticked box 1 in section 3, send a copy of your letter to the LEA asking them to make an assessment.

You will be able to send further documents at a later date if you want.

Your signatures ....

....

Date ....

Please return this form together with any supporting documents to the address below:

Special Educational Needs Tribunal
Secretariat
71 Victoria Street
LONDON SW1H 0HW
Telephone: 0171-925 6925 Facsimile: 0171-925 6926

Appendix 2: Statutes

Education Act 1996 (c. 56)

An Act to amend and consolidate the Education Act 1944 and certain other enactments relating to education, with amendments to give effect to recommendations of the Law Commission. [24th July 1996]

Be it enacted by the Queen's most Excellent Majesty, by and with the advice and consent of the Lords Spiritual and Temporal, and Commons, in this present Parliament assembled, and by the authority of the same, as follows:

* * * *

PART IV

CHILDREN WITH SPECIAL EDUCATIONAL NEEDS

Introductory

Meaning of "special educational needs" and "special educational provision", etc.

312.—(1) A child has "special educational needs" for the purposes of this Act, if he has a learning difficulty which calls for special educational provision to be made for him.

(2) Subject to subsection (3) (and except for the purposes of section 15(5)) a child has a "learning difficulty" for the purposes of this Act if—

- (a) he has a significantly greater difficulty in learning than the majority of children of his age,
- (b) he has a disability which either prevents or hinders him from making use of educational facilities of a kind generally provided for children of his age in schools within the area of the local education authority, or
- (c) he is under the age of five years and is, or would be if special educational provision were not made for him, likely to fall within paragraph (a) or (b) when of or over that age.

(3) A child is not to be taken as having a learning difficulty solely because the language (or form of the language) in which he is, or will be, taught is different from a language (or form of a language) which has at any time been spoken in his home.

(4) In this Act, "special educational provision" means—

(a) in relation to a child who has attained the age of two years, educational provision which is additional to, or otherwise different from, the educational provision made generally for children of his age in schools maintained by the local education authority (other than special schools) or grant-maintained schools in their area, and
(b) in relation to a child under that age, educational provision of any kind.

(5) In this Part—

"child" includes any person who has not attained the age of 19 years and is a registered pupil at a school;
"maintained school" means any county or voluntary school or any maintained special school not established in a hospital.

Code of practice

Code of Practice

313.—(1) The Secretary of State shall issue, and may from time to time revise, a code of practice giving practical guidance in respect of the discharge by local education authorities and the governing bodies of maintained or grant-maintained schools, or grant-maintained special schools, of their functions under this Part.

(2) It shall be the duty of—

(a) local education authorities, and such governing bodies, exercising functions under this Part, and
(b) any other person exercising any function for the purpose of the discharge by local education authorities, and such governing bodies, of functions under this Part,

to have regard to the provisions of the code.

(3) On any appeal under this Part to the Tribunal, the Tribunal shall have regard to any provision of the code which appears to the Tribunal to be relevant to any question arising on the appeal.

(4) The Secretary of State shall publish the code as for the time being in force.

(5) In this Part "the Tribunal" means the Special Education Needs Tribunal.

Making and approval of code

314.—(1) Where the Secretary of State proposes to issue or revise a code of practice, he shall prepare a draft of the code (or revised code).

(2) The Secretary of State shall consult such persons about the draft as he thinks fit and shall consider any representations made by them.

(3) If he determines to proceed with the draft (either in its original form or with such modifications as he thinks fit) he shall lay it before both Houses of Parliament.

(4) If the draft is approved by resolution of each House, the Secretary of State shall issue the code in the form of the draft and the code shall come into effect on such day as the Secretary of State may by order appoint.

Special educational provision: general

Review of arrangements

315.—(1) A local education authority shall keep under review the arrangements made by them for special educational provision.

(2) In doing so the authority shall, to the extent that it appears necessary or desirable for the purpose of co-ordinating provision for children with special educational needs, consult the funding authority and the governing bodies of county, voluntary, maintained special and grant-maintained schools in their area.

Children with special educational needs normally to be educated in mainstream schools

316.—(1) Any person exercising any functions under this Part in respect of a child with special educational needs who should be educated in a school shall secure that, if the conditions mentioned in subsection (2) are satisfied, the child is educated in a school which is not a special school unless that is incompatible with the wishes of his parent.

(2) The conditions are that educating the child in a school which is not a special school is compatible with—

- (a) his receiving the special educational provision which his learning difficulty calls for,
- (b) the provision of efficient education for the children with whom he will be educated, and
- (c) the efficient use of resources.

Duties of governing body or LEA in relation to pupils with special educational needs

317.—(1) The governing body, in the case of a county, voluntary or grant-maintained school, and the local education authority, in the case of a maintained nursery school, shall—

- (a) use their best endeavours, in exercising their functions in relation to the school, to secure that if any registered pupil has special educational needs the special educational provision which his learning difficulty calls for is made,
- (b) secure that, where the responsible person has been informed by the local education authority that a registered pupil has special educational needs, those needs are made known to all who are likely to teach him, and
- (c) secure that the teachers in the school are aware of the importance of identifying, and providing for, those registered pupils who have special educational needs.

(2) In subsection (I)(b) "the responsible person" means—

- (a) in the case of a county, voluntary or grant-maintained school, the head teacher or the appropriate governor (that is, the chairman of the governing body or, where the governing body have designated another governor for the purposes of this paragraph, that other governor), and

(b) in the case of a nursery school, the head teacher.

(3) To the extent that it appears necessary or desirable for the purpose of co-ordinating provision for children with special educational needs—

(a) the governing bodies of county, voluntary and grant-maintained schools shall, in exercising functions relating to the provision for such children, consult the local education authority, the funding authority and the governing bodies of other such schools, and

(b) in relation to maintained nursery schools, the local education authority shall, in exercising those functions, consult the funding authority and the governing bodies of county, voluntary and grant-maintained schools.

(4) Where a child who has special educational needs is being educated in a county, voluntary or grant-maintained school or a maintained nursery school, those concerned with making special educational provision for the child shall secure, so far as is reasonably practicable and is compatible with—

(a) the child receiving the special educational provision which his learning difficulty calls for,

(b) the provision of efficient education for the children with whom he will be educated, and

(c) the efficient use of resources,

that the child engages in the activities of the school together with children who do not have special educational needs.

(5) The annual report for each county, voluntary, maintained special or grant-maintained school shall include a report containing such information as may be prescribed about the implementation of the governing body's policy for pupils with special educational needs.

(6) The annual report for each county, voluntary or grant-maintained school shall also include a report containing information as to—

(a) the arrangements for the admission of disabled pupils;

(b) the steps taken to prevent disabled pupils from being treated less favourably than other pupils; and

(c) the facilities provided to assist access to the school by disabled pupils;

and for this purpose "disabled pupils" means pupils who are disabled persons for the purposes of the Disability Discrimination Act 1995.

(7) In this section "annual report" means the report prepared under the articles of government for the school in accordance with section 161 or, as the case may be, paragraph 7 of Schedule 23.

Provision of goods and services in connection with special educational needs

318.—(1) A local education authority may for the purpose only of assisting—

(a) the governing bodies of county, voluntary or grant-maintained schools (in their or any other area) in the performance of the governing bodies' duties under section 317(1)(a), or

(b) the governing bodies of maintained or grant-maintained special schools (in their or any other area) in the performance of the governing bodies' duties,

supply goods or services to those bodies.

(2) The terms on which goods or services are supplied by local education authorities under this section—

(a) to the governing bodies of grant-maintained schools or grant-maintained special schools, or

(b) to the governing bodies of county, voluntary or maintained special schools,

in any other area may, in such circumstances as may be prescribed, include such terms as to payment as may be prescribed.

(3) A local education authority may supply goods or services to any authority or other person (other than a governing body within subsection (1)) for the purpose only of assisting them in making for any child in respect of whose education grants are (or are to be) made under arrangements under section 1 of the Nursery Education and Grant-Maintained Schools Act 1996 any special education provision which any learning difficulty of the child calls for.

(4) This section is without prejudice to the generality of any other power of local education authorities to supply goods or services.

Special educational provision otherwise than in schools

319.—(1) Where a local education authority are satisfied that it would be inappropriate for—

(a) the special educational provision which a learning difficulty of a child in their area calls for, or

(b) any part of any such provision, to be made in a school, they may arrange for the provision (or, as the case may be, for that part of it) to be made otherwise than in a school.

(2) Before making an arrangement under this section, a local education authority shall consult the child's parent.

Provision outside England and Wales for certain children

320.—(1) A local education authority may make such arrangements as they think fit to enable a child for whom they maintain a statement under section 324 to attend an institution outside England and Wales which specialises in providing for children with special needs.

(2) In subsection (1) "children with special needs" means children who have particular needs which would be special educational needs if those children were in England and Wales.

(3) Where a local education authority make arrangements under this section in respect of a child, those arrangements may in particular include contributing to or paying—

- (a) fees charged by the institution,
- (b) expenses reasonably incurred in maintaining him while he is at the institution or travelling to or from it,
- (c) his travelling expenses, and
- (d) expenses reasonably incurred by any person accompanying him while he is travelling or staying at the institution.

(4) This section is without prejudice to any other powers of a local education authority.

Identification and assessment of children with special educational needs

General duty of local education authority towards children for whom they are responsible

321.—(1) A local education authority shall exercise their powers with a view to securing that, of the children for whom they are responsible, they identify those to whom subsection (2) below applies.

(2) This subsection applies to a child if—

- (a) he has special educational needs, and
- (b) it is necessary for the authority to determine the special educational provision which any learning difficulty he may have calls for.

(3) For the purposes of this Part a local education authority are responsible for a child if he is in their area and—

- (a) he is a registered pupil at a maintained, grant-maintained or grant-maintained special school,
- (b) education is provided for him at a school which is not a maintained, grant-maintained or grant-maintained special school but is so provided at the expense of the authority or the funding authority,
- (c) he does not come within paragraph (a) or (b) above but is a registered pupil at a school and has been brought to the authority's attention as having (or probably having) special educational needs, or
- (d) he is not a registered pupil at a school, is not under the age of two years or

over compulsory school age and has been brought to their attention as having (or probably having) special educational needs.

Duty of District Health Authority or local authority to help local education authority

322.—(1) Where it appears to a local education authority that any Health Authority or local authority could, by taking any specified action, help in the exercise of any of their functions under this Part, they may request the help of the authority, specifying the action in question.

(2) An authority whose help is so requested shall comply with the request unless—

(a) they consider that the help requested is not necessary for the purpose of the exercise by the local education authority of those functions, or
(b) subsection (3) applies.

(3) This subsection applies—

(a) in the case of a Health Authority, if that authority consider that, having regard to the resources available to them for the purpose of the exercise of their functions under the National Health Service Act 1977, it is not reasonable for them to comply with the request, or
(b) in the case of a local authority, if that authority consider that the request is not compatible with their own statutory or other duties and obligations or unduly prejudices the discharge of any of their functions.

(4) Regulations may provide that, where an authority are under a duty by virtue of subsection (a) above to comply with a request to help a local education authority in the making of an assessment under section 323 or a statement under section 324 they must, subject to prescribed exceptions, comply with the request within the prescribed period.

(5) In this section, "local authority" means a county council, a county borough council, district council (other than one for an area for which there is a county council), a London borough council or the Common Council of the City of London.

Assessment of educational needs

323.—(1) Where a local education authority are of the opinion that a child for whom they are responsible falls, or probably falls, within subsection (2) they shall serve a notice on the child's parent informing him—

(a) that they propose to make an assessment of the child's educational needs,
(b) of the procedure to be followed in making the assessment,
(c) of the name of the officer of the authority from whom further information may be obtained, and
(d) of the parent's right to make representations, and submit written evidence, to the authority within such period (which shall not be less than

29 days beginning with the date on which the notice is served) as may be specified in the notice.

(2) A child falls within this subsection if—

(a) he has special educational needs, and
(b) it is necessary for the authority to determine the special educational provision which any learning difficulty he may have calls for.

(3) Where—

(a) a local education authority have served a notice under subsection (1) and the period specified in the notice in accordance with subsection (1)(d) has expired, and
(b) the authority remain of the opinion, after taking into account any representations made and any evidence submitted to them in response to the notice, that the child falls, or probably falls, within subsection (2),

they shall make an assessment of his educational needs.

(4) Where a local education authority decide to make an assessment under this section, they shall give notice in writing to the child's parent of that decision and of their reasons for making it.

(5) Schedule 26 to this Act in relation to the making of assessments under this section.

(6) Where, at any time after serving a notice under subsection (1) a local education authority decide not to assess the educational needs of the child concerned they shall give notice in writing to the child's parent of their decision.

Statement of special educational needs

324.—(1) If, in the light of an assessment under section 323 of any child's educational needs and of any representations made by the child's parent in pursuance of Schedule 27, it is necessary for the local education authority to determine the special educational provision which any learning difficulty he may have calls for, the authority shall make and maintain a statement of his special educational needs.

(2) The statement shall be in such form and contain such information as may be prescribed.

(3) In particular, the statement shall—

(a) give details of the authority's assessment of the child's special educational needs, and
(b) specify the special educational provision to be made for the purpose of meeting those needs, including the particulars required by subsection (4).

(4) The statement shall—

(a) specify the type of school or other institution which the local education authority consider would be appropriate for the child,
(b) if they are not required under Schedule 27 to specify the name of any school in the statement, specify the name of any school or institution (whether in the United Kingdom or elsewhere) which they consider

would be appropriate for the child and should be specified in the statement, and

(c) specify any provision for the child for which they make arrangements under section 319 and which they consider should be specified in the statement.

(5) Where a local education authority maintain a statement under this section, then—

(a) unless the child's parent has made suitable arrangements, the authority—

(i) shall arrange that the special educational provision specified in the statement is made for the child, and

(ii) may arrange that any non-educational provision specified in the statement is made for him in such manner as they consider appropriate, and

(b) if the name of a maintained, grant-maintained or grant-maintained special school is specified in the statement, the governing body of the school shall admit the child to the school.

(6) Subsection (5)(b) above does not affect any power to exclude from a school a pupil who is already a registered pupil there.

(7) Schedule 27 has effect in relation to the making and maintenance of statements under this section.

Appeal against decision not to make statement

325.—(1) If, after making an assessment under section 323 of the educational needs of any child for whom no statement is maintained under section 324, the local education authority do not propose to make such a statement, they shall give notice in writing of their decision, and of the effect of subsection (2) below, to the child's parent.

(2) In such a case, the child's parent may appeal to the Tribunal against the decision.

(3) On an appeal under this section, the Tribunal may—

(a) dismiss the appeal,

(b) order the local education authority to make and maintain such a statement, or

(c) remit the case to the authority for them to reconsider whether, having regard to any observations made by the Tribunal, it is necessary for the authority to determine the special educational provision which any learning difficulty the child may have calls for.

Appeal against contents of statement

326.—(1) The parent of a child for whom a local education authority maintain a statement under section 324 may—

(a) when the statement is first made,

(b) where the description in the statement of the authority's assessment of the child's special educational needs, or the special educational provision specified in the statement, is amended, or

(c) where, after conducting an assessment of the educational needs of the child under section 323, the local education authority determine not to amend the statement,

appeal to the Tribunal against the description in the statement of the authority's assessment of the child's special educational needs, the special educational provision specified in the statement or, if no school is named in the statement, that fact.

(2) Subsection (1)(b) above does not apply where the amendment is made in pursuance of—

(a) paragraph 8 (change of named school) or 11(3)(b) (amendment ordered by Tribunal) of Schedule 27, or
(b) directions under section 442 (revocation of school attendance order);

and subsection (1)(c) does not apply to a determination made following the service of notice under paragraph 10 (amendment by the LEA) of Schedule 27 of a proposal to amend the statement.

(3) On an appeal under this section, the Tribunal may—

(a) dismiss the appeal,
(b) order the authority to amend the statement, so far as it describes the authority's assessment of the child's special educational needs or specifies the special educational provision, and make such other consequential amendments to the statement as the Tribunal think fit, or
(c) order the authority to cease to maintain the statement.

(4) On an appeal under this section the Tribunal shall not order the local education authority to specify the name of any school in the statement (either in substitution for an existing name or in a case where no school is named) unless—

(a) the parent has expressed a preference for the school in pursuance of arrangements under paragraph 3 (choice of school) of Schedule 27, or
(b) in the proceedings the parent, the local education authority, or both have proposed the school.

(5) Before determining any appeal under this section the Tribunal may, with the agreement of the parties, correct any deficiency in the statement.

Access for local education authority to certain schools

327.—(1) This section applies where—

(a) a local education authority maintain a statement for a child under section 324, and
(b) in pursuance of the statement education is provided for the child at—
    (i) a school maintained by another local education authority,
    (ii) a grant-maintained school, or
    (iii) a grant-maintained special school.

(2) Any person authorised by the local education authority shall be entitled to have access at any reasonable time to the premises of any such school for the purpose of monitoring the special educational provision made in pursuance of the statement for the child at the school.

Reviews of educational needs

328.—(1) Regulations may prescribe the frequency with which assessments under section 323 are to be repeated in respect of children for whom statements are maintained under section 324.

(2) Where—

- (a) the parent of a child for whom a statement is maintained under section 324 asks the local education authority to arrange for an assessment to be made in respect of the child under section 323,
- (b) no such assessment has been made within the period of six months ending with the date on which the request is made, and
- (c) it is necessary for the authority to make a further assessment under section 323,

the authority shall comply with the request.

(3) If in any case where subsection (2)(a) and (b) applies the authority determine not to comply with the request—

- (a) they shall give notice of that fact and of the effect of paragraph (b) below to the child's parent, and
- (b) the parent may appeal to the Tribunal against the determination.

(4) On an appeal under subsection (3) above the Tribunal may—

- (a) dismiss the appeal, or
- (b) order the authority to arrange for an assessment to be made in respect of the child under section 323.

(5) A statement under section 324 shall be reviewed by the local education authority—

- (a) on the making of an assessment in respect of the child concerned under section 323, and
- (b) in any event, within the period of 12 months beginning with the making of the statement or, as the case may be, with the previous review.

(6) Regulations may make provision—

- (a) as to the manner in which reviews of such statements are to be conducted,
- (b) as to the participation in such reviews of such persons as may be prescribed, and
- (c) in connection with such other matters relating to such reviews as the Secretary of State considers appropriate.

Assessment of educational needs at request of child's parent

329.—(1) Where—

(a) the parent of a child for whom a local education authority are responsible but for whom no statement is maintained under section 324 asks the authority to arrange for an assessment to be made in respect of the child under section 323,
(b) no such assessment has been made within the period of six months ending with the date on which the request is made, and
(c) it is necessary for the authority to make an assessment under that section,

the authority shall comply with the request.

(2) If in any case where subsection (1)(a) and (b) applies the authority determine not to comply with the request—

(a) they shall give notice of that fact and of the effect of paragraph (b) below to the child's parent, and
(b) the parent may appeal to the Tribunal against the determination.

(3) On an appeal under subsection (2) above the Tribunal may—

(a) dismiss the appeal, or
(b) order the authority to arrange for an assessment to be made in respect of the child under section 323.

Assessment of educational needs at request of governing body of grant-maintained school

330.—(1) Where in the case of a child for whom a local education authority are responsible but for whom no statement is maintained under section 324—

(a) a grant-maintained school is specified in a direction in respect of the child under section 431 (direction to admit child to specified school),
(b) the governing body of the school ask the authority to arrange for an assessment to be made in respect of the child under section 323, and
(c) no such assessment has been made within the period of six months ending with the date on which the request is made,

the local education authority shall serve a notice under subsection (2) on the child's parent.

(2) The notice shall inform the child's parent—

(a) that the local education authority propose to make an assessment of the child's educational needs,
(b) of the procedure to be followed in making the assessment,
(c) of the name of the officer of the authority from whom further information may be obtained, and
(d) of the parent's right to make representations, and submit written evidence, to the authority within such period (which must not be less

than 29 days beginning with the date on which the notice is served) as may be specified in the notice.

(3) Where—

- (a) a local education authority have served a notice under subsection (2) and the period specified in the notice in accordance with subsection (2)(d) has expired, and
- (b) the authority are of the opinion, after taking into account any representations made and any evidence submitted to them in response to the notice, that the child falls, or probably falls, within subsection (4),

they shall make an assessment of his educational needs under section 323.

(4) A child falls within this subsection if—

- (a) he has special educational needs, and
- (b) it is necessary to determine the special educational provision which any learning difficulty he may have calls for.

(5) Where a local education authority decide in pursuance of this section to make an assessment under section 323, they shall give notice in writing to the child's parent, and to the governing body of the grant-maintained school, of that decision and of their reasons for making it.

(6) Where, at any time after serving a notice under subsection (2), a local education authority decide not to assess the educational needs of the child concerned, they shall give notice in writing to the child's parent and to the governing body of the grant-maintained school of their decision.

Assessment of educational needs of children under two

331.—(1) Where a local education authority are of the opinion that a child in their area who is under the age of two years falls, or probably falls, within subsection (2) below—

- (a) they may, with the consent of his parent, make an assessment of the child's educational needs, and
- (b) they shall make such an assessment if requested to do so by his parent.

(2) A child falls within this subsection if—

- (a) he has special educational needs, and
- (b) it is necessary for the authority to determine the special educational provision which any learning difficulty he may have calls for.

(3) An assessment under this section shall be made in such manner as the authority consider appropriate.

(4) After making an assessment under this section, the authority—

- (a) may make a statement of the child's special educational needs, and
- (b) may maintain that statement,

in such manner as they consider appropriate.

Duty of Health Authority or National Health Service trust to notify parent etc.

332.—(1) This section applies where a Health Authority or a National Health Service trust, in the course of exercising any of their functions in relation to a child who is under the age of five, form the opinion that he has (or probably has) special educational needs.

(2) The Authority or trust—

(a) shall inform the child's parent of their opinion and of their duty under paragraph (b), and

(b) after giving the parent an opportunity to discuss that opinion with an officer of the Authority or trust, shall bring it to the attention of the appropriate local education authority.

(3) If the Authority or trust are of the opinion that a particular voluntary organisation is likely to be able to give the parent advice or assistance in connection with any special educational needs that the child may have, they shall inform the parent accordingly.

Special Educational Needs Tribunal

Constitution of Tribunal

333.—(1) There shall continue to be a tribunal, known as the Special Educational Needs Tribunal, which shall exercise the jurisdiction conferred on it by this Part.

(2) There shall be appointed—

(a) a President of the Tribunal (referred to in this Part as "the President"),

(b) a panel of persons (referred to in this Part as "the chairmen's panel") who may serve as chairman of the Tribunal, and

(c) a panel of persons (referred to in this Part as "the lay panel") who may serve as the other two members of the Tribunal apart from the chairman.

(3) The President and the members of the chairmen's panel shall each be appointed by the Lord Chancellor.

(4) The members of the lay panel shall each be appointed by the Secretary of State.

(5) Regulations may—

(a) provide for the jurisdiction of the Tribunal to be exercised by such number of tribunals as may be determined from time to time by the President, and

(b) make such other provision in connection with the establishment and continuation of the Tribunal as the Secretary of State considers necessary or desirable.

(6) The Secretary of State may, with the consent of the Treasury, provide such staff and accommodation as the Tribunal may require.

The President and members of the panels

334.—(1) No person may be appointed President or member of the chairmen's panel unless he has a seven year general qualification (within the meaning of section 71 of the Courts and Legal Services Act 1990).

(2) No person may be appointed member of the lay panel unless he satisfies such requirements as may be prescribed.

(3) If, in the opinion of the Lord Chancellor, the President is unfit to continue in office or is incapable of performing his duties, the Lord Chancellor may revoke his appointment.

(4) Each member of the chairmen's panel or lay panel shall hold and vacate office under the terms of the instrument under which he is appointed.

(5) The President or a member of the chairmen's panel or lay panel—

(a) may resign office by notice in writing to the Lord Chancellor or (as the case may be) the Secretary of State, and
(b) is eligible for re-appointment if he ceases to hold office.

Remuneration and expenses

335.—(1) The Secretary of State may pay to the President, and to any other person in respect of his service as a member of the Tribunal, such remuneration and allowances as the Secretary of State may, with the consent of the Treasury, determine.

(2) The Secretary of State may defray the expenses of the Tribunal to such amount as he may, with the consent of the Treasury, determine.

Tribunal procedure

336.—(1) Regulations may make provision about the proceedings of the Tribunal on an appeal under this Part and the initiation of such an appeal.

(2) The regulations may, in particular, include provision—

(a) as to the period within which, and the manner in which, appeals are to be instituted,
(b) where the jurisdiction of the Tribunal is being exercised by more than one tribunal—
    (i) for determining by which tribunal any appeal is to be heard, and
    (ii) for the transfer of proceedings from one tribunal to another,
(c) for enabling any functions which relate to matters preliminary or incidental to an appeal to be performed by the President, or by the chairman,
(d) for the holding of hearings in private in prescribed circumstances,
(e) for hearings to be conducted in the absence of any member, other than the chairman,
(f) as to the persons who may appear on behalf of the parties,

(g) for granting any person such discovery or inspection of documents or right to further particulars as might be granted by a county court,
(h) requiring persons to attend to give evidence and produce documents,
(i) for authorising the administration of oaths to witnesses,
(j) for the determination of appeals without a hearing in prescribed circumstances,
(k) as to the withdrawal of appeals,
(l) for the award of costs or expenses,
(m) for taxing or otherwise settling any such costs or expenses (and, in particular, for enabling such costs to be taxed in the county court),
(n) for the registration and proof of decisions and orders, and
(o) for enabling the Tribunal to review its decisions, or revoke or vary its orders, in such circumstances as may be determined in accordance with the regulations.

(3) The Secretary of State may pay such allowances for the purpose of or in connection with the attendance of persons at the Tribunal as he may, with the consent of the Treasury, determine.

(4) Part I of the Arbitration Act 1996 shall not apply to any proceedings before the Tribunal but regulations may make provision corresponding to any provision of that Act.

(5) Any person who without reasonable excuse fails to comply with—

(a) any requirement in respect of the discovery or inspection of documents imposed by the regulations by virtue of subsection (2)(g), or
(b) any requirement imposed by the regulations by virtue of subsection (2)(h),

is guilty of an offence.

(6) A person guilty of an offence under subsection (5) is liable on summary conviction to a fine not exceeding level 3 on the standard scale.

Special schools and independent schools

Special schools

337.—(1) A school which is specially organised to make special educational provision for pupils with special educational needs and is for the time being approved by the Secretary of State under section 342 shall be known as a special school.

(2) There are three categories of special school—

(a) maintained special schools;
(b) grant-maintained special schools; and
(c) special schools which are neither maintained nor grant-maintained schools.

(3) A special school is a maintained special school if it is maintained by a local education authority.

(4) A special school is a grant-maintained special school if it is conducted by a governing body incorporated in pursuance of proposals for the purpose—

(a) made by the funding authority under section 339 of this Act (or section 183 of the Education Act 1993), or
(b) made under section 345 of this Act (or section 186 of that Act).

Approval of special schools

342.—(1) The Secretary of State may approve under this section any school which is specially organised to make special educational provision for pupils with special educational needs, (and which is not a maintained or grant-maintained school), and may give his approval before or after the school is established.

(2) Regulations may make provision as to the requirements which are to be complied with as a condition of approval under subsection (1) above.

(3) Any school which—

(a) is established in pursuance of proposals approved under section 340 (or section 184 of the Education Act 1993), or
(b) was a special school immediately before 1st April 1994 (the date when section 184 of the Act came into force),

shall be treated, subject to subsection (4) below, as approved under this section.

(4) Regulations may make provision as to—

(a) the requirements which are to be complied with by a school while approved under this section, and
(b) the withdrawal of approval from a school (including approval treated as given under subsection (3)) at the request of the proprietor or on the ground that there has been a failure to comply with any prescribed requirement.

(5) Without prejudice to the generality of subsections (2) and (4), the requirements which may be imposed by the regulations include requirements—

(a) which call for arrangements to be approved by the Secretary of State, or
(b) as to the organisation of any special school as a primary school or as a secondary school.

(6) Regulations shall make provision for securing that, so far as practicable, every pupil attending a special school—

(a) receives religious education and attends religious worship, or
(b) is withdrawn from receiving such education or from attendance at such worship in accordance with the wishes of his parent.

(7) Where approval is withdrawn from a maintained special school or grant-maintained special school, the local education authority or, as the case may be, the governing body shall serve under section 339 notice of their proposals to discontinue the school.

(8) For the purposes of proposals made under subsection (7)—

(a) that section 339 shall have effect as if the school had not ceased to be a special school on the withdrawal of the approval, and

(b) section 340 shall have effect as if subsections (1) to (3), and the reference in subsection (4) to the rejection of proposals, were omitted.

Approval of independent schools

347.—(1) The Secretary of State may approve an independent school as suitable for the admission of children for whom statements are maintained under section 324.

(2) Regulations may make provision as to—

(a) the requirements which are to be complied with by a school as a condition of its approval under this section,

(b) the requirements which are to be complied with by a school while an approval under this section is in force in respect of it, and

(c) the withdrawal of approval from a school at the request of the proprietor or on the ground that there has been a failure to comply with any prescribed requirement.

(3) An approval under this section may be given subject to such conditions (in addition to those prescribed) as the Secretary of State sees fit to impose.

(4) In any case where there is a failure to comply with such a condition imposed under subsection (3) above, the Secretary of State may withdraw his approval.

(5) No person shall so exercise his functions under this Part that a child with special educational needs is educated in an independent school unless—

(a) the school is for the time being approved by the Secretary of State as suitable for the admission of children for whom statements are maintained under section 324, or

(b) the Secretary of State consents to the child being educated there.

Provision of special education at non-maintained schools

348.—(1) This section applies where—

(a) special educational provision in respect of a child with special educational needs is made at a school which is not a maintained school, and

(b) either the name of the school is specified in a statement in respect of the child under section 324 or the local education authority are satisfied—

(i) that his interests require the necessary special educational provision to be made for him at a school which is not a maintained school, and

(ii) that it is appropriate for the child to be provided with education at the particular school.

(2) Where this subsection applies, the local education authority shall pay the whole of the fees payable in respect of the education provided for the child at the school, and if—

(a) board and lodging are provided for him at the school, and

(b) the authority are satisfied that the necessary special educational provision cannot be provided for him at the school unless the board and lodging are also provided,

the authority shall pay the whole of the fees payable in respect of the board and lodging.

(3) In this section, "maintained school" means—

(a) a school maintained by a local education authority,
(b) a grant-maintained school, and
(c) a grant-maintained special school.

SCHEDULE 27
MAKING AND MAINTENANCE OF STATEMENTS UNDER SECTION 324

Introductory

1.—In this Schedule, "statement" means a statement of a child's special educational needs under section 324.

Copy of proposed statement

2.—Before making a statement, a local education authority shall serve on the parent of the child concerned—

(a) a copy of the proposed statement, and
(b) a written notice explaining the arrangements under paragraph 3, the effect of paragraph 4 and the right to appeal under section 326 and containing such other information as may be prescribed,

but the copy of the proposed statement shall not specify any matter in pursuance of section 324(4) of this Act or any prescribed matter.

Choice of school

3.—(1) Every local education authority shall make arrangements for enabling a parent on whom a copy of a proposed statement has been served under paragraph 2 to express a preference as to the maintained, grant-maintained or grant-maintained special school at which he wishes education to be provided for his child and to give reasons for his preference.

(2) Any such preference must be expressed or made within the period of 15 days beginning—

(a) with the date on which the written notice mentioned in paragraph 2(b) was served on the parent, or
(b) if a meeting has (or meetings have) been arranged under paragraph 4(1)(b) or (2), with the date fixed for that meeting (or the last of those meetings).

(3) Where a local education authority make a statement in a case where the parent of the child concerned has expressed a preference in pursuance of such

arrangements as to the school at which he wishes education to be provided for his child, they shall specify the name of that school in the statement unless—

(a) the school is unsuitable to the child's age, ability or aptitude or to his special educational needs, or
(b) the attendance of the child at the school would be incompatible with the provision of efficient education for the children with whom he would be educated or the efficient use of resources.

(4) A local education authority shall, before specifying the name of any maintained, grant-maintained or grant-maintained special school in a statement, consult the governing body of the school and, if the school is maintained by another local education authority, that authority.

Representations

4.—(1) A parent on whom a copy of a proposed statement has been served under paragraph 2 may—

(a) make representations (or further representations) to the local education authority about the content of the statement, and
(b) require the authority to arrange a meeting between him and an officer of the authority at which the statement can be discussed.

(2) Where a parent, having attended a meeting arranged by a local education authority under sub-paragraph (1)(b), disagrees with any part of the assessment in question, he may require the authority to arrange such meeting or meetings as they consider will enable him to discuss the relevant advice with the appropriate person or persons.

(3) In this paragraph—

"relevant advice" means such of the advice given to the authority in connection with the assessment as they consider to be relevant to that part of the assessment with which the parent disagrees, and
"appropriate person" means the person who gave the relevant advice or any other person who, in the opinion of the authority, is the appropriate person to discuss it with the parent.

(4) Any representations under sub-paragraph (1)(a) above must be made within the period of 15 days beginning—

(a) with the date on which the written notice mentioned in paragraph 2(b) was served on the parent, or
(b) if a meeting has (or meetings have) been arranged under sub-paragraph (1)(b) or (2), with the date fixed for that meeting (or the last of those meetings).

(5) A requirement under sub-paragraph (1)(b) above must be made within the period of 15 days beginning with the date on which the written notice mentioned in paragraph 2(b) was served on the parent.

(6) A requirement under sub-paragraph (2) must be made within the period of15 days beginning with the date fixed for the meeting arranged under sub-paragraph (1)(b).

Making the statement

5.—(1) Where representations are made to a local education authority under paragraph 4(1)(a), the authority shall not make the statement until they have considered the representations and the period or the last of the periods allowed by paragraph 4 above for making requirements or further representations has expired.

(2) The statement may be in the form originally proposed (except as to the matters required to be excluded from the copy of the proposed statement) or in a form modified in the light of the representations.

(3) Regulations may provide that, where a local education authority are under a duty (subject to compliance with the preceding requirements of this Schedule) to make a statement, the duty, or any step required to be taken for performance of the duty, must, subject to prescribed exceptions, be performed within the prescribed period.

(4) Such provision shall not relieve the authority of the duty to make a statement, or take any step, which has not been performed or taken within that period.

Service of statement

6.—Where a local education authority make a statement they shall serve a copy of the statement on the parent of the child concerned and shall give notice in writing to him—

(a) of his right under section 326(1) to appeal against—

 (i) the description in the statement of the authority's assessment of the child's special educational needs,
 (ii) the special educational provision specified in the statement or,
 (iii) if no school is named in the statement, that fact, and

(b) of the name of the person to whom he may apply for information and advice about the child's special educational needs.

Keeping, disclosure and transfer of statements

7.—(1) Regulations may make provision as to the keeping and disclosure of statements.

(2) Regulations may make provision, where a local education authority become responsible for a child for whom a statement is maintained by another authority, for the transfer of the statement to them and for Part IV to have effect as if the duty to maintain the transferred statement were their duty.

Change of named school

8.—(1) Sub-paragraph (2) applies where—

(a) the parent of a child for whom a statement is maintained which specifies the name of a school or institution asks the local education authority to substitute for that name the name of a maintained, grant-maintained or grant-maintained special school specified by the parent, and

(b) the request is not made less than 12 months after—

(i) an earlier request under this paragraph,

(ii) the service of a copy of the statement under paragraph 6,

(iii) if the statement has been amended, the date when notice of the amendment is given under paragraph 10(3)(b), or

(iv) if the parent has appealed to the Tribunal under section 326 or this paragraph, the date when the appeal is concluded,

whichever is the later.

(2) The local education authority shall comply with the request unless—

(a) the school is unsuitable to the child's age, ability or aptitude or to his special educational needs, or

(b) the attendance of the child at the school would be incompatible with the provision of efficient education for the children with whom he would be educated or the efficient use of resources.

(3) Where the local education authority determine not to comply with the request—

(a) they shall give notice of that fact and of the effect of paragraph (b) below to the parent of the child, and

(b) the parent of the child may appeal to the Tribunal against the determination.

(4) On the appeal the Tribunal may—

(a) dismiss the appeal, or

(b) order the local education authority to substitute for the name of the school or other institution specified in the statement the name of the school specified by the parent.

(5) Regulations may provide that, where a local education authority are under a duty to comply with a request under this paragraph, the duty must, subject to prescribed exceptions, be performed within the prescribed period.

(6) Such provision shall not relieve the authority of the duty to comply with such a request which has not been complied with within that period.

Procedure for amending or ceasing to maintain a statement

9.—(1) A local education authority may not amend, or cease to maintain, a statement except in accordance with paragraph 10 or 11.

(2) Sub-paragraph (1) above does not apply where the local education authority—

(a) cease to maintain a statement for a child who has ceased to be a child for whom they are responsible,
(b) amend a statement in pursuance of paragraph 8,
(c) are ordered to cease to maintain a statement under section 326(3)(c), or
(d) amend a statement in pursuance of directions under section 442 (revocation of school attendance order).

10.—(1) Before amending a statement, a local education authority shall serve on the parent of the child concerned a notice informing him—

(a) of their proposal, and
(b) of his right to make representations under sub-paragraph (2).

(2) A parent on whom a notice has been served under sub-paragraph (1) may, within the period of 15 days beginning with the date on which the notice is served, make representations to the local education authority about their proposal.

(3) The local education authority—

(a) shall consider any representations made to them under sub-paragraph (2) and
(b) on taking a decision on the proposal to which the representations relate, shall give notice in writing to the parent of their decision.

(4) Where a local education authority make an amendment under this paragraph to the description in a statement of the authority's assessment of a child's special educational needs or to the special educational provision specified in a statement, they shall give notice in writing to the parent of his right under section 326(1) to appeal against—

(a) the description in the statement of the authority's assessment of the child's special educational needs,
(b) the special educational provision specified in the statement or,
(c) if no school is named in the statement, that fact.

(5) A local education authority may only amend a statement under this paragraph within the prescribed period beginning with the service of the notice under sub-paragraph (1).

11.—(1) A local education authority may cease to maintain a statement only if it is no longer necessary to maintain it.

(2) Where the local education authority determine to cease to maintain a statement—

(a) they shall give notice of that fact and of the effect of paragraph (b) below to the parent of the child, and

(b) the parent of the child may appeal to the Tribunal against the determination.

(3) On an appeal under this paragraph the Tribunal may—

(a) dismiss the appeal, or
(b) order the local education authority to continue to maintain the statement in its existing form or with such amendments of—

(i) the description in the statement of the authority's assessment of the child's special educational needs, or
(ii) the special educational provision specified in the statement,

and such other consequential amendments, as the Tribunal may determine.

(4) Except where the parent of the child appeals to the Tribunal under this paragraph, a local education authority may only cease to maintain a statement under this paragraph within the prescribed period beginning with the service of the notice under sub-paragraph (2).

Further and Higher Education Act 1992 (C. 13)

An Act to make new provision about further and higher education.

[6th March 1992]

Be it enacted by the Queen's most Excellent Majesty, by and with the advice and consent of the Lords Spiritual and Temporal, and Commons, in this present Parliament assembled, and by the authority of the same as follows:

PART I
FURTHER EDUCATION
CHAPTER 1
RESPONSIBILITY FOR FURTHER EDUCATION

The new funding councils

The Further Education Funding Councils

1.—(1) There shall be established—

(a) a body corporate to be known as the Further Education Funding Council for England to exercise in relation to England the functions conferred on them, and
(b) a body corporate to be known as the Further Education Funding Council for Wales to exercise in relation to Wales the functions conferred on them.

(2) The Further Education Funding Council for England shall consist of not less than twelve nor more than fifteen members appointed by the Secretary of State, of whom one shall be so appointed as chairman.

(3) The Further Education Funding Council for Wales shall consist of not less

than eight nor more than twelve members appointed by the Secretary of State, of whom one shall be so appointed as chairman.

(4) In appointing the members of a council the Secretary Of State—

(a) shall have regard to the desirability of including persons who appear to him to have experience of, and to have shown capacity in, the provision of education or to have held, and to have shown capacity in, any position carrying responsibility for the provision of education and, in appointing such persons, he shall have regard to the desirability of their being currently engaged in the provision of further education or in carrying responsibility for such provision, and

(b) shall have regard to the desirability of including persons who appear to him to have experience of, and to have shown capacity in, industrial, commercial or financial matters or the practice of any profession.

(5) In this Part of this Act any reference to a council is to a further education funding council.

(6) References in the Education Acts to the appropriate further education funding council, in relation to any educational institution—

(a) where the institution mainly serves the population of England, are to the Further Education Funding Council for England and, where the institution mainly serves the population of Wales, are to the Further Education Funding Council for Wales, and

(b) where the institution receives financial support from a further education funding council, are to that council also (if different).

(7) Any dispute as to whether any functions are exercisable by one of the councils shall be determined by the Secretary of State.

(8) Schedule 1 to this Act has effect with respect to each of the councils.

The new further education sector

Full-time education for 16 to 18 year-olds

2.—(1) It shall be the duty of each council to secure the provision for the population of their area of sufficient facilities for education to which this subsection applies, that is, full-time education suitable to the requirements of persons over compulsory school age who have not attained the age of nineteen years.

(2) That duty extends to all persons among that population who may want such education and have not attained the age of nineteen years.

(3) A council shall discharge that duty so as—

(a) to secure that the facilities are provided at such places, are of such character and are so equipped as to be sufficient to meet the reasonable needs of all persons to whom the duty extends, and

(b) to take account of the different abilities and aptitudes of such persons.

(4) A council may secure the provision of facilities for education to which subsection (1) above applies for persons to whom that duty does not extend.

(5) A council shall discharge their functions under this section so as to make the most effective use of the council's resources and, in particular to avoid provision which might give rise to disproportionate expenditure.

(6) In discharging those functions a council shall have regard to any education to which subsection (1) above applies provided by schools maintained by local education authorities, grant-maintained schools, special schools not maintained by local education authorities, city technology colleges or city colleges for the technology of the arts.

Part-time education, and full-time education for those over 18

3.—(1) It shall be the duty of each council to secure the provision for the population of their area of adequate facilities for education to which this subsection applies, that is—

(a) part-time education suitable to the requirements of persons of any age over compulsory school age, and

(b) full-time education suitable to the requirements of persons who have attained the age of nineteen years,

where the education is provided by means of a course of a description mentioned in Schedule 2 to this Act.

(2) A council shall discharge that duty so as—

(a) to secure that facilities are provided at such places, are of such character and are so equipped as to meet the reasonable need for education to which subsection (1) above applies, and

(b) to take account of the different abilities and aptitudes of persons among that population.

(3) A council may secure the provision of facilities for education to which subsection (1) above applies where they are not under a duty to do so.

(4) A council shall discharge their functions under this section so as to make the most effective use of their resources and, in particular, to avoid provision which might give rise to disproportionate expenditure.

(5) In discharging those functions a council shall have regard to any education to which subsection (1) above applies provided by institutions outside the further education sector or higher education sector.

(6) The Secretary of State may by order amend Schedule 2 to this Act.

Persons with learning difficulties

4.—(1) In exercising their functions under sections 2 and 3 of this Act, each council shall (subject to the provisions of those sections) do so in accordance with subsections (2) to (4) below.

(2) Each council shall have regard to the requirements of persons having learning difficulties.

(3) A council shall, if they are satisfied in the case of any person among the

population of their area who has a learning difficulty and is over compulsory school age but has not attained the age of twenty-five years, that—

(a) the facilities available in institutions within the further education sector or the higher education sector are not adequate for him, and
(b) it is in his best interests to do so,

secure provision for him at an institution outside those sectors.

(4) A council shall, if they are satisfied that they cannot secure such provision for a person as they are required to secure under subsection (3) above unless they also secure the provision of boarding accommodation for him, secure the provision of boarding accommodation for him.

(5) In exercising their functions under sections 2 and 3 of this Act in the case of any person who has a learning difficulty and is over compulsory school age, a council may—

(a) if they are satisfied that the facilities available in institutions within the further education sector or the higher education sector are not adequate for him, secure provision for him at an institution outside those sectors, and
(b) secure the provision of boarding accommodation for him.

(6) Subject to subsection (7), below, for the purposes of this section a person has a "learning difficulty" if—

(a) he has a significantly greater difficulty in learning than the majority of persons of his age, or
(b) he has a disability which either prevents or hinders him from making use of facilities of a kind generally provided by institutions within the further education sector for persons of his age.

(7) A person is not to be taken as having a learning difficulty solely because the language (or form of the language) in which he is, or will be, taught is different from a language (or form of a language) which has at any time been spoken in his home.

SCHEDULE 2
COURSES OF FURTHER EDUCATION

The description of courses of further education referred to in section 3(1) of this Act are the following—

(a) a course which prepares students to obtain a vocational qualification which is, or falls within a class, for the time being approved for the purposes of this sub-paragraph by the Secretary of State,
(b) a course which prepares students to qualify for—

    (i) the General Certificate of Secondary Education, or
    (ii) the General Certificate of Education at Advanced Level or Advanced Supplementary Level (including Special Papers),

(c) a course for the time being approved for the purposes of this sub-paragraph by the Secretary of State which prepares students for entry to a course of higher education,

(d) a course which prepares students for entry to another course falling within paragraph (a) to (c) above,

(e) a course for basic literacy in English,

(f) a course to improve the knowledge of English of those for whom English is not the language spoken at home,

(g) a course to teach the basic principles of mathematics,

(h) in relation to Wales, a course for proficiency or literacy in Welsh,

(j) a course to teach independent living and communication skills to persons having learning difficulties which prepares them for entry to another course falling within paragraphs (d) to (h) above.

Appendix 3: Statutory Instruments

The Education (Special Educational Needs) Regulations 1994 (S.I. 1994 No. 1047)

ARRANGEMENT OF REGULATIONS

PART I
General

PART II
Assessments

PART III
Statements

PART IV
Revocation and Transitional Provisions

SCHEDULE

In exercise of the powers conferred on the Secretary of State by sections 166(4), 168(2), 172(6), 301(6) of, and paragraphs 2 and 3 of Schedule 9 and paragraphs 5, 7, and 8 of Schedule 10 to the Education Act 1993, and by section 19 and paragraphs 1 and 3 of Schedule 1 to the Education Act 1981 the Secretary of State for Education, as respects England, and the Secretary of State for Wales, as respects Wales, hereby make the following Regulations:—

PART I
GENERAL

Title and commencement

1. These Regulations may be cited as the Education (Special Educational Needs) Regulations 1994 and shall come into force on 1st September 1994.

Interpretation

2. (1) In these Regulations—

"the Act" means the Education Act 1993;
"authority" means a local education authority;
"district health authority" has the same meaning as in the National Health Service Act 1977;
"head teacher" includes any person to whom the duties or functions of a head teacher under these Regulations have been delegated by the head teacher in accordance with regulation 3;
"social services authority" means a local authority for the purposes of the Local Authority Social Services Act 1970 acting in the discharge of such functions as are referred to in section 2(1) of that Act;
"target" means the knowledge, skills and understanding which a child is expected to have by the end of a particular period;
"transition plan" means a document prepared pursuant to regulation 16(9) or 17(9) which sets out the arrangements which an authority consider appropriate for a young person during the period when he is aged 14 to 19 years, including arrangements for special educational provision and for any other necessary provision, for suitable employment and accommodation and

for leisure activities, and which will facilitate a satisfactory transition from childhood to adulthood;

"working day" means a day other than a Saturday, Sunday, Christmas Day, Good Friday or Bank Holiday within the meaning of the Banking and Financial Dealings Act 1971;

"the 1981 Act" means the Education Act 1981;

"the 1983 Regulations" means the Education (Special Educational Needs) Regulations 1983.

(2) In these Regulations any reference to the district health authority or the social services authority is, in relation to a particular child, a reference to the district health authority or social services authority in whose area that child lives.

(3) Where a thing is required to be done under these Regulations—

(a) within a period after an action is taken, the day on which that action was taken shall not be counted in the calculation of that period; and
(b) within a period and the last day of that period is not a working day, the period shall be extended to include the following working day.

(4) References in these Regulations to a section are references to a section of the Act.

(5) References in these Regulations to a regulation are references to a regulation in these Regulations and references to a Schedule are references to the Schedule to these Regulations.

Delegation of functions

3. Where a head teacher has any functions or duties under these Regulations he may delegate those functions or duties—

(a) generally to a member of the staff of the school who is a qualified teacher [within the meaning of section 218 of the Education Reform Act 1988], or
(b) in a particular case to a member of the staff of the school who teaches the child in question.

AMENDMENT

Reg. 3(a) was amended by the Education (Special Education Needs) (Amendment) Regulations 1995 with effect from August 14, 1995.

Service of documents

4. (1) Where any provision in Part III of the Act or in these Regulations authorises or requires any document to be served or sent to a person or any written notice to be given to a person the document may be served or sent or the notice may be given by properly addressing, pre-paying and posting a letter containing the document or notice.

(2) For the purposes of this regulation, the proper address of a person is—

(a) in the case of the child's parent, his last known address;

(b) in the case of a head teacher or other member of the staff of a school, the school's address;
(c) in the case of any other person, the last known address of the place where he carries on his business, profession or other employment.

(3) Where first class post is used, the document or notice shall be treated as served, sent or given on the second working day after the date of posting, unless the contrary is shown.

(4) Where second class post is used, the document or notice shall be treated as served, sent or given on the fourth working day after the date of posting, unless the contrary is shown.

(5) The date of posting shall be presumed, unless the contrary is shown, to be the date shown in the post-mark on the envelope in which the document is contained.

PART II
ASSESSMENTS

Notices relating to assessment

5. (1) Where under section 167(1) or 174(2) an authority give notice to a child's parent that they propose to make an assessment, or under section 167(4) give notice to a child's parent of their decision to make an assessment, they shall send copies of the relevant notice to—

(a) the social services authority,
(b) the district health authority, and
(c) if the child is registered at a school, the head teacher of that school.

(2) Where a copy of a notice is sent under paragraph (1) an endorsement on the copy or a notice accompanying that copy shall inform the recipient what help the authority are likely to request.

(3) Where under section 172(2) or 173(1) a child's parent asks the authority to arrange for an assessment to be made the authority shall give notice in writing to the persons referred to in paragraph (1)(a) to (c) of the fact that the request has been made and inform them what help they are likely to request.

Advice to be sought

6. (1) For the purpose of making an assessment under section 167 an authority shall seek—

(a) advice from the child's parent;
(b) educational advice as provided for in regulation 7;
(c) medical advice from the district health authority as provided for in regulation 8;
(d) psychological advice as provided for in regulation 9;
(e) advice from the social services authority; and
(f) any other advice which the authority consider appropriate for the purpose of arriving at a satisfactory assessment.

(2) The advice referred to in paragraph (1) shall be written advice relating to—

(a) the educational, medical, psychological or other features of the case (according to the nature of the advice sought) which appear to be relevant to the child's educational needs (including his likely future needs);
(b) how those features could affect the child's educational needs, and
(c) the provision which is appropriate for the child in light of those features of the child's case, whether by way of special educational provision or non-educational provision, but not relating to any matter which is required to be specified in a statement by virtue of section 168(4)(b).

(3) A person from whom the advice referred to in paragraph (1) is sought may in connection therewith consult such persons as it appears to him expedient to consult; and he shall consult such persons, if any, as are specified in the particular case by the authority as persons who have relevant knowledge of, or information relating to, the child.

(4) When seeking the advice referred to in paragraph (1)(b) to (f) an authority shall provide the person from whom it is sought with copies of—

(a) any representations made by the parent, and
(b) any evidence submitted by, or at the request of, the parent under section 167(1)(d).

(5) The authority need not seek the advice referred to in paragraph (1)(b), (c), (d), (e) or (f) if—

(a) the authority have obtained advice under paragraph (1)(b), (c), (d), (e) or (f) respectively within the preceding 12 months, and
(b) the authority, the person from whom the advice was obtained and the child's parent are satisfied that the existing advice is sufficient for the purpose of arriving at a satisfactory assessment.

Educational advice

7. (1) The educational advice referred to in regulation 6(1)(b) shall, subject to paragraphs (2) to (5), be sought—

(a) from the head teacher of each school which the child is currently attending or which he has attended at any time within the preceding 18 months;
(b) if advice cannot be obtained from a head teacher of a school which the child is currently attending (because the child is not attending a school or otherwise) from a person who the authority are satisfied has experience of teaching children with special educational needs or knowledge of the differing provision which may be called for in different cases to meet those needs;
(c) if the child is not currently attending a school and if advice obtained under subparagraph (b) is not advice from such a person, from a person responsible for educational provision for him; and

(d) if any of the child's parents is a serving member of Her Majesty's armed forces, from the Service Children's Education Authority.

(2) The advice sought as provided in paragraph (1)[(a) to (c)] shall not be sought from any person who is not a qualified teacher within the meaning of section 218 of the Education Reform Act 1988.

(3) The advice sought from a head teacher as provided in paragraph (1)(a) shall, if the head teacher has not himself taught the child within the preceding 18 months, be advice given after consultation with a teacher who has so taught the child.

(4) The advice sought from a head teacher as provided in paragraph (1)(a) shall include advice relating to the steps which have been taken by the school to identify and assess the special educational needs of the child and to make provision for the purpose of meeting those needs.

(5) Where it appears to the authority, in consequence of medical advice or otherwise, that the child in question is—

(a) hearing impaired, or
(b) visually impaired, or
(c) both hearing impaired and visually impaired,

and any person from whom advice is sought as provided in paragraph (1) is not qualified to teach pupils who are so impaired then the advice sought shall be advice given after consultation with a person who is so qualified.

(6) For the purposes of paragraph (5) a person shall be considered to be qualified to teach pupils who are hearing impaired or visually impaired or who are both hearing impaired and visually impaired if he is qualified to be employed at a school as a teacher of a class for pupils who are so impaired otherwise than to give instruction in a craft, trade, or domestic subject.

(7) Paragraphs (3) and (5) are without prejudice to regulation 6(3).

AMENDMENT

The words in square brackets in Reg. 7(2) were added by The Education (Special Education Needs) (Amendment) Regulations 1995 with effect from August 14, 1995.

Medical advice

8. The advice referred to in paragraph 6(1)(c) shall be sought from the district health authority, who shall obtain the advice from a fully registered medical practitioner.

Psychological advice

9. (1) The psychological advice referred to in regulation 6(1)(d) shall be sought from a person—

(a) regularly employed by the authority as an educational psychologist, or
(b) engaged by the authority as an educational psychologist in the case in question.

(2) The advice sought from a person as provided in paragraph (1) shall, if that

person has reason to believe that another psychologist has relevant knowledge of, or information relating to, the child, be advice given after consultation with that other psychologist.

(3) Paragraph (2) is without prejudice to regulation 6(3).

Matters to be taken into account in making an assessment

10. When making an assessment an authority shall take into consideration—

(a) any representations made by the child's parent under section 167(1)(d);
(b) any evidence submitted by, or at the request of, the child's parent under section 167(1)(d); and
(c) the advice obtained under regulation 6.

Time limits

11. (1) Where under section 167(1) the authority serve a notice on the child's parent informing him that they propose to make an assessment of the child's educational needs under section 167 they shall within 6 weeks of the date of service of the notice give notice to the child's parent—

(a) under section 167(4) of their decision to make an assessment, and of their reasons for making that decision, or
(b) under section 167(6) of their decision not to assess the educational needs of the child.

(2) Where under section 174(2) the authority serve a notice on the child's parent informing him that they propose to make an assessment of the child's educational needs under section 167 they shall within 6 weeks of the date of service of the notice give notice to the child's parent and to the governing body of the grant-maintained school which asked the authority to make an assessment—

(a) under section 174(5) of their decision to make an assessment and their reasons for making that decision, or
(b) under section 174(6) of their decision not to assess the educational needs of the child.

(3) Where under sections 172(2) or 173(1) a parent asks the authority to arrange for an assessment to be made under section 167 they shall within 6 weeks of the date of receipt of the request give notice to the child's parent—

(a) under section 167(4) of their decision to make an assessment, or
(b) under section 172(3)(a) or 173(2)(a) respectively of their decision not to comply with the request and of the parent's right to appeal to the Tribunal against the determination.

(4) An authority need not comply with the time limits referred to in paragraphs (1) to (3) if it is impractical to do so because—

(a) the authority have requested advice from the head teacher of a school during a period beginning one week before any date on which that school was closed for a continuous period of not less than 4 weeks from that date and ending one week before the date on which it re-opens;

(b) exceptional personal circumstances affect the child or his parent during the 6 week period referred to in paragraphs (1) to (3); or

(c) the child or his parent are absent from the area of the authority for a continuous period of not less than 4 weeks during the 6 week period referred to in paragraphs (1) to (3).

(5) Subject to paragraph (6), where under section 167(4) an authority have given notice to the child's parent of their decision to make an assessment they shall complete that assessment within 10 weeks of the date on which such notice was given.

(6) An authority need not comply with the time limit referred to in paragraph (5) if it is impractical to do so because—

(a) in exceptional cases after receiving advice sought under regulation 6 it is necessary for the authority to seek further advice;

(b) the child's parent has indicated to the authority that he wishes to provide advice to the authority after the expiry of 6 weeks from the date on which a request for such advice under regulation 6(a) was received, and the authority have agreed to consider such advice before completing the assessment;

(c) the authority have requested advice from the head teacher of a school under regulation 6(1)(b) during a period beginning one week before any date on which that school was closed for a continuous period of not less than 4 weeks from that date and ending one week before the date on which it re-opens;

(d) the authority have requested advice from a district health authority or a social services authority under [regulation 6(1)(c)] or (e) respectively and the district health authority or the social services authority have not complied with that request within 6 weeks from the date on which it was made;

(e) exceptional personal circumstances affect the child or his parent during the 10 week period referred to in paragraph (5);

(f) the child or his parent are absent from the area of the authority for a continuous period of not less than 4 weeks during the 10 week period referred to in paragraph (5); or

(g) the child fails to keep an appointment for an examination or a test during the 10 week period referred to in paragraph (5).

(7) Subject to paragraph (8), where an authority have requested advice from a district health authority or a social services authority under regulation 6(1)(c) or (e) respectively they shall comply with that request within 6 weeks of the date on which they receive it.

(8) A district health authority or a social services authority need not comply with the time limit referred to in paragraph (7) if it is impractical to do so because—

(a) exceptional personal circumstances affect the child or his parent during the 6 week period referred to in paragraph (7);

(b) the child or his parent are absent from the area of the authority for a continuous period of not less than 4 weeks during the 6 week period referred to in paragraph (7);

(c) the child fails to keep an appointment for an examination or a test made by the district health authority or the social services authority respectively during the 6 week period referred to in paragraph (7); or

(d) they have not before the date on which a copy of a notice has been served on them in accordance with regulation 5(1) or a notice has been served on them in accordance with regulation 5(3) produced or maintained any information or records relevant to the assessment of the child under section 167.

AMENDMENT

Reg. 11(6)(d) was amended by the Education (Special Education Needs) (Amendment) Regulations 1994 with effect from September 1, 1994.

PART III

STATEMENTS

Notice accompanying a proposed statement

12. The notice which shall accompany a copy of a proposed statement served on the parent pursuant to paragraph 2 of Schedule 10 to the Act shall be in a form substantially corresponding to that set out in Part A of the Schedule and shall contain the information therein specified.

Statement of special educational needs

13. A statement of a child's special educational needs made under section 168(1) shall be in a form substantially corresponding to that set out in Part B of the Schedule, shall contain the information therein specified, and shall be dated and authenticated by the signature of a duly authorised officer of the authority concerned.

Time limits

14. (1) Where under section 167 an authority have made an assessment of the educational needs of a child for whom no statement is maintained they shall within two weeks of the date on which the assessment was completed either—

(a) serve a copy of a proposed statement and a written notice on the child's parent under paragraph 2 of Schedule 10 to the Act, or

(b) give notice in writing to the child's parent under section 169(1) that they have decided not to make a statement and that he may appeal against that decision to, the Tribunal.

(2) Where under section 167 an authority have made an assessment of the educational needs of a child for whom a statement is maintained they shall within two weeks of the date on which the assessment was completed—

(a) under paragraph 10(1) of Schedule 10 to the Act serve on the child's parent a notice that they propose to amend the statement and of his right to make representations;

(b) under paragraph 11(2) of Schedule 10 to the Act give notice to the child's parent that they have determined to cease to maintain the statement and of his right of appeal to the Tribunal; or

(c) serve on the child's parent a notice which informs him that they have determined not to amend the statement and their reasons for that determination, which is accompanied by copies of the professional advice obtained during the assessment, and which informs the child's parent that under section 170(1)(c) he may appeal to the Tribunal against the description in the statement of the authority's assessment of the child's special educational needs, the special educational provision specified in the statement or, if no school is named in the statement, that fact.

(3) Subject to paragraph (4), where an authority have served a copy of a proposed statement on the child's parent under paragraph 2 of Schedule 10 to the Act they shall within 8 weeks of the date on which the proposed statement was served serve a copy of the completed statement and a written notice on the child's parent under paragraph 6 of that Schedule, or give notice to the child's parent that they have decided not to make a statement.

(4) The authority need not comply with the time limit referred to in paragraph (3) if it is impractical to do so because—

(a) exceptional personal circumstances affect the child or his parent during the 8 week period referred to in paragraph (3);

(b) the child or his parent are absent from the area of the authority for a continuous period of not less than 4 weeks during the 8 week period referred to in paragraph (3);

(c) the child's parent indicates that he wishes to make representations to the authority about the content of the statement under paragraph 4(1)(a) of Schedule 10 to the Act after the expiry of the 15 day period for making such representations provided for in paragraph 4(4) of that Schedule;

(d) a meeting between the child's parent and an officer of the authority has been held pursuant to paragraph 4(1)(b) of Schedule 10 to the Act and the child's parent has required that another such meeting be arranged or under paragraph 4(2) of that Schedule has required a meeting with the appropriate person under to be arranged; or

(e) the authority have sent a written request to the Secretary of State seeking his consent under section 189(5)(b) to the child being educated at an independent school which is not approved by him and such consent has not been received by the authority within two weeks of the date on which the request was sent.

(5) Where under paragraph 8(1) of Schedule 10 to the Act the child's parent asks the authority to substitute for the name of a school or institution specified in a statement the name of another school specified by him and where the condition

referred to in paragraph 8(1)(b) of that Schedule has been satisfied the authority shall within 8 weeks of the date on which the request was received either—

(a) comply with the request; or
(b) give notice to the child's parent under paragraph 8(3) of that Schedule that they have determined not to comply with the request and that he may appeal against that determination to the Tribunal.

(6) Where under paragraph 10(1) of Schedule 10 to the Act an authority serve a notice on the child's parent informing him of their proposal to amend a statement they shall not amend the statement after the expiry of 8 weeks from the date on which the notice was served.

(7) Where under paragraph 11(2) of Schedule 10 to the Act an authority give notice to the child's parent that they have determined to cease to maintain a statement they shall not cease to maintain the statement—

(a) before the expiry of the prescribed period during which the parent may appeal to the Tribunal against the determination, or
(b) after the expiry of 4 weeks from the end of that period.

Review of statement where child not aged 14 attends school

15. (1) This regulation applies where—

(a) an authority review a statement under section 172(5) other than on the making of an assessment,
(b) the child concerned attends a school, and
(c) regulation 16 does not apply.

(2) The authority shall by notice in writing require the head teacher of the child's school to submit a report to them under this regulation by a specified date not less than two months from the date the notice is given and shall send a copy of the notice to the child's parent.

(3) The head teacher shall for the purpose of preparing the report referred to in paragraph (2) seek advice as to the matters referred to in paragraph (4) from—

(a) the child's parent;
(b) any person whose advice the authority consider appropriate for the purpose of arriving at a satisfactory report and whom they specify in the notice referred to in paragraph (2), and
(c) any person whose advice the head teacher considers appropriate for the purpose of arriving at a satisfactory report.

(4) The advice referred to in paragraph (3) shall be written advice as to—

(a) the child's progress towards meeting the objectives specified in the statement;
(b) the child's progress towards attaining any targets established in furtherance of the objectives specified in the statement;
(c) where the school is not established in a hospital and is a maintained, grant-maintained or grant-maintained special school, the application of the provisions of the National Curriculum to the child;

(d) where the school is not established in a hospital and is a maintained, grant-maintained or grant-maintained special school, the application of any provisions substituted for the provisions of the National Curriculum in order to maintain a balanced and broadly based curriculum;
(e) where appropriate, and in any case where a transition plan exists, any matters which are the appropriate subject of such a plan;
(f) whether the statement continues to be appropriate;
(g) any amendments to the statement which would be appropriate; and
(h) whether the authority should cease to maintain the statement.

(5) The notice referred to in paragraph (2) shall require the head teacher to invite the following persons to attend a meeting to be held on a date before the report referred to in that paragraph is submitted—

(a) the representative of the authority specified in the notice,
(b) the child's parent,
(c) a member or members of the staff of the school who teach the child or who are otherwise responsible for the provision of education for the child whose attendance the head teacher considers appropriate,
(d) any other person whose attendance the head teacher considers appropriate, and
(e) any person whose attendance the authority consider appropriate and who is specified in the notice.

(6) The head teacher shall not later than two weeks before the date on which a meeting referred to in paragraph (5) is to be held send to all the persons invited to that meeting copies of the advice he has received pursuant to his request under paragraph (3) and by written notice accompanying the copies shall request the recipients to submit to him before or at the meeting written comments on that advice and any other advice which they think appropriate.

(7) The meeting referred to in paragraph (5) shall consider—

(a) the matters referred to in paragraph (4); and
(b) any significant changes in the child's circumstances since the date on which the statement was made or last reviewed.

(8) The meeting shall recommend—

(a) any steps which it concludes ought to be taken, including whether the authority should amend or cease to maintain the statement,
(b) any targets to be established in furtherance of the objectives specified in the statement which it concludes the child ought to meet during the period until the next review, and
(c) where a transition plan exists, the matters which it concludes ought to be included in that plan.

(9) If the meeting cannot agree the recommendations to be made under paragraph (8) the persons who attended the meeting shall make differing recommendations as appears necessary to each of them.

(10) The report to be submitted under paragraph (2) shall be completed after the meeting is held and shall include the head teacher's assessment of the matters

referred to in paragraph (7) and his recommendations as to the matters referred to in paragraph (8), and shall refer to any difference between his assessment and recommendations and those of the meeting.

(11) When the head teacher submits his report to the authority under paragraph (2) he shall at the same time send copies to—

(a) the child's parent,
(b) the persons from whom the head teacher sought advice under paragraph (3),
(c) the persons who were invited to attend the meeting in accordance with paragraph (5),
(d) any other person to whom the authority consider it appropriate that a copy be sent and to whom they direct him to send a copy, and
(e) any other person to whom the head teacher considers it appropriate that a copy be sent.

(12) The authority shall review the statement under section 172(5) in light of the report and any other information or advice which they consider relevant, shall make written recommendations as to the matters referred to in paragraph (8)(a) and (b) and, where a transition plan exists, shall amend the plan as they consider appropriate.

(13) The authority shall within one week of completing the review under section 172(5) send copies of the recommendations and any transition plan referred to in paragraph (12) to—

(a) the child's parent;
(b) the head teacher;
(c) the persons from whom the head teacher sought advice under paragraph (3);
(d) the persons who were invited to attend the meeting in accordance with paragraph (5), and
(e) any other person to whom the authority consider it appropriate that a copy be sent.

Review of statement where child aged 14 attends school

16. (1) This regulation applies where—

(a) an authority review a statement under section 172(5) other than on the making of an assessment,
(b) the child concerned attends a school, and
(c) the review is the first review commenced after the child has attained the age of 14 years.

(2) The authority shall for the purpose of preparing a report under this regulation by notice in writing require the head teacher of the child's school to seek the advice referred to in regulation 15(4), including in all cases advice as to the matters referred to in regulation 15(4)(e), from—

(a) the child's parent,

(b) any person whose advice the authority consider appropriate for the purpose of arriving at a satisfactory report and whom they specify in the notice referred to above, and
(c) any person whose advice the head teacher considers appropriate for the purpose of arriving at a satisfactory report.

(3) The authority shall invite the following persons to attend a meeting to be held on a date before the review referred to in paragraph (1) is required to be completed—

(a) the child's parent;
(b) a member or members of the staff of the school who teach the child or who are otherwise responsible for the provision of education for the child whose attendance the head teacher considers appropriate and whom he has asked the authority to invite;
(c) a representative of the social services authority;
(d) a person providing careers services under sections 8 to 10 of the Employment and Training Act 1973(a);
(e) any person whose attendance the head teacher considers appropriate and whom he has asked the authority to invite; and
(f) any person whose attendance the authority consider appropriate.

(4) The head teacher shall not later than two weeks before the date on which the meeting referred to in paragraph (3) is to be held serve on all the persons invited to attend that meeting copies of the advice he has received pursuant to his request under paragraph (2) and shall by written notice request the recipients to submit to him before or at the meeting written comments on that advice and any other advice which they think appropriate.

(5) A representative of the authority shall attend the meeting.

(6) The meeting shall consider the matters referred to in regulation 15(7), in all cases including the matters referred to in regulation 15(4)(e), and shall make recommendations in accordance with regulation 15(8) and (9), in all cases including recommendations as to the matters referred to in regulation 15(8)(c).

(7) The report to be prepared by the authority under paragraph (2) shall be completed after the meeting, shall contain the authority's assessment of the matters required to be considered by the meeting and their recommendations as to the matters required to be recommended by it and shall refer to any difference between their assessment and recommendations and those of the meeting.

(8) The authority shall within one week of the date on which the meeting was held send copies of the report completed under paragraph (7) to—

(a) the child's parent;
(b) the head teacher;
(c) the persons from whom the head teacher sought advice under paragraph (2);
(d) the persons who were invited to attend the meeting under paragraph (3); and
(e) any person to whom they consider it appropriate to send a copy.

(9) The authority shall review the statement under section 172(5) in light of the

report and any other information or advice which it considers relevant, shall make written recommendations as to the matters referred to in regulation 15(8)(a) and (b), and shall prepare a transition plan.

(10) The authority shall within one week of completing the review under section 172(5) send copies of the recommendations and the transition plan referred to in paragraph (9) to the persons referred to in paragraph (8).

Review of statement where child does not attend school

17. (1) This regulation applies where an authority review a statement under section 172(5) other than on the making of an assessment and the child concerned does not attend a school.

(2) The authority shall prepare a report addressing the matters referred to in regulation 15(4), including the matters referred to in regulation 15(4)(e) in any case where the review referred to in paragraph (1) is commenced after the child has attained the age of 14 years or older, and for that purpose shall seek advice on those matters from the child's parent and any other person whose advice they consider appropriate in the case in question for the purpose of arriving at a satisfactory report.

(3) The authority shall invite the following persons to attend a meeting to be held on a date before the review referred to in paragraph (1) is required to be completed—

- (a) the child's parent;
- (b) where the review referred to in paragraph (1) is the first review commenced after the child has attained the age of 14 years, a representative of the social services authority;
- (c) where subparagraph (b) applies, a person providing careers services under sections 8 to 10 of the Employment and Training Act 1973; and
- (d) any person or persons whose attendance the authority consider appropriate.

(4) The authority shall not later than two weeks before the date on which the meeting referred to in paragraph (3) is to be held send to all the persons invited to that meeting a copy of the report which they propose to make under paragraph (2) and by written notice accompanying the copies shall request the recipients to submit to the authority written comments on the report and any other advice which they think appropriate.

(5) A representative of the authority shall attend the meeting.

(6) The meeting shall consider the matters referred to in regulation 15(7), including in any case where the review is commenced after the child has attained the age of 14 years the matters referred to in regulation 15(4)(e), and shall make recommendations in accordance with regulation 15(8) and (9), including in any case where the child has attained the age of 14 years or older as aforesaid recommendations as to the matters referred to in regulation 15(8)(c).

(7) The report prepared by the authority under paragraph (2) shall be completed after the meeting referred to in paragraph (3) is held, shall contain the authority's assessment of the matters required to be considered by the meeting and their

recommendations as to the matters required to be recommended by it, and shall refer to any difference between their assessment and recommendations and those of the meeting.

(8) The authority shall within one week of the date on which the meeting referred to in paragraph (3) was held send copies of the report completed under paragraph (7) to—

(a) the child's parent;
(b) the persons from whom they sought advice under paragraph (2);
(c) the persons who were invited to attend the meeting under paragraph (3); and
(d) any person to whom they consider it appropriate to send a copy.

(9) The authority shall review the statement under section 172(5) in light of the report and any other information or advice which it considers relevant, shall make written recommendations as to the matters referred to in regulation 15(8)(a) and (b), in any case where the review is the first review commenced after the child has attained the age of 14 years prepare a transition plan, and in any case where a transition plan exists amend the plan as they consider appropriate.

(10) The authority shall within one week of completing the review under section 172(5) send copies of the recommendations and any transition plan referred to in paragraph (9) to the persons referred to in paragraph (8).

Transfer of statements

18. (1) This regulation applies where a child in respect of whom a statement is maintained moves from the area of the authority which maintains the statement ("the old authority") into that of another ("the new authority").

(2) The old authority shall transfer the statement to the new authority, and from the date of the transfer—

(a) the statement shall be treated for the purposes of the new authority's duties and functions under Part III of the Act and these Regulations as if it had been made by the new authority on the date on which it was made by the old authority, and
(b) where the new authority make an assessment under section 167 and the old authority have supplied the new authority with advice obtained in pursuance of a previous assessment regulation 6(5) shall apply as if the new authority had obtained the advice on the date on which the old authority obtained it.

(3) The new authority shall within 6 weeks of the date of the transfer serve a notice on the child's parent informing him—

(a) that the statement has been transferred,
(b) whether they proposed to make an assessment under section 167, and
(c) when they propose to review the statement in accordance with paragraph (4).

(4) The new authority shall review the statement under section 172(5) before the expiry of whichever of the following two periods expires later—

(a) the period of twelve months beginning with the making of the statement, or as the case may be, with the previous review, or
(b) the period of three months beginning with the date of the transfer.

(5) Where by virtue of the transfer the new authority come under a duty to arrange the child's attendance at a school specified in the statement but in light of the child's move that attendance is no longer practicable the new authority may arrange for the child's attendance at another school appropriate for the child until such time as it is possible to amend the statement in accordance with paragraph 10 of Schedule 10 to the Act.

Restriction on disclosure of statements

19. (1) Subject to the provisions of the Act and of these Regulations, a statement in respect of a child shall not be disclosed without the parent's consent except—

(a) to persons to whom, in the opinion of the authority concerned, the statement should be disclosed in the interests of the child;
(b) for the purposes of any appeal under the Act;
(c) for the purposes of educational research which, in the opinion of the authority, may advance the education of children with special educational needs, if, but only if, the person engaged in that research undertakes not to publish anything contained in, or derived from, a statement otherwise than in a form which does not identify any individual concerned including, in particular, the child concerned and his parent;
(d) on the order of any court or for the purposes of any criminal proceedings;
(e) for the purposes of any investigation under Part III of the Local Government Act 1974 (investigation of maladministration)(a);
(f) to the Secretary of State when he requests such disclosure for the purposes of deciding whether to give directions or make an order under section 68 or 99 of the Education Act 1944(b);
(g) for the purposes of an assessment of the needs of the child with respect to the provision of any statutory services for him being carried out by officers of a social services authority by virtue of arrangements made under section 5(5) of the Disabled Persons (Services, Consultation and Representation) Act 1986(c);
(h) for the purposes of a local authority in the performance of their duties under sections 22(3)(a), 85(4)(a), 86(3)(a) and 87(3) of the Children Act 1989(d); or
(i) to one of Her Majesty's Inspectors of Schools, or to a registered inspector or a member of an inspection team, who requests the right to inspect or take copies of a statement in accordance with section 3(3) of or paragraph 7 of Schedule 2 to the Education (Schools) Act 1992(e) respectively.

(2) The arrangements for keeping such statements shall be such as to ensure, so far as is reasonably practicable, that unauthorised persons do not have access to them.

(3) In this regulation any reference to a statement includes a reference to any representations, evidence, advice or information which is set out in the appendices to a statement.

PART IV
REVOCATION AND TRANSITIONAL PROVISIONS

Revocation of the 1983 Regulations

20. Subject to regulation 21, the 1983 Regulations, the Education (Special Educational Needs) (Amendment) Regulations 1988(f) and the Education (Special Educational Needs) (Amendment) Regulations 1990(g) are hereby revoked.

Transitional provisions

21. (1) Subject to the following provisions of this regulation references in these Regulations to anything done under the Act or these Regulations shall be read in relation to the times, circumstances or purposes in relation to which a corresponding provision of the 1981 Act or the 1983 Regulations had effect and so far as the nature of the reference permits as including a reference to that corresponding provision.

(2) Regulations 3 to 8 of the 1983 Regulations shall continue to apply in relation to any assessment where before 1st September 1994 in pursuance of section 5(5) of the 1981 Act the authority notify the parent that they have decided to make an assessment, and Part II of these Regulations shall not apply in relation to any such assessment.

(3) Where regulations 3 to 8 of the 1983 Regulations continue to apply in relation to any assessment but the authority have not before 1st January 1995—

(a) notified the parent of their decision that they are not required to determine the special educational provision of the child in accordance with section 5(7) of the 1981 Act, or

(b) served on the parent a copy of a proposed statement in accordance with section 7(3) of the 1981 Act

Part II of these Regulations shall apply in relation to the assessment from 1st January 1995 as if on that date the authority had given notice to the parent under section 167(4) of their decision to make an assessment.

(4) Where in accordance with paragraph (3) above Part II of these Regulations applies in relation to an assessment the authority shall obtain advice in accordance with Part II, but advice obtained in accordance with the 1983 Regulations shall be considered to have been obtained under Part II if such advice is appropriate for the purpose of arriving at a satisfactory assessment under that Part.

(5) Where before 1st September 1994 in accordance with section 5(3) of the 1981 Act the authority have served notice on the child's parent that they propose to make

an assessment but they have not before that date notified the parent under section 5(5) of the 1981 Act that they have decided to make the assessment or notified them that they have decided not to make the assessment, the authority shall decide whether or not to make the assessment in accordance with section 167 and not later than 13th October 1994 give notice to the child's parent—

(a) under section 167(4) of their decision to make an assessment, and of their reasons for making that decision, or
(b) under section 167(6) of their decision not to assess the educational needs of the child,

and Part II of these Regulations shall apply to any such assessment.

(6) Where before 1st September 1994 in accordance with section 9 of the 1981 Act a parent has asked the authority to arrange for an assessment to be made of the child's educational needs but the authority have not before that date notified the parent under section 5(5) of the 1981 Act that they have decided to make the assessment or notified them that they have decided not to make the assessment, the authority shall decide whether or not to make the assessment in accordance with section 167 and not later than 13th October 1994 give notice to the child's parent—

(a) under section 167(4) of their decision to make an assessment, or
(b) under section 172(3)(a) or 173(2)(a) of their decision not to comply with the request and of the parent's right to appeal to the Tribunal against the determination,

and Part II of these Regulations shall apply to any such assessment.

(7) Regulation 10 of the 1983 Regulations shall continue to apply to the making of any statement where before 1st January 1995 the authority have served on the parent a copy of a proposed statement in accordance with section 7(3) of the 1981 Act, and regulations 12, 13 and 14(1) to (4) of these Regulations shall not apply to making of any such statement.

(8) Regulation 14(6) and (7) shall not apply in relation to a proposal to amend or cease to maintain a statement where an authority serve a notice under paragraph 6 of Schedule 1 to the 1981 Act before 1st September 1994.

(9) Regulations 15 to 17 shall not apply to any review of a statement which is required to be completed before 1st December 1994.

(10) Regulations 15 to 17 shall apply to a review of a statement which is not required to be completed before 1st December 1994, but where the statement was made under the 1981 Act they shall apply with any necessary modifications, including the following:

(a) where the review is the first review [to which regulations 15 to 17 apply]

 (i) the authority shall seek advice as to the objectives which the special educational provision for the child should meet rather than as to the child's progress towards meeting the objectives specified in the statement;
 (ii) the authority shall seek advice as to the targets which should be established in furtherance of those objectives rather than as to the child's progress towards attaining any such targets;

(iii) where the child has attained the age of 14 years before the date on which the review is commenced the authority shall in any event seek advice as to any matters which are the appropriate subject of a transition plan;

(iv) the meeting held in accordance with regulation 15(7), 16(6) or 17(6) shall consider the matters referred to in those regulations as modified by subparagraphs (i) to (iii) above as appropriate, and shall make recommendations under regulation 15(8), 16(7) or 17(7) but including recommendations as to the objectives referred to in subparagraph (i), the targets referred to in subparagraph (ii) and where appropriate the transition plan referred to in paragraph (iii); and

(v) the authority shall review the statement in accordance with regulation 15(12), 16(9) or 17(9), shall make recommendations as to the matters referred to in those regulations read in light of the modifications in this subparagraph, shall prepare a transition plan where subparagraph (iii) above applies, and shall in any event specify the objectives referred to in subparagraph (i) above;

and

(b) where the review is not the first review [to which regulations 15 to 17 apply] any reference to objectives shall include a reference to objectives specified in accordance with subparagraph (a)(v) above in addition to objectives specified in a statement.

(11) Subject to paragraphs (12) and (13), regulation 12 of the 1983 Regulations shall continue to apply in relation to a transfer on a date before 1st September 1994, and regulation 18 of these Regulations shall not apply in relation to such a transfer.

(12) Notwithstanding paragraph (11), where a statement has been transferred on a date before 1st September 1994 and the new authority has not before that date either—

(a) in pursuance of section 5(3) of the 1981 Act served a notice on the child's parent that they propose to make an assessment, or

(b) in pursuance of regulation 12(4) of the 1983 Regulations notified the child's parent that they do not propose to make an assessment,

they shall comply with regulation 18(3) of these Regulations before 13th October 1994.

(13) Notwithstanding paragraph (11), where a statement has been transferred on a date before 1st September 1994 the new authority shall review the statement under section 172(5) before the expiry of whichever of the following two periods expires later—

(a) the period of twelve months beginning with the making of the statement, or as the case may be, with the previous review, or

(b) the period ending on 30th November 1994.

(14) Regulation 11 of the 1983 Regulations shall not apply to statements made before or after 1st September 1994 and regulation 19 of these Regulations shall

apply, except that a statement may be disclosed for the purposes of any appeal under section 8 of the 1981 Act(a) as well as for the purposes of any appeal under the Act.

AMENDMENT

Regs. 21(10)(a) and (b) were amended by The Education (Special Education Needs) (Amendment) Regulations 1995 with effect from August 14, 1995.

SCHEDULE
PART A

Notice to Parent

To: [name and address of parent]

1. Accompanying this notice is a copy of a statement of the special educational needs of [*name of child*] which [*name of authority*] ("the authority") propose to make under the Education Act 1993.

2. You may express a preference for the maintained, grant-maintained or grant-maintained special school you wish your child to attend and may give reasons for your preference.

3. If you wish to express such a preference you must do so not later than 15 days from the date on which you receive this notice and the copy of the statement or 15 days from the date on which you last attend a meeting in accordance with paragraph 10 or 11 below, whichever is later. If the 15th day falls on a weekend or a bank holiday you must do so not later than the following working day.

4. If you express a preference in accordance with paragraphs 2 and 3 above the authority are required to specify the name of the school you prefer in the statement, and accordingly to arrange special educational provision at that school, unless—

(a) the school is unsuitable to your child's age, ability or aptitude or to his/her special educational needs, or

(b) the attendance of your child at the school would be incompatible with the provision of efficient education for the children with whom he/she would be educated or the efficient use of resources.

5. The authority will normally arrange special educational provision in a maintained, grant-maintained or grant-maintained special school. However, if you believe that the authority should arrange special educational provision for your child at a non-maintained special school or an independent school you may make representations to that effect.

6. The following maintained, grant-maintained and grant-maintained special schools provide [*primary/secondary*] education in the area of the authority:

[*Here list all maintained, grant-maintained, and grant-maintained special schools in the authority's area which provide primary education, or list all such schools which provide secondary education, depending on whether the child requires primary or secondary education. Alternatively, list the required information in a list attached to this notice*].

7. A list of the non-maintained special schools which make special educational provision for pupils with special educational needs in England and Wales and are approved by the Secretary of State for Education or the Secretary of State for Wales is attached to this notice.

8. A list of the independent schools in England and Wales which are approved by the Secretary of State for Education or the Secretary of State for Wales as suitable for the admission of children for whom statements of special educational needs are maintained is attached to this notice.

9. You are entitled to make representations to the authority about the content of the statement. If you wish to make such representations you must do so not later than 15 days from the date on which you receive this notice, or 15 days from the date on which you last attended a meeting in accordance with the next paragraph, whichever is the later date.

10. You are entitled, not later than 15 days from the date on which you receive this notice, to require the authority to arrange a meeting between you and an officer of the authority at which any part of the statement, or all of it, may be discussed. In particular, any advice on which the statement is based may be discussed.

11. If having attended a meeting in accordance with paragraph 10 above you still disagree with any part of the assessment in question, you may within 15 days of the date of the meeting require the authority to arrange a meeting or meetings to discuss the advice which they consider relevant to the part of the assessment you disagree with. They will arrange for the person who gave the advice, or some other person whom they think appropriate, to attend the meeting.

12. If at the conclusion of the procedure referred to above the authority serve on you a statement with which you disagree you may appeal to the Special Educational Needs Tribunal against the description of your child's special educational needs, against the special educational provision specified including the school named, or, if no school is named, against that fact.

13. All correspondence with the authority should be addressed to the officer responsible for this case:

[*Here set out name, address and telephone number of case officer, and any reference number which should be quoted*]

[*Date*]

[*Signature of officer responsible*]

PART B

Statement of Special Educational Needs
Part 1: Introduction

1. In accordance with section 168 of the Education Act 1993 ("the Act") and the Education (Special Educational Needs) Regulations 1994 ("the Regulations"), the following statement is made by [*here set out name of authority*] ("the authority") in respect of the child whose name and other particulars are mentioned below.

Child	
Surname	Other names ....
	....
Home address	
....	Sex ....
....	
....	Religion....................................
Date of birth	Home language ....
Child's parent or person responsible	
Surname	Other names ....
Home address	....
....	Relationship to child.....................
....	....
Telephone No	

2. When assessing the child's special educational needs the authority took into consideration in accordance with [regulation 10] of the Regulations, the representations, evidence and advice set out in the Appendices to this statement.

AMENDMENT

Para. 2 of Part I of Part B in the Schedule was amended by The Education (Special Educational Needs) (Amendment) Regulations 1994 with effect from September 1, 1994.

PART 2: SPECIAL EDUCATIONAL NEEDS

[*Here set out the child's special educational needs, in terms of the child's learning difficulties which call for special educational provision, as assessed by the authority.*]

PART 3: SPECIAL EDUCATIONAL PROVISION

Objectives

[*Here specify the objectives which the special educational provision for the child should aim to meet.*]

Educational provision to meet needs and objectives

[*Here specify the special educational provision which the authority consider appropriate to meet the needs specified in Part 2 and to meet the objectives specified in this Part, and in particular specify—*

(a) *any appropriate facilities and equipment, staffing arrangements and curriculum,*
(b) *any appropriate modifications to the application of the National Curriculum,*
(c) *any appropriate exclusions from the application of the National Curriculum, in detail, and the provision which it is proposed to substitute for any such exclusions in order to maintain a balanced and broadly based curriculum; and*
(d) *where residential accommodation is appropriate, that fact.*]

Monitoring

[*Here specify the arrangements to be made for—*

(a) *regularly monitoring progress in meeting the objectives specified in this Part,*
(b) *establishing targets in furtherance of those objectives,*
(c) *regularly monitoring the targets referred to in (b),*
(d) *regularly monitoring the appropriateness of any modifications to the application of the National Curriculum, and*
(e) *regularly monitoring the appropriateness of any provision substituted for exclusions from the application of the National Curriculum.*

Here also specify any special arrangements for reviewing this statement.]

PART 4: PLACEMENT

[*Here specify—*

(a) *the type of school which the authority consider appropriate for the child and the name of the school for which the parent has expressed a preference or, where the authority are required to specify the name of a school, the name of the school which they consider would be appropriate for the child and should be specified, or*
(b) *the provision for his education otherwise than at a school which the authority consider appropriate.*]

PART 5: NON-EDUCATIONAL NEEDS

[*Here specify the non-educational needs of the child for which the authority consider provision is appropriate if the child is to properly benefit from the special educational provision specified in Part 3.*]

PART 6: NON-EDUCATIONAL PROVISION

[*Here specify any non-educational provision which the authority propose to make available or which they are satisfied will be made available by a district health authority, a social services authority or some other body, including the arrangements for its provision. Also specify the objectives of the provision, and the arrangements for monitoring progress in meeting those objectives.*]

Date

A duly authorised officer of the authority

Appendix A: Parental Representations

[*Here set out any written representations made by the parent of the child under section 167(1)(d) of or paragraph 4(1) of Schedule 10 to the Act and a summary which the parent has accepted as accurate of any oral representations so made or record that no such representations were made.*]

Appendix B: Parental Evidence

[*Here set out any written evidence either submitted by the parent of the child under section 167(1)(d) of the Act or record that no such evidence was submitted.*]

Appendix C: Advice from the Child's Parent

[*Here set out the advice obtained under regulation 6(1)(a).*]

Appendix D: Educational Advice

[*Here set out the advice obtained under regulation 6(1)(b).*]

Appendix E: Medical Advice

[*Here set out the advice obtained under regulation 6(1)(c).*]

Appendix F: Psychological Advice

[*Here set out the advice obtained under regulation 6(1)(d).*]

Appendix G: Advice from the Social Services Authority

[*Here set out the advice obtained under regulation 6(1)(e).*]

Appendix H: Other Advice Obtained by the Authority

[*Here set out the advice obtained under regulation 6(1)(f).*]

The Education (Special Educational Needs) (Information) Regulations 1994

(S.I. 1994 No. 1048)

In exercise of the powers conferred on the Secretary of State by section 8(5) and (7) of the Education Act 1980 and sections 153(1), 161(5) and 305(1) of, and paragraph 14 of Schedule 11 to, the Education Act 1993, the Secretary of State for Education, as respects England, and the Secretary of State for Wales, as respects Wales, hereby make the following Regulations:

Citation and commencement

1. These Regulations may be cited as the Education (Special Educational Needs) (Information) Regulations 1994 and shall come into force on 1st September 1994.

Publication of information about special educational needs

2. (1) The governing body of each county, voluntary, or grant-maintained school, shall publish information about the matters set out in Schedule 1.

(2) The governing body of each maintained or grant-maintained special school, other than a special school established in a hospital, shall publish information about the matters set out in Schedule 2.

(3) The governing body of each maintained or grant-maintained special school which is established in a hospital shall publish information about the matters set out in Schedule 3.

Manner of publication of information

3. (1) The information referred to in regulation 2 shall be published in a single document by making copies available free of charge—

(a) for distribution—

(i) to parents of pupils or prospective pupils, and
(ii) to the local education authority, District Health Authority or funding authority for the area in which the school is situated,

who or which request a copy at the school or through the post; and

(b) for reference at the school.

(2) The first occasion on which copies of the document referred to in paragraph (1) above are made available in accordance with that paragraph shall be no later than 1st August 1995.

Publication of information – supplementary

4. Where the information referred to in regulation 2 is to be published by the local education authority with the agreement of the government body pursuant to section 8(6) of the Education Act 1980, it shall be supplied to them by the governing body and shall be published without material alteration.

Annual reports

5. (1) The annual report for each county, voluntary, maintained special, grant-maintained or grant-maintained special school shall include a report containing the information about the implementation of the governing body's policy for pupils with special educational needs as specified in Schedule 4.

(2) Paragraph (1) above shall apply in relation to the first annual report prepared after 1st August 1995 and to each annual report prepared thereafter.

Modification of the Education Act 1993 in relation to grant-maintained special schools

6. The provision of Part II, Chapter X and Part III of the Education Act 1993 set out in paragraphs (a) and (b) below shall have effect with the modifications as therein stated—

(a) section 153 (provision of information by governing body) shall apply to the governing body of a grant-maintained special school; and

(b) section 161(5) (duties of governing body etc. in relation to pupils with special educational needs) shall apply to each grant-maintained special school and the reference in that subsection to "annual report" shall include a report prepared under the articles of government of a grant-maintained special school.

SCHEDULE 1
INFORMATION FROM COUNTY, VOLUNTARY AND GRANT-MAINTAINED SCHOOLS

BASIC INFORMATION ABOUT THE SCHOOL'S SPECIAL EDUCATIONAL PROVISION

1. The objectives of the governing body in making provision for pupils with special educational needs, and a description of how the governing body's special educational needs policy will contribute towards meeting those objectives.
2. The name of the person who is responsible for co-ordinating the day to day provision of education for pupils with special educational needs at the school (whether or not the person is known as the SEN co-ordinator).
3. The arrangements which have been made for co-ordinating the

provision of education for pupils with special educational needs at the school.

4. The admission arrangements for pupils with special educational needs who do not have a statement in so far as they differ from the arrangements for other pupils.
5. The kinds of provision for special educational needs in which the school specialises and any special units.
6. Facilities for pupils with special educational needs at the school including facilities which increase or assist access to the school by pupils who are disabled.

INFORMATION ABOUT THE SCHOOL'S POLICIES FOR THE IDENTIFICATION, ASSESSMENT AND PROVISION FOR ALL PUPILS WITH SPECIAL EDUCATIONAL NEEDS

7. How resources are allocated to and amongst pupils with special educational needs.
8. How pupils with special educational needs are identified and their needs determined and reviewed.
9. Arrangements for providing access by pupils with special educational needs to a balanced and broadly based curriculum (including the National Curriculum).
10. How pupils with special educational needs engage in the activities of the school together with pupils who do not have special educational needs.
11. How the governing body evaluate the success of the education which is provided at the school to pupils with special educational needs.
12. Any arrangements made by the governing body relating to the treatment of complaints from parents of pupils with special educational needs concerning the provision made at the school.

INFORMATION ABOUT THE SCHOOL'S STAFFING POLICIES AND PARTNERSHIP WITH BODIES BEYOND THE SCHOOL

13. Any arrangements made by the governing body relating to in-service training for staff in relation to special educational needs.
14. The use made of teachers and facilities from outside the school including links with support services for special educational needs.
15. The role played by the parents of pupils with special educational needs.
16. Any links with other schools, including special schools, and the provision made for the transition of pupils with special educational needs between schools or between the school and the next stage of life or education.
17. Links with child health services, social services and educational welfare services and any voluntary organisations which work on behalf of children with special educational needs.

Schedule 2
Information from Maintained and Grant-Maintained Special Schools

BASIC INFORMATION ABOUT THE SCHOOL'S SPECIAL EDUCATIONAL PROVISION

1. The objectives of the governing body in making provision for pupils with special educational needs, and a description of how the governing body's special educational needs policy will contribute towards meeting those objectives.
2. The kinds of special educational needs for which provision is made at the school.
3. Facilities for pupils at the school including facilities which increase or assist access to the school by pupils who are disabled.

INFORMATION ABOUT THE SCHOOL'S POLICIES FOR THE ASSESSMENT AND PROVISION FOR ALL PUPILS WITH SPECIAL EDUCATIONAL NEEDS

4. How resources are allocated amongst pupils.
5. How the needs of pupils are identified and reviewed.
6. Arrangements for providing access by pupils to a balanced and broadly based curriculum (including the National Curriculum).
7. How the governing body evaluate the success of the education which is provided at the school to pupils.
8. Any arrangements made by the governing body relating to the treatment of complaints from parents of pupils concerning the provisions made at the school.

INFORMATION ABOUT THE SCHOOL'S STAFFING POLICIES AND PARTNERSHIP WITH BODIES BEYOND THE SCHOOL

9. Any arrangements made by the governing body relating to in-service training for staff in relation to special educational needs.
10. The use made of teachers and facilities from outside the school including links with support services for special educational needs.
11. The role played by parents of pupils.
12. Any links with other schools, and any arrangements for managing the transition of pupils between schools or between the school and the next stage of life or education.
13. Links with child health services, social services and educational welfare services and any voluntary organisations which work on behalf of children with special educational needs.

Schedule 3
Information from Special Schools in Hospitals

1. The name of the person who is responsible for co-ordinating the day to day provision of education for pupils with special educational needs at the school (whether or not the person is known as the SEN co-ordinator).
2. How pupils with special educational needs are identified and their needs determined and reviewed.
3. How resources are allocated to and amongst pupils with special educational needs.
4. How the educational progress of pupils with special educational needs is monitored.
5. How the contents of a pupil's statement are ascertained and made known to staff.
6. The arrangements for ensuring continuity of the educational provision set out in a pupil's statement differentiating where necessary between long stay and short stay patients.
7. Arrangements for providing access to pupils with special educational needs to a balanced and broadly based curriculum.
8. The use made of teachers and facilities from outside the school including links with support services for special educational needs.

SCHEDULE 4
INFORMATION IN ANNUAL REPORT

1. The success of the governing body's special educational needs policies in the period since the last annual report.
2. Significant changes in the governing body's policy on pupils with special educational needs since the last annual report.
3. The outcome of any consultation carried out under section 161(3) of the Education Act 1993.
4. How resources have been allocated to and amongst pupils with special educational needs since the last annual report.

The Special Educational Needs Tribunal Regulations 1995

(S.I. 1995 No. 3113)

ARRANGEMENT OF REGULATIONS

PART I
GENERAL

PART 2
MAKING AN APPEAL TO THE TRIBUNAL AND REPLY BY THE AUTHORITY
(A) THE PARENT

(B) THE REPLY BY THE AUTHORITY

PART 3
PREPARATION FOR A HEARING

PART 4
THE DETERMINATION OF APPEALS

PART 5
ADDITIONAL POWERS OF AND PROVISIONS RELATING TO THE TRIBUNAL

The Secretary of State for Education and Employment, in respect of England,

and the Secretary of State for Wales, in respect of Wales, in exercise of the powers conferred by sections 177(5), 178(2), 180(1) and (2), 301(6) and 305(1) of the Education Act 1993, and after consultation with the Council on Tribunals in accordance with section 8 of the Tribunals and Inquiries Act 1992, hereby make the following Regulations:

PART 1
GENERAL

Citation and commencement

1. These Regulations may be cited as the Special Educational Needs Tribunal Regulations 1995 and shall come into force on 1st January 1996.

Interpretation

2. In these Regulations, unless the context otherwise requires—

"the 1993 Act" means the Education Act 1993;
"the authority" means the local education authority which made the disputed decision;
"child" means the child in respect of whom the appeal is brought;
"disputed decision" means the decision or determination in respect of which the appeal is brought;
"the clerk to the tribunal" means the person appointed by the Secretary of the Tribunal to act in that capacity at one or more hearings;
"hearing" means a sitting of the tribunal duly constituted for the purpose of receiving evidence, hearing addresses and witnesses or doing anything lawfully requisite to enable the tribunal to reach a decision on any question;
"parent" means a parent who has made an appeal to the Special Educational Needs Tribunal under the 1993 Act;
"records" means the records of the Special Educational Needs Tribunal;
"the Secretary of the Tribunal" means the person for the time being acting as the Secretary of the office of the Special Educational Needs Tribunal;
"the tribunal" means the Special Educational Needs Tribunal but where the President has determined pursuant to regulation 4(1) that the jurisdiction of the Special Educational Needs Tribunal is to be exercised by more than one tribunal, it means, in relation to any proceedings, the tribunal to which the proceedings have been referred by the President;
"working day", except in regulation 24, means any day other than—

(a) a Saturday, a Sunday, Christmas Day, Good Friday or a day which is a bank holiday within the meaning of the Banking and Financial Dealings Act 1971; or
(b) a day in August.

Members of lay panel

3. No person may be appointed as a member of the lay panel unless the Secretary of State is satisfied that he has knowledge and experience in respect of—

(a) children with special educational needs; or
(b) local government.

Establishment of tribunals

4. (1) Such number of tribunals shall be established to exercise the jurisdiction of the Special Educational Needs Tribunal as the President may from time to time determine.

(2) The tribunals shall sit at such times and in such places as may from time to time be determined by the President.

Membership of tribunal

5. (1) Subject to the provisions of regulation 28(5), the tribunal shall consist of a chairman and two other members.

(2) For each hearing—

(a) the chairman shall be the President or a person selected from the chairman's panel by the President; and
(b) the two other members of the tribunal other than the chairman shall be selected from the lay panel by the President.

Proof of documents and certification of decisions

6. (1) A document purporting to be a document issued by the Secretary of the Tribunal on behalf of the Special Educational Needs Tribunal shall, unless the contrary is proved, be deemed to be a document so issued.

(2) A document purporting to be certified by the Secretary of the Tribunal to be a true copy of a document containing a decision of the tribunal shall, unless the contrary is proved, be sufficient evidence of matters contained therein.

PART 2
MAKING AN APPEAL TO THE TRIBUNAL AND REPLY BY THE AUTHORITY

(A) THE PARENT

Notice of appeal

7. (1) An appeal to the Special Educational Needs Tribunal shall be made by notice which—

(a) shall state—

(i) the name and address of the parent making the appeal and if more than one address is given, the address to which the tribunal should send replies or notices concerning the appeal;
(ii) the name of the child;
(iii) that the notice is a notice of appeal;
(iv) the name of the authority which made the disputed decision and the date on which the parent was notified of it;
(v) the grounds of the appeal;
(vi) if the parent seeks an order that a school (other than one already named in the statement of special educational needs relating to the child) be named in the child's statement, the name and address of that school;

(b) shall be accompanied by—

(i) a copy of the notice of the disputed decision;
(ii) where the appeal is made under section 170 of, or paragraph 8 of Schedule 10 to, the 1993 Act, a copy of the statement of special educational needs relating to the child; and

(c) may state the name, address and profession of any representative of the parent to whom the tribunal should (subject to any notice under regulation 42(2)(a)) send replies or notices concerning the appeal instead of the parent.

(2) The parent shall sign the notice of appeal.

(3) The parent must deliver the notice of appeal to the Secretary of the Tribunal so that it is received no later than the first working day after the expiry of 2 months from the date on which the authority gave him notice, under Part III of the 1993 Act, that he had a right of appeal.

Response, and supplementary provisions

8. (1) If the authority delivers a reply under regulation 12 the parent may deliver a written response to it.

(2) A response under paragraph (1) above must be delivered to the Secretary of the Tribunal not later than 15 working days from the date on which the parent receives a copy of the authority's written reply from the Secretary of the Tribunal.

(3) Subject to paragraph (5) below a response under paragraph (1) shall include all written evidence which the parent wishes to submit to the tribunal (unless such evidence was delivered with the notice of appeal);

(4) The parent may in exceptional cases (in addition to delivering a response under paragraph (1) above—

(a) with the permission of the President, at any time before the hearing; or
(b) with the permission of the tribunal at the hearing itself—

amend the notice of appeal or any response, deliver a supplementary statement of grounds of appeal or amend a supplementary statement of grounds of appeal.

(5) The parent may in exceptional cases—

(a) with the permission of the President at any time within 15 working days from the date on which a response under paragraph (2) above could have been delivered, or
(b) with the permission of the tribunal at the hearing itself—

deliver written evidence (if he has not previously done so) or further written evidence.

(6) The parent shall deliver a copy of every amendment and supplementary statement made under paragraph 4(a) above and any written evidence delivered under paragraph (5)(a) above to the Secretary of the Tribunal.

Withdrawal of appeal

9. The parent may—

(a) at any time before the hearing of the appeal withdraw his appeal by sending to the Secretary of the Tribunal a notice signed by him stating that he withdraws his appeal;
(b) at the hearing of the appeal, withdraw his appeal.

Further action by parent

10. (1) The parent shall supply the Secretary of the Tribunal with the information requested in the enquiry made under regulation 17.

(2) If the parent does not intend to attend or be represented at the hearing, he may, not less than 5 working days before the hearing, send to the Secretary of the Tribunal additional written representations in support of his appeal.

Representatives of the parent: further provisions

11. (1) Where a parent has not stated the name of a representative in the notice of appeal pursuant to regulation 7(1)(c) he may at any time before the hearing notify the Secretary of the Tribunal in writing of the name, address and profession of a representative to whom the tribunal should (subject to any notice under regulation 42(2)(a)) send any subsequent documents or notices concerning the appeal instead of to the parent;

(2) Where a parent has stated the name of a representative, whether in the notice of appeal pursuant to regulation 7(1)(c) or pursuant to paragraph (1) above, he may at any time notify the Secretary of the Tribunal in writing—

(a) of the name, address and profession of a new representative of the parent to whom the tribunal should send documents or notices concerning the appeal instead of to the representative previously notified; or
(b) that no person is acting as a representative of the parent and accordingly any subsequent documents or notices concerning the appeal should be sent to the parent himself.

(3) If the person named by the parent as a representative under regulation 7(1)(c)

or paragraphs (1) or (2)(a) above notifies the Secretary of the Tribunal in writing that he is not prepared, or is no longer prepared, to act in that capacity—

(a) the Secretary of the Tribunal shall notify the parent, and
(b) any subsequent documents or notices concerning the appeal shall be sent to the parent himself.

(4) At a hearing, the parent may conduct his case himself (with assistance from one person if he wishes) or may appear and be represented by one person whether or not legally qualified:

Provided that, if the President gives permission before the hearing or the tribunal gives permission at the hearing, the parent may obtain assistance or be presented by more than one person.

(B) THE REPLY BY THE AUTHORITY

Action by the authority on receipt of a notice of appeal

12. (1) An authority which receives a copy of a notice of appeal shall deliver to the Secretary of the Tribunal a written reply acknowledging service upon it of the notice of appeal and stating—

(a) whether or not the authority intends to oppose the appeal and, if it does intend to oppose the appeal, the grounds on which it relies; and
(b) the name and profession of the representative of the authority and the address for service of the authority for the purposes of the appeal.

(2) The authority's reply shall include—

(a) a statement summarising the facts relating to the disputed decision;
(b) if they are not part of the decision, the reasons for the disputed decision; and
(c) subject to regulation 13(3) all written evidence which the authority wishes to submit to the tribunal.

(3) Every such reply shall be signed by an officer of the authority who is authorised to sign such documents and shall be delivered to the Secretary of the Tribunal not later than 20 working days after the date on which the copy of the notice of appeal was received by the authority from the Secretary of the Tribunal.

Amendment of reply by the authority

13. (1) The authority, if it has delivered a reply pursuant to regulation 12, may, in exceptional cases—

(a) with the permission of the President at any time before the hearing; or
(b) with the permission of the tribunal at the hearing itself

amend its reply, deliver a supplementary reply or amend a supplementary reply.
(2) The President or, as the case may be, the tribunal may give permission under

paragraph (1) above on such terms as he or it thinks fit including the payment of costs or expenses.

(3) The authority may, in exceptional cases—

(a) with the permission of the President at any time within 15 working days from the date on which the parent could have delivered a response under regulation 8(1); or

(b) with the permission of the tribunal at the hearing itself

deliver written evidence (if it has not previously done so) or further written evidence.

(4) The authority shall send a copy of every amendment and supplementary statement made before the hearing to the Secretary of the Tribunal.

Failure to reply and absence of opposition

14. If no reply is received by the Secretary of the Tribunal within the time appointed by regulation 12(3) or if the authority states in writing that it does not resist the appeal, or withdraws its opposition to the appeal the tribunal shall—

(a) determine the appeal on the basis of the notice of appeal without a hearing; or

(b) without notifying the authority hold a hearing at which the authority is not represented.

Representation at hearing and further action by the authority

15. (1) At a hearing or part of a hearing the authority may be represented by one person whether or not legally qualified:

Provided that if the President gives permission before the hearing or the tribunal gives permission at the hearing the authority may be represented by more than one person.

(2) The authority shall supply the Secretary of the Tribunal with the information requested in the enquiry made under Regulation 17.

(3) If the authority does not intend to attend or be represented at the hearing it may, not less than 5 working days before the hearing, send to the Secretary of the Tribunal additional written representations in support of its reply.

PART 3

PREPARATION FOR A HEARING

Acknowledgement of appeal and service of documents by the Secretary of the Tribunal

16. (1) Upon receiving a notice of appeal the Secretary of the Tribunal shall—

(a) enter particulars of it in the records;

(b) send to the parent—

ACKNOWLEDGEMENT OF APPEAL AND SERVICE OF DOCUMENTS BY THE SECRETARY OF THE TRIBUNAL

(i) an acknowledgement of its receipt and a note of the case number entered in the records;
(ii) a note of the address to which notices and communications of the Tribunal should be sent; and
(iii) notification that advice about the appeal procedure may be obtained from the office of the Special Educational Needs Tribunal;

(c) subject to paragraph (6) below, send to the authority—

(i) a copy of the notice of appeal and any accompanying papers;
(ii) a note of the address to which notices and communications to the Special Educational Needs Tribunal or to the Secretary of the Tribunal should be sent, and
(iii) a notice stating the time for replying and the consequences of failure to do so.

(2) Where the Secretary of the Tribunal is of the opinion that, on the basis of the notice of appeal, the parent is asking the Special Educational Needs Tribunal to do something which it cannot, he may give notice of that effect to the parent stating the reasons for his opinion and informing him that the notice of appeal will not be entered in the records unless the parent notifies the Secretary of the Tribunal that he wishes to proceed with it.

(3) Where the Secretary of the Tribunal is of the opinion that there is an obvious error in the notice of appeal—

(a) he may correct that error and if he does so shall notify the parent accordingly and such notification shall state the effect of sub-paragraph (b) below; and
(b) unless within 5 working days the parent notifies the Secretary of the Tribunal that he objects to the correction, the notice of appeal as so corrected shall be treated as the notice of appeal for the purposes of these Regulations.

(4) An appeal, as respects which a notice has been given under paragraph (2) above, shall only be treated as having been received for the purposes of paragraph (1) when the parent notifies the Secretary of the Tribunal that he wishes to proceed with it.

(5) Subject to paragraph (6) below, the Secretary of the Tribunal shall forthwith send a copy of a reply by the authority under regulation 12 and of a response under regulation 8 together with any amendments or supplementary statements, written representations, written evidence or other documents received from a party, to the other party to the proceedings.

(6) If a notice of appeal, reply by the authority under regulation 12 or response by the parent under regulation 8 is delivered to the Secretary of the Tribunal after the time prescribed by these Regulations, the Secretary of the Tribunal shall defer the sending of the copies referred to in paragraph (1)(c) or (5) above pending a decision by the President as to an extension of the time limit pursuant to regulation 41.

Enquiries by the Secretary of the Tribunal

17. The Secretary of the Tribunal shall, at any time after he has received the notice of appeal—

(a) enquire of each party—

(i) whether or not the party intends to attend the hearing;
(ii) whether the party wishes to be represented at the hearing in accordance with regulation 11(4) or 15(1) and if so the name of the representative;
(iii) whether the party wishes the hearing to be in public;
(iv) whether the party intends to call witnesses and if so the names of the proposed witnesses; and
(v) whether the party or a witness will require the assistance of an interpreter; and

(b) enquire of the parent whether he wishes any persons (other than a person who will represent him or any witness which he proposes to call) to attend the hearing if the hearing is to be in private and if so the names of such persons.

Directions in preparation for a hearing

18. (1) The President may at any time before the hearing give such directions (including the issue of a witness summons) as are provided in this Part of these Regulations to enable the parties to prepare for the hearing or to assist the tribunal to determine the issues.

(2) Directions given pursuant to regulations 20 and 21 may be given on the application of a party or of the President's own motion.

(3) A witness summons issued pursuant to regulation 22 may only be issued on the application of a party.

(4) An application by a party for directions shall be made in writing to the Secretary of the Tribunal and, unless it is accompanied by the written consent of the other party, shall be served by the Secretary of the Tribunal on that other party. If the other party objects to the directions sought, the President shall consider the objection and, if he considers it necessary for the determination of the application, shall give the parties an opportunity of appearing before him.

(5) Directions containing a requirement under this Part of these Regulations shall, as appropriate—

(a) include a statement of the possible consequences for the appeal, as provided by regulation 23, of a party's failure to comply with the requirement within the time allowed by the President; and
(b) contain a reference to the fact that, under section 180(5) of the 1993 Act, any person who without reasonable excuse fails to comply with requirements regarding discovery or inspection of documents, or regarding attendance to give evidence and procedure documents, shall be liable on summary conviction to a fine not exceeding level 3 on the

standard scale and shall, unless the person to whom the direction is addressed had an opportunity of objecting to the direction, contain a statement to the effect that that person may apply to the President under regulation 19 to vary or set aside the direction.

Varying or setting aside of directions

19. Where a person to whom a direction (including any summons) given under this Part of these Regulations is addressed had no opportunity to object to the giving of such direction, he may apply to the President, by notice to the Secretary of the Tribunal, to vary it or set it aside, but the President shall not so do without first notifying the person who applied for the direction and considering any representations made by him.

Particulars and supplementary statements

20. The President may give directions requiring any party to provide such particulars or supplementary statements as may be reasonably required for the determination of the appeal.

Disclosure of documents and other material

21. (1) The President may give directions requiring a party to deliver to the tribunal any document or other material which the tribunal may require and which it is in the power of that party to deliver. The President shall make such provision as he thinks necessary to supply copies of any document obtained under this paragraph to the other party to the proceedings, and it shall be a condition of such supply that that party shall use such a document only for the purposes of the appeal.

(2) The President may grant to a party such discovery or inspection of documents (including the taking of copies) as might be granted by a county court.

Summoning of witnesses

22. The President may by summons require any person in England and Wales to attend as a witness at a hearing of an appeal at such time and place as may be specified in the summons and at the hearing to answer any questions or produce any documents or other material in his custody or under his control which relate to any matter in question in the appeal:

Provided that—

(a) no person shall be compelled to give any evidence or produce any document or other material that he could not be compelled to give or produce at a trial of an action in a Court of law;

(b) in exercising the powers conferred by this regulation, the President shall take into account the need to protect any matter that relates to intimate personal or financial circumstances or consists of information communicated or obtained in confidence;

(c) no person shall be required to attend in obedience to such a summons unless he has been given at least 5 working days' notice of the hearing or, if less than 5 working days, he has informed the President that he accepts such notice as he has been given; and

(d) no person shall be required in obedience to such a summons to attend and give evidence or to produce any document unless the necessary expenses of his attendance are paid or tendered to him.

Failure to comply with directions

23. (1) If a party has not complied with a direction to it under this Part of these Regulations within the time specified in the direction the tribunal may—

(a) where the party in default is the parent, dismiss the appeal without a hearing;

(b) where a party in default is the authority, determine the appeal without a hearing; or

(c) hold a hearing (without notifying the party in default) at which the party in default is not represented or, where the parties have been notified of the hearing under regulation 24, direct that neither the party in default nor any person whom he intends should represent him be entitled to attend the hearing;

(2) In this regulation "the party in default" means the party which has failed to comply with the direction.

Notice of place and time of hearing and adjournments

24. (1) Subject to the provisions of regulation 25, the Secretary of the Tribunal shall, after consultation with the parties, fix the time and place of the hearing and send to each party a notice that the hearing is to be at such time and place.

(2) The notice referred to in paragraph (1) above shall be sent—

(a) not less than 5 working days before the date fixed for the hearing where the hearing is held under regulation 14, 31 or 36;

(b) not less than 10 working days before the date fixed for the hearing in any other case

or within such shorter period before the date fixed for the hearing as the parties may agree.

(3) The Secretary of the Tribunal shall include in or with the notice of hearing—

(a) information and guidance, in a form approved by the President, as to attendance at the hearing of the parties and witnesses, the bringing of documents, and the right of representation or assistance as provided by regulation 11(4) or 15(1); and

(b) a statement explaining the possible consequences of non-attendance and of the right of—

(i) a parent; and
(ii) the authority, if it has presented a reply,

who does not attend and is not represented, to make representations in writing.

(4) The tribunal may alter the time and place of any hearing and the Secretary of the Tribunal shall give the parties not less than 5 working days (or such shorter time as the parties agree) notice of the altered hearing date:

Provided that any altered hearing date shall not (unless the parties agree) be before the date notified under paragraph (1).

(5) The tribunal may from time to time adjourn the hearing and, if the time and place of the adjourned hearing are announced before the adjournment, no further notice shall be required.

(6) Nothing in paragraphs (1) or (4) above shall oblige the Secretary of the Tribunal to consult, or send a notice to any party who by virtue of any provision of these Regulations is not entitled to be represented at the hearing.

(7) In this regulation "working day" means any day other than a Saturday, a Sunday, Christmas Day, Good Friday or a day which is a bank holiday within the meaning of the Banking and Financial Dealings Act 1971.

PART 4
DETERMINATION OF APPEALS

Power to determine an appeal without a hearing

25. (1) The tribunal may—

(a) if the parties so agree in writing; or
(b) in the circumstances described in regulations 14 and 23,

determine an appeal or any particular issue without a hearing.

(2) The provisions of regulation 27(2) shall apply in respect of the determination of an appeal, or any particular issue, under this regulation.

Hearings to be in private: exceptions

26. (1) A hearing by the tribunal shall be in private unless—

(a) both the parent and the authority request that the hearing be in public; or
(b) the President, at any time before the hearing, or the tribunal at the hearing, orders that the hearing should be in public.

(2) The following persons (as well as the parties and their representatives and witnesses) shall be entitled to attend the hearing of an appeal, even though it is in private—

(a) subject to the provisions of paragraph (8), below, any person named by the parent in response to the enquiry under regulation 17(b) unless the President has determined that any such person should not be entitled to attend the hearing and notified the parent accordingly;
(b) a parent of the child who is not a party to the appeal;

(c) the clerk to the tribunal and the Secretary of the Tribunal;
(d) the President and any member of the chairman's or lay panel (when not sitting as members of the tribunal);
(e) a member of the Council on Tribunals;
(f) any person undergoing training as a member of the chairman's or lay panel or as a clerk to the tribunal;
(g) any person acting on behalf of the President in the training or supervision of clerks to tribunals;
(h) an interpreter.

(3) The tribunal, with the consent of the parties or their representatives actually present, may permit any other person to attend the hearing of an appeal which is held in private.

(4) Without prejudice to any other powers it may have, the tribunal may exclude from the hearing, or part of it, any person whose conduct has disrupted or is likely, in the opinion of the tribunal, to disrupt the hearing.

(5) For the purposes of arriving at its decision a tribunal shall, and for the purposes of discussing any question of procedure may, notwithstanding anything contained in these Regulations, order all persons to withdraw from the sitting of the tribunal other than the members of the tribunal or any of the persons mentioned in paragraph 2(c) to (f) above.

(6) Except as provided in paragraph (7) below none of the persons mentioned in paragraphs (2) or (3) above shall, save in the case of the clerk to the tribunal or an interpreter as their respective duties require, take any part in the hearing or (where entitled or permitted to remain) in the deliberations of the tribunal.

(7) The tribunal may permit a parent of the child who is not a party to the appeal to address the tribunal on the subject matter of the appeal.

(8) Where the parent has named more than two persons in response to the enquiry under regulation 17(b) only two persons shall be entitled to attend the hearing unless the President has given permission before the hearing or the tribunal gives permission at the hearing for a greater number to attend.

Failure of parties to attend hearing

27. (1) If a party fails to attend or be represented at a hearing of which he has been duly notified, the tribunal may—

(a) unless it is satisfied that there is sufficient reason for such absence, hear and determine the appeal in the party's absence; or
(b) adjourn the hearing.

(2) Before disposing of an appeal in the absence of a party, the tribunal shall consider any representations in writing submitted by that party in response to the notice of hearing and, for the purpose of this regulation the notice of appeal, any reply by the authority under regulations 12 or 13 and any response by the parent under regulation 8 shall be treated as representations in writing.

Procedure at hearing

28. (1) At the beginning of the hearing the chairman shall explain the order of proceeding which the tribunal proposes to adopt.

(2) The tribunal shall conduct the hearing in such manner as it considers most suitable to the clarification of the issues and generally to the just handling of the proceedings; it shall, so far as appears to it appropriate, seek to avoid formality in its proceedings.

(3) The tribunal shall determine the order in which the parties are heard and the issues determined.

(4) The tribunal may, if it is satisfied that it is just and reasonable to do so, permit a party to rely on grounds not stated in his notice of appeal or, as the case may be, his reply or response and to adduce any evidence not presented to the authority before or at the time it took the disputed decision.

(5) If at or after the commencement of any hearing a member of the tribunal other than the chairman is absent, the hearing may, with the consent of the parties, be conducted by the other two members and in that event the tribunal shall be deemed to be properly constituted and the decision of the tribunal shall be taken by those two members.

Evidence at hearing

29. (1) In the course of the hearing the parties shall be entitled to give evidence, to call witnesses, to question any witnesses and to address the tribunal both on the evidence and generally on the subject matter of the appeal:

> Provided that neither party shall be entitled to call more than two witnesses to give evidence orally (in addition to any witnesses whose attendance is required pursuant to paragraph (2) below) unless the President has given permission before the hearing or the tribunal gives permission at the hearing.

(2) Evidence before the tribunal may be given orally or by written statement, but the tribunal may at any stage of the proceedings require the personal attendance of any maker of any written statement:

> Provided that neither party shall be entitled to give evidence by written statement if such evidence was not submitted with the notice of appeal or submitted in accordance with regulation 8 or (as appropriate) regulations 12 or 13.

(3) The tribunal may receive evidence of any fact which appears to the tribunal to be relevant.

(4) The tribunal may require any witness to give evidence on oath or affirmation, and for that purpose there may be administered an oath or affirmation in due form, or may require any evidence given by written statement to be given by affidavit.

Decision of the tribunal

30. (1) A decision of the tribunal may be taken by a majority and where the tribunal is constituted by two members only under regulation 28(5) the chairman shall have a second or casting vote.

(2) The decision of the tribunal may be given orally at the end of the hearing or reserved and, in any event, whether there has been a hearing or not shall be recorded forthwith in a document which, save in the case of a decision by consent, shall also contain, or have annexed to it, a statement of the reasons (in summary form) for the tribunal's decision, and each such document shall be signed and dated by the chairman.

(3) Neither a decision given orally nor the document referred to in paragraph (2) above shall contain any reference to the decision being by majority (if that be the case) or to any opinion of a minority.

(4) Every decision of the tribunal shall be entered in the records.

(5) As soon as may be the Secretary of the Tribunal shall send a copy of the document referred to in paragraph (2) above to each party, accompanied by guidance, in a form approved by the President, about the circumstances in which there is a right to appeal against a tribunal decision and the procedure to be followed.

(6) Where, under regulations 7(1)(c), or 11(1) or (2)(a) a parent has stated the name of a representative the Secretary of the Tribunal shall (notwithstanding regulation 42) send a copy of the documents referred to in paragraph (5) above to the parent as well as to the representative.

(7) Every decision shall be treated as having been made on the date on which a copy of the document recording it is sent to the parent (whether or not the decision has been previously announced at the end of the hearing).

Review of the tribunal's decision

31. (1) Any party may apply to the Secretary of the Tribunal for the decision of the tribunal to be reviewed on the grounds that—

- (a) its decision was wrongly made as a result of an error on the part of the tribunal staff;
- (b) a party, who was entitled to be heard at a hearing but failed to appear or to be represented, had good and sufficient reason for failing to appear;
- (c) there was an obvious error in the decision of the tribunal which decided the case; or
- (d) the interests of justice require.

(2) An application for the purpose of paragraph (1) above shall be made not later than 10 working days after the date on which the decision was sent to the parties and shall be in writing stating the grounds in full.

(3) An application for the purposes of paragraph (1) above may be refused by the President, or by the chairman of the tribunal which decided the case, if in his opinion it has no reasonable prospect of success, but if such an application is not refused—

(a) the parties shall have an opportunity to be heard on the application for review; and
(b) the review shall be determined by the tribunal which decided the case or, where it is not practicable for it to be heard by that tribunal, by a tribunal appointed by the President.

(4) The tribunal may of its own motion review its decision on any of the grounds referred to in sub-paragraphs (a) to (d) of paragraph (1) above, and if it proposes to do so—

(a) it shall serve notice on the parties not later than ten working days after the date on which the decision was sent to the parties; and
(b) the parties shall have an opportunity to be heard on the proposal for review.

(5) If, on the application of a party under paragraphs (1) to (3) above or of its own motion under paragraph (4) above the tribunal is satisfied as to any of the grounds referred to in sub-paragraphs (a) to (d) of paragraph (1) above, the tribunal may review and, by certificate under the chairman's hand, set aside or vary the relevant decision.

(6) If, having reviewed the decision, the decision is set aside, the tribunal shall substitute such decision as it thinks fit or order a rehearing before either the same or a differently constituted tribunal.

(7) If any decision is set aside or varied under this regulation or altered in any way by order of a superior court, the Secretary of the Tribunal shall alter the entry in the records to conform with the chairman's certificate or order of a superior court and shall notify the parties accordingly.

Review of the President's decision

32. (1) If, on the application of a party to the Secretary of the Tribunal or of his own motion the President is satisfied that—

(a) a decision by him was wrongly made as a result of an error on the part of the tribunal staff;
(b) there was an obvious error in his decision; or
(c) the interests of justice require,

the President may review and set aside or vary the relevant decision of his.

(2) An application for the purposes of paragraph (1) above shall be made not later than 10 working days after the date on which the party making the application was notified of the decision and shall be in writing stating the grounds in full. Where the President proposes to review his decision of his own motion he shall serve notice of that proposal on the parties within the same period.

(3) The parties shall have an opportunity to be heard on any application or proposal for review under this regulation and the review shall be determined by the President.

(4) If any decision is set aside or varied under this regulation the Secretary of the Tribunal shall alter the entry in the records and shall notify the parties accordingly.

Orders for costs and expenses

33. (1) The tribunal shall not normally make an order in respect of costs and expenses, but may, subject to paragraph (2) below, make such an order—

- (a) against a party (including any party who has withdrawn his appeal or reply) if it is of the opinion that that party has acted frivolously or vexatiously or that his conduct in making, pursuing or resisting an appeal was wholly unreasonable;
- (b) against a party which has failed to attend or be represented at a hearing of which he has been duly notified;
- (c) against the authority where it has not delivered a written reply under regulation 12; or
- (d) against the authority, where it considers that the disputed decision was wholly unreasonable.

(2) Any order in respect of costs and expenses may be made—

- (a) as respects any costs or expenses incurred, or any allowances paid; or
- (b) as respects the whole, or any part, of any allowance (other than allowances paid to members of tribunals) paid by the Secretary of State under section 180(3) of the 1993 Act to any person for the purposes of, or in connection with, his attendance at the tribunal.

(3) No order shall be made under paragraph (1) above against a party without first giving that party an opportunity of making representations against the making of the order.

(4) An order under paragraph (1) above may require the party against whom it is made to pay the other party either a specified sum in respect of the costs and expenses incurred by that other party in connection with the proceedings or the whole or part of such costs as taxed (if not otherwise agreed).

(5) Any costs required by an order under this regulation to be taxed may be taxed in the county court according to such of the scales prescribed by the county court rules for proceedings in the county court as shall be directed in the order.

PART 5
ADDITIONAL POWERS OF AND PROVISIONS RELATING TO THE TRIBUNAL

Transfer of proceedings

34. Where it appears to the President that an appeal pending before a tribunal could be determined more conveniently in another tribunal he may at any time, upon the application of a party or of his own motion, direct that the said proceedings be transferred so as to be determined in that other tribunal:

Provided that no such direction shall be given unless notice has been sent to all parties concerned giving them an opportunity to show cause why such a direction should not be given.

Miscellaneous powers of the tribunal

35. (1) Subject to the provisions of the 1993 Act and these Regulations, a tribunal may regulate its own procedure.

(2) A tribunal may, if it thinks fit, if both parties agree in writing upon the terms of a decision to be made by the tribunal, decide accordingly.

Power to strike out

36. (1) The Secretary of the Tribunal shall, at any stage of the proceedings if the authority applies or the President so directs serve a notice on the parent stating that it appears that the appeal should be struck out on one or both of the grounds specified in paragraph (2) below or for want of prosecution.

(2) The grounds referred to in paragraph (1) above are that—

(a) the appeal is not, or is no longer, within the jurisdiction of the Special Educational Needs Tribunal;

(b) the notice of the appeal is, or the appeal is or has become, scandalous, frivolous or vexatious.

(3) The notice under paragraph (1) above shall state that the parent may make representations in accordance with paragraph (8) below.

(4) The tribunal, after considering any representations duly made, may order that the appeal should be struck out on one or both of the grounds specified in paragraph (2) above or for want of prosecution.

(5) The tribunal may make such an order without holding a hearing unless either party requests the opportunity to make oral representations, and if the tribunal holds a hearing it may be held at the beginning of the hearing of the substantive appeal.

(6) The President may, if he thinks fit, at any stage of the proceedings order that a reply, response or statement should be struck out or amended on the grounds that it is scandalous, frivolous and vexatious.

(7) Before making an order under paragraph (6) above, the President shall give to the party against whom he proposes to make the order a notice inviting representations and shall consider any representations duly made.

(8) For the purposes of this regulation—

(a) a notice inviting representations must inform the recipient that he may, within a period (not being less than 5 working days) specified in the notice, either make written representations or request an opportunity to make oral representations;

(b) representations are duly made if—

(i) in the case of written representations, they are made within the period so specified; and

(ii) in the case of oral representations, the party proposing to make them has requested an opportunity to do so within the period so specified.

Power to exercise powers of President and Chairman

37. (1) An act required or authorised by these Regulations to be done by the President may be done by a member of the chairman's panel authorised by the President.

(2) Where, pursuant to paragraph (1) above, a member of the chairman's panel carries out the function under regulation 5(2) of selecting the chairman of a tribunal, he may select himself.

(3) Where, pursuant to paragraph (1) above a member of the chairman's panel makes a decision, regulation 32 shall apply in relation to that decision taking the reference in that regulation to the President as a reference to the member of the chairman's panel by whom the decision was taken.

(4) Subject to regulation 39(6) in the event of the death or incapacity of the chairman following the decision of the tribunal in any matter, the functions of the chairman, for the completion of the proceedings, including any review of the decision, may be exercised by the President or any member of the chairman's panel.

The Secretary of the Tribunal

38. A function of the Secretary of the Tribunal may be performed by another member of the staff of the Tribunal authorised for the purpose of carrying out that function by the President.

Irregularities

39. (1) An irregularity resulting from failure to comply with any provisions of these Regulations or of any direction of the tribunal before the tribunal has reached its decision shall not of itself render the proceedings void.

(2) Where any such irregularity comes to the attention of the tribunal, the tribunal may, and shall, if it considers that any person may have been prejudiced by the irregularity, give such directions as it thinks just before reaching its decision to cure or waive the irregularity.

(3) Clerical mistakes in any document recording a decision of the tribunal or a direction or decision of the President produced by or on behalf of the tribunal or errors arising in such documents from accidental slips or omissions may at any time be corrected by the chairman or the President (as the case may be) by certificate under his hand.

(4) The Secretary of the Tribunal shall as soon as may be send a copy of any corrected document containing reasons for the tribunal's decision, to each party.

(5) Where under regulations 7(1)(c) or 11(1) or (2)(a) a parent has stated the name of a representative the Secretary of the Tribunal shall (notwithstanding

regulation 42) send a copy of the document referred to in paragraph (4) above to the parent as well as to the representative.

(6) Where by these Regulations a document is required to be signed by the chairman but by reason of death or incapacity the chairman is unable to sign such a document, it shall be signed by the other members of the tribunal, who shall certify that the chairman is unable to sign.

Method of sending, delivering or serving notices and documents

40. (1) A notice given under these Regulations shall be in writing and where under these Regulations provision is made for a party to notify the Secretary of the Tribunal of any matter he shall do so in writing.

(2) All notices and documents required by these Regulations to be sent or delivered to the Secretary of the Tribunal or the tribunal may be sent by post or by facsimile or delivered to or at the office of the Special Educational Needs Tribunal or such other office as may be notified by the Secretary of the Tribunal to the parties.

(3) All notices and documents required or authorised by these Regulations to be sent or given to any person mentioned in sub-paragraph (a) or (b) below may (subject to paragraph (5) below) either be sent by first class post or by facsimile or delivered to or at—

(a) in the case of a notice or document directed to a party—

(i) his address for service specified in the notice of appeal or in a written reply or in a notice under paragraph (4) below, or

(ii) if no address for service has been so specified his last known address; and

(b) in the case of a notice or document directed to any person other than a party, his address or place of business or if such a person is a corporation, the corporation's registered or principal office and if sent or given to the authorised representative of a party shall be deemed to have been sent or given to that party.

(4) A party may at any time by notice of the Secretary of the Tribunal change his address for service under these Regulations.

(5) The recorded delivery service shall be used instead of the first class post for service of a summons issued under regulation 22 requiring the attendance of a witness.

(6) A notice or document sent by the Secretary of the Tribunal by post in accordance with these Regulations, and not returned, shall be taken to have been delivered to the addressee on the second working day after it was posted.

(7) A notice or document sent by facsimile shall be taken to have been delivered when it is received in legible form.

(8) Where for any sufficient reason service of any document or notice cannot be effected in the manner prescribed under this regulation, the President may dispense with service or make an order for substituted service in such manner as he may

deem fit and such service shall have the same effect as service in the manner prescribed under this regulation.

Extensions of time

41. (1) Where, pursuant to any provision of these Regulations anything is required to be done by a party within a period of time the President may, on the application of the party in question or of his own motion, in exceptional circumstances extend any period of time.

(2) Where a period of time has been extended pursuant to paragraph (1) above any reference in these Regulations to that period of time shall be construed as a reference to the period of time as so extended.

Parent's representative

42. (1) Subject to paragraph (2) below where, pursuant to regulations 7(1)(c) or 11(1) or 2(a) a parent has stated the name of a representative, any reference in Parts 3, 4 or 5 of these Regulations (however expressed) to sending documents to, or giving notice to, the parent shall be construed as a reference to sending documents to or giving notice to the representative and any such reference to sending documents to or giving notice to a party or the parties shall in the context of the parent be likewise construed as a reference to sending documents to, or giving notice to the representative.

(2) Paragraph (1) above does not apply if—

(a) the parent has notified the Secretary of the Tribunal that he does not wish it to apply;

(b) the parent has notified the Secretary of the Tribunal under regulation 11(2)(b) that no person is acting as a representative; or

(c) the representative named has notified the Secretary of the Tribunal under regulation 11(3) that he is not prepared or no longer prepared to act in that capacity.

Revocation and Transitional Provisions

43. (1) The Special Educational Needs Tribunal Regulations 1994(a) (in this regulation referred to as "the 1994 Regulations") are hereby revoked.

(2) Notwithstanding paragraph (1) above—

(a) any notice of appeal received before 1st March 1996 may comply either with regulation 7 of the 1994 Regulations or with regulation 7 of these Regulations; and

(b) the 1994 Regulations shall continue to apply in relation to any appeal where the notice of appeal was entered in the records under regulation 17(2) of the 1994 Regulations before 1st January 1996.

Index